Charles Maurice Davies

Heterodox London

Phases of free thought in the metropolis

Charles Maurice Davies

Heterodox London
Phases of free thought in the metropolis

ISBN/EAN: 9783337276287

Printed in Europe, USA, Canada, Australia, Japan

Cover: Foto ©Thomas Meinert / pixelio.de

More available books at **www.hansebooks.com**

HETERODOX LONDON:

OR,

PHASES OF FREE THOUGHT IN THE METROPOLIS.

BY

REV. CHARLES MAURICE DAVIES, D.D.

AUTHOR OF "ORTHODOX" AND "UNORTHODOX LONDON," ETC.

"PROVE ALL THINGS: HOLD FAST THAT WHICH IS GOOD."

IN TWO VOLUMES.

VOL. II.

LONDON:
TINSLEY BROTHERS, 8, CATHERINE STREET, STRAND.
1874.

[All rights of Translation and Reproduction are reserved.]

LONDON :
SAVILL, EDWARDS AND CO., PRINTERS, CHANDOS STREET,
COVENT GARDEN.

CONTENTS.

	PAGE
A Sunday Séance	1
A Spiritual Organization	12
An Inspirational Speaker	42
Modern Mysticism	90
Mr. Bradlaugh versus God	116
The Literature of Infidelity	147
The Ritual of Infidelity	165
Mr. Bradlaugh on Toryism	188
The Land and Labour League	210
The Kansas Co-operative Colony	234
At Sunday School	242
Spouting at Cogers' Hall	264
Somers Town on Bible Slavery	273
Vegetarianism	282
West-End Secularism	315
Irishism	319
The Victoria Institute on Atheism and Pantheism	330
An Atheist's Funeral	397

INTRODUCTION.

THE great advantage which I expect individually to gain by this examination of outlying forms of belief is the confirmation or modification of my own previous convictions. Once admit the function of Private Judgment, and it is quite impossible to hold a creed on such tenure without freest comparison thereof with other claimants on one's belief. Without further reference to my own convictions, which it would be irrelevant and therefore impertinent to thrust on my readers, except in so far as may be necessary to the elucidation of my subject, I proceed nevertheless to quote some passages from a sermon I preached in the church where I was curate (St. George's, Campden Hill, Kensington) just before I commenced the inquiries which resulted in the present volumes. I do this, not at all by way of self-glorification, but, on the contrary, to show how idle it is to dogmatize on these matters without proper data; and how completely the clerical life cuts one off from the accumulation of such data. I spoke the words (pp. x. xi. *below*) in all honesty then; but I am convinced that they are now ruinously wrong. The processes by which such conviction has been forced in upon my mind have been glanced at *passim*, but are more particularly adverted to at pp. 128, 391.

I feel certain that, as an institution based on the exercise of Free Judgment and an open Bible, the Church of England must stand on the defensive, and have a Christian Evidence Society in something more than name, officered with her very best men, if she is to hold her own against the advancing tide of Free-thought—as it is specifically termed.

I find that I have, then, in the following words, depreciated—as I fancy most of the clergy do—the magnitude of the task before them, and especially the method of argumentation which I now see must be used for its accomplishment. The sermon was nearly the last I preached before relinquishing my curacy:—

The Duty of Faith towards Unbelief.

"*Blessed are they that have not seen, and yet have believed.*"—St. John xx. 29.

Some short time ago, when I was preaching on another subject, I set aside this one for subsequent inquiry—the attitude of Faith towards Unbelief. How ought Christians to comport themselves to such persons as openly avow unbelief in the doctrines of

Christianity, or even the existence and providential superintendence of God?

It becomes necessary for me to redeem my promise of treating this subject to-night if at all.

The question presents itself to us at every step, is utterly different from that which regulates our conduct towards nominal Christians.

There we can come forward with a strong point in our favour. We can say, "You are inconsistent; you profess to believe in God, yet in works you deny Him." That is the staple subject of nine-tenths of our sermons. We exhort our hearers to walk worthy of their vocation, to discharge vows voluntarily assumed, to be true to their colours as good soldiers of Christ.

But these people *are* consistent. Their self-chosen ground is logic. They say I do not believe in God. Either I am a reluctant doubter, or I dogmatically deny His existence; or, again, granting God as a necessary first cause, I deny His superintending providence, or the Revelation of Himself by Jesus Christ.

They *could*, of course, consistently go on and question the Bible's code of morals; but, in fairness be it said, they do not generally do this. No; they arrive (so they say) at the same end by a different road. Reason dictates to them what Faith prescribes to the believer. Worship and Prayer are, of necessity, meaningless to them; but morality—such moral duties as honesty, sobriety, temperance, chastity are rigidly observed and forcibly inculcated.

If they were wicked profligate people, as the unbelievers of another age *were*, the case would be easier. We could say look at the results of your doctrines. But they are not. They are decent respectable people, in no way distinguishable from Christians as far as practice goes; and the question becomes a very difficult one indeed as to what should be the course adopted by a person who, firmly believing himself, feels that when he is converted, there devolves upon him the duty of converting others—of strengthening his brethren. It is to that very practical question I ask your attention for a few moments. Not only is it in itself pertinent but it is part of a much larger one still—namely, how Christians ought to behave in reference to all forms of faith and practice which they regard as wrong—in reference, that is, to sin. Depend upon it, the most fatal mistake that can possibly be made, is to use hard words: to talk to the sinner as though he were enjoying some luxury which we begrudged him. Do we not all of us know Christians whose Christianity seems to exhaust itself in finding out that other people are wrong, and then, instead of trying to set them right, calling them hard names, and adopting that very course which is sure to harden them in their own opinions or practices?

You must fix in your mind this fact, which lies on

the very surface of the Gospel, that sin is a moral disease, much more deserving our pity than any bodily ailment—certainly not calling for vituperation or harshness in the treatment.

Look, Christians, to your great example, Christ. See him face to face with the sinful woman—one whose name was a by-word about the streets, and whose very presence shocked that good Simon, the Pharisee. See Him in presence of the adulteress, driving out her accusers with that awful scathing irony—"Let him without sin be the first to cast the stone." Nay, see Him at the very last, speaking so gently to the thief on the Cross that people are almost afraid to dwell upon the sweet words—"To-day shalt thou be with me in Paradise"—lest they seem to sanction what is called a deathbed repentance.

But we are speaking now, not of moral sin or obliquity, but of the intellectual failing—I use that word advisedly—of unbelief. Look at those words to Thomas the Doubter, the ideal sceptic. There is not a word of what is termed rebuke in them. Not one whit more—if so much—than that with which the Great Master received the credulity of Nathanael, who believed Christ's Messianic claims because, forsooth, Jesus said He saw him under the fig-tree, before Simon called him. The whole tenor of Christ's words to Thomas is one of compassionate sympathy —not of rebuke or vituperation.

Fix this preliminary fact in your mind, then—that

it is no more use to tell a man to believe than to tell him to be strong, or to have an ear for music. One man has Faith, and another has not; as truly so as one man is in robust health, and another an invalid.

Of course there is such a thing as shutting one's eyes to conviction, just as it is possible to ruin one's bodily health by excesses. That, however, is not the point we are considering—but where a man, like Thomas, simply says, "I cannot believe."

But then, in the second place, you will say, Taking this type of St. Thomas, if I am not to abuse the Doubter, I may—nay, I *must*—try to convince him—to reason him out of his doubts. Your very comparison of feeble health suggests this. The physician does not leave the sick man to recover in the course of nature. He gives him medicine to heal his sickness.

Accepting, of course, the case alluded to in the text as typical, there is this to be said. If you were quite sure that you could bring to bear that kind and amount of evidence which Christ did—and which was, in fact, demonstration, then, by all means, argue with the Doubter. But when can you? I believe that more harm has been done by weak friends and injudicious advocates than by all the open enemies Christianity ever had. However much we may any of us sympathize with the spirit which animated the Christian Evidence Society to go and meet Infidelity on its own ground, we still cannot, with any truth, say that it has been successful. I have been present at discussions between Doubters and Believers, and not, for obvious reasons, taking myself as an average listener—but supposing it possible to have a thoroughly unprejudiced person there, I felt very dubious indeed as to where such a person would say the weight of evidence lay.

We come back once more to the point from whence we set out then. Faith, though it may be strengthened by argument, does not originally come of argument, any more than of volition. That appears the great mistake of the intellectual advocates of the Bible. They seem to think that they can inspire a saving faith in its teachings, just as they can in any fact of common life. Infidelity itself is forced to confess that the *facts* of the Bible are every day receiving new corroborations. It is not these the Doubter questions; it is their supernatural origin: and this, I hold, no amount of argumentation will ever prove.

This is really only the same as saying that no amount of medicine will ever cure the sick man, unless the principle of life be there. It can aid that; but it cannot inspire it. If it is absent the man will die, in spite of all medicines.

Do we mean, then, that we are simply to leave the Doubter to his fate? We seem to have cut the ground from beneath our feet when we say that we are neither to denounce unbelief, nor to argue against it.

With the example of Christ and St. Thomas before us, and also having taken unbelief as equivalent to spiritual sickness, it is quite certain *that* is not the course we would suggest.

It appears to me that, in our treatment of these cases—that is, in our conduct with reference to those who do not believe in God or Christianity—we leave out altogether the cardinal idea of the *supernatural character of Faith.*

I dislike technical terms of theology when I can avoid them; but we seem to forget that there is such a thing as "*preventing* grace."

Thomas, remember, though in the episode of the text we see him as a sceptic, was *no* Doubter, but a tried and trained Apostle. Christ, who knew that man's soul, as God knows yours and mine, to its very depths and abysses, knew that the principle of Faith, the principle of spiritual life, remember, was there, or all the demonstration in the world would have been useless. Do you think the prints of the nails or the scar of the spear would have convinced Pilate or Caiaphas? Not at all. They would only have said it was a clever imposture.

Call to mind, too, a case which I doubt not has occurred to many of you in your commonest experience of life. When some dear one droops and fades before your eyes; when you see health's hues die out of the cheek, and youth become feeble and decrepid as palsied age, you send for the most skilled specialist money can procure; and as he bends over the panting chest or feels the languid pulse, you tremble to hear him say "I can do nothing; the physician's work is over, because the life-giving principle is virtually gone"—and then you have to summon *us* to prepare for a higher life which no death can ever touch.

Do you not perceive to what this tends? We see a man before us who either will not (if we like to use that phrase) or *cannot* believe. We want to impart to that man the simple Christian faith which is our greatest stay and comfort here, and which we know he will want, O so sadly! when his call comes to go from this world to another.

What shall we do? *Blame* such an one? Surely not so, with the tender example of Christ and St. Thomas before us. We may venture to ask, as He did, *Is* seeing the only mode of believing? We may even moralize—How blessed it would be for you if you *could* believe without seeing. But, O brethren, for Christ's sake, literally for the sake of our Blessed Master, no hard names. No saying, Stand by, for I am holier than thou; no thanking God we are not as other men, or even as these publicans.

Shall we reason with them?—It were hard to say No, if we feel that we have the intellectual skill to fence their doubts, or if we are quite sure that we have the evidence at hand that will satisfy them—not that satisfied *us*, mind, but that will satisfy them. Only remember that if we argue and fail to convince them, they will be sure to claim a victory, and to be confirmed in their doubt.

What I would rather advise—nay, rather what I feel our Master teaches—is this, go to your closet, and kneel down and wrestle in prayer to God for that one. Don't call this leaving him to his fate. You believe in what is called the dynamical force of prayer, do you not? Intercessory prayer is exactly what we have been speaking of as *medicine for a sin-sick soul*. You may blame a man for not believing; you may argue with him and deem your reasoning unanswerable—and yet fail. He *cannot* believe. Your logic does not touch his case. Kneel down and pray, "God, give that weak and wavering soul strength to believe and live!" that is more the attitude for a Christian believer—I mean a believer in God, not a believer in self.

Do you not remember some solemn words Christ spoke to this effect to another apostle, who was really a more habitual doubter than St. Thomas—I mean St. Peter? He said Satan had desired to have him that he might sift him as wheat; but He had done what? Rated him soundly for his frequent wavering?—No. Commenced a course of evidential instruction?—Not at all. He had prayed the Father that his faith fail not. And when he was converted, he was, in like manner, to strengthen his brethren who may in their turn be wavering. Not by abuse; not by logic or rhetoric; but by praying to God for them.

Praying and living; for life is prayer. Do you know the great stumbling-block of the Doubter? If you don't, I can tell you. It is *the inconsistent lives of Christians*. He says, and dare we say it is unfairly, " You, with all your apparatus of Bible, Church, sacrament, service, sermon—I know not what—live no better than I with my conscience void of offence towards God and man."

It used to be the fashion to point to the Doubter's deathbed, and triumphantly say, " Look there—if unbelief helps man to live, it will not help him to die." They have their array of philosophical deaths ready to hand; and, on the other side, they point us to the deathbed terrors of the conscience-stricken Christian, and turn back the argument upon ourselves.

To pray for the Doubter, and at the same time not to silence his doubt by the quiet protest of our own holy lives, is just like giving the sick man wholesome medicine while you keep him prisoned in a poisonous atmosphere. You see this is one more instance, then, where the real Christian, like his Master, does not strive or cry, does not break the bruised reed, or quench the smoking flax. Harsh denunciations and hot arguments are the world's methods. Quiet prayer and unobtrusive piety are Christ's. What is that before which unbelievers of every class bow down in unwilling homage?—The historical fact of Christ's moral teaching, which no casuistry can call in question. There is a path in which we can all follow Him. Tell the unbeliever to come to you, and you will show him what God has done for your soul. That your belief in God and Christ and your Bible and Church does not make you intolerant, or incline you to be argumentative; that it inspires, on the other hand, a chord of sympathy with all *his* doubts and difficulties. It is not supercilious pity that you feel; such pity would be offensive. It is not that you echo out the Psalmist's dictum, "The fool hath said in his heart 'There is no God.'" They are not fools that are saying it now. They are the world's intellectual masters. But you feel your faith in God has been a comfort and a stay to you in difficulties. You do not feel that it has forced you to dwarf your intellectual faculties, or pause for one moment in the course of practical progress. On the contrary, you feel it has helped you on in all of these. And so you will not venture to question a creed that you feel is as honest on the negative side as yours on the positive—will not say that "Doubt is devil-born." You will not presume to argue with those you freely confess your intellectual superiors. But you *will* dare to pray in secret for them. You *will* try to show them what Christ has done for you; and if all this fails, you will do no more than your Master did when commenting on the long withholden recognition of His apostle

—hope on still, and say (Christ said no more) "How blessed it would be if you *could* believe!"

I am quite content to incur the imputation either of egotism, or that which is technically termed "padding," if I convince my clerical brethren that something more is necessary than prayer and piety in these days of enlightened doubt, and that is to be able to give to every one that asks a reason for the hope that is in us. I depreciated such machinery when I preached my sermon; perhaps I unduly exalt it since I wrote my book, and that the truth, as is so often the case, lies somewhere between the two extremes.

A word again on the subject of the quotations which I have been forced to put into this volume, and which cannot fail to be as painful and offensive to those who read as they have been to myself in writing them. It was incumbent on me to *show how far the mischief has gone*, and especially to illustrate forcibly the inevitable connexion between dogmatic atheism and political disaffection. Mr. Bradlaugh's ironical Letter to the Prince of Wales is the final outcome of the doctrines held by its writer; or at least there was only one stronger expression still—not penned by Mr. Bradlaugh, but sold at his Lecture Hall—and this I could not bring myself to quote. I entreat those who feel outraged by the publication of such matter to believe that I have only tolerated it, after most careful deliberation, as a serious and unpleasant duty.

HETERODOX LONDON.

A SUNDAY SÉANCE.

It may perhaps appear to some persons that, in this and other works I have written on kindred subjects, I give too prominent a place to Modern Spiritualism. I do so advisedly, however. I stated at the outset, and I here repeat, that Modern Spiritualism is rising—nay, has risen—into the rank of a religion to an extent of which few persons are aware. The very fact that, in dealing with each part of my threefold subject, I have felt bound to treat of this new claimant on our regards, may be taken in evidence both of its ubiquity and its Protean character. As an "unorthodox" system—if it were to be considered a religious system at all—its place was clear enough; but we also found it claiming a niche in the temple of Orthodoxy. There is, I mean, a Christian Spiritualism widely prevalent in all the various religious bodies, not even excepting the Roman Catholic, but claiming particular notice from me as spreading widely over the Established Church. I have already narrated my experiences at a Sunday Evening Séance, which was preceded by a religious service, where the officiating minister was a clergyman of the Church of England; and my present paper will detail some further sittings with this same circle; though here it will be found the religious and theological teaching assumes such a shape as to justify its comprehension in a work bearing the title of Heterodox London. The proceedings of this particular body I mean, which had so far only slipped the moorings of discipline, have now cut themselves quite aloof from distinctive Christian doctrine, and the teachings appear to me to be rapidly gravitating towards that goal which is reached by so many different approaches—namely, a Pure Theism.

But here I am beset by a difficulty which more or less attends every one who would describe the outcome of an inceptive or nascent creed; its professors are still in a Church-in-the-Catacombs kind of state, and to let in daylight upon them may be to do them serious injury. "Never mind, as long as the truth gains by it," I fancy I hear some enthusiastic defender of orthodoxy exclaim; but, it must be remembered, I am indebted to the courtesy of these good people—for I am sure they are good even if mistaken —in that I have been allowed to be present at their services and séances. They utterly disclaim all idea of propagandism (though I suppose no one ever held a creed tenaciously which he did not wish to spread), and therefore some amount of reticence will still be imposed upon me in reference to these phases of faith. For instance, all references to personality or locality I must not only forego, but seek to conceal and mislead my readers. I vouch, however, for facts; and I repeat my conviction that any account which proposes to be a vivid sketch of heterodoxy in 1874, and from which a picture of existing practices in Modern Spiritualism should be absent, must be meagre and unfaithful.

Although, then, I heard by a side-wind that my previous report on the Sunday Evening Séance had given some little offence, I did not find that I was utterly excommunicated. In fact, the clergyman himself, who would be most likely to be injured in respect of his bishop and congregation by such publicity, took no umbrage at all; so with respect to other objectors I did not trouble myself much; and found I had done no very serious damage from the fact of my receiving two cards, one inviting me to a service and spirit-séance, over the former of which the clergyman in question, and over the latter a distinguished American medium, was to preside; while another similar card, bearing date for the following Sunday, invited me to a celebration of the Lord's Supper, to be followed by an exercise of the gifts of magnetic healing. This promised to be heterodoxy, and no mistake; so I need scarcely say I thankfully accepted both invitations.

The address to which I was thus led was in central London, being, in point of fact, the residence of the lady-medium herself. I entered an old-fashioned panelled parlour, which I found arranged as a chapel, a recess, wherein stood an antique oak sideboard, serving the purpose of a quasi-sacrarium. Over the face of this article of furniture was spread a red velvet frontal, with a medallion of an ecclesiastical design worked in the centre. On the sideboard were, first, a large standard crucifix, wreathed with a garland of forget-me-nots—whether natural or artificial I could not determine—and two large lighted wax *bougies*, which were necessary, as the windows were carefully shuttered and curtained, and there was no other light in the room, with the single exception of a deep red sanctuary-lamp suspended above the kneeling-cushion in front of the "altar." On the table, or sideboard itself, were numerous little photographs, presumably of friends of those accustomed to sit there, and a very small flagon and chalice of white polished metal— I fancy silver. The chairs for the congregation, about fifty in number, all fronted the altar; and there were already two or three ladies occupying them; but the room was so dark that I could not at all see what they were like, and they were, moreover, all engaged in private prayer or in reading. In fact, the whole scene looked like a private chapel in a Roman Catholic convent. At right angles to these chairs, and on both sides of the altar—I shall call it so throughout—ran two short forms which I rightly surmised were for the choir; and in the corner farthest from the door was a plain oak lectern, with a small harmonium behind it.

Gradually the chairs were pretty well filled—a boy in the passage keeping the door ajar so as to prevent the necessity of new-comers knocking or ringing. There seemed to be no scrutiny as to those who came; but I noticed that each one on entering made his or her way to the chimney-piece, and dropped some coin into an alms-box on which was inscribed "For Expenses." I found afterwards that all the admissions were by private invitation, and there was a tacit understanding that every one who came should contribute according to ability. I appreciated the delicacy which had not informed me upon this detail. I am very much mistaken if I did not hear the clink of gold coin more than once, as some richly-dressed and jewelled lady passed to her place during the quarter of an hour's waiting which intervened between my arrival and the beginning of the service.

At half-past three—the appointed time—a lady came in and went to the harmonium, playing a soft simple air, while the clergyman entered in white surplice only, preceded by four children similarly attired, two little boys, and two girls of ten or eleven, the latter with long golden hair streaming over their white garment. One of these carried a fuming pot of fragrant incense, which she placed on the altar, the clergyman kneeling in front, and the children prettily grouped two on either side of him. All remained for a long time in silent devotion.

Proceedings commenced with the singing of a beautiful Metrical Litany, which I believe I am right in saying had been written by the clergyman himself, or rather compiled from many of those which had cropped up during the then recent Mission Week. The air was a very taking one; and I recognised it as a familiar one at Roman Catholic Benediction Services. It was sung antiphonally, one verse by the clergyman, the other by the choir and congregation, an accompaniment being played throughout. I noticed that all Trinitarian passages had been carefully expunged whenever the suffrages had been taken from orthodox sources. It ran, as far as I can recollect, thus :—

A Sunday Séance.

Priest.

Maker of the starry height,
From amid our earthly night,
When we draw Thy presence near,
Hear us, Holy Spirit, hear.

People.

(Repeat the same verse.)

Priest.

When we feel our heart within
Leading on to works of sin,
Thou our blinded gaze canst clear—
Hear us, Holy Spirit, hear.

People.

Let Thy grace in bounteous shower,
Fall with Absolution's power.
Nought with Thee as guide we fear—
Hear us, Holy Spirit, hear.

Priest (pianissimo).

When in silent grief we bend
Losing some departed friend,
Teach us that they still are near—
Hear us, Holy Spirit, hear.

People.

Open Thou the weeper's eye,
Make the mourner's teardrops dry;
Keep our parted ones still dear—
Hear us, Holy Spirit, hear.

Priest.

When the thorny path is trod,
Link us closely still to God.
When the storm breaks dark and drear—
Hear us, Holy Spirit, hear.

People.

In all time of our distress,
In the hour of joyfulness,
Thee alike we would revere—
Hear us, Holy Spirit, hear.

A few Collects followed, and one longer prayer, of a deeply spiritual character; but I did not recognise it as coming from any book of devotion with which I was acquainted. Then a second hymn was sung to the tune known as "Melcombe," to which the "O Salutaris Hostia" is generally set in the Benediction Service. The clergyman then passed to the lectern, and read the Parable of the Rich Man and Lazarus, on which he made no comment, except so far as to justify the alteration he adopted in reading the solemn story, where he changed the word "Hell" to "Hades"—"In Hades he lift up his eyes," &c.— as he said it was desirable to leave more time for the séance. He therefore gave out a third hymn, and pronounced the beautiful Old Testament Benediction; after which he took off his surplice, and, clad in his cassock, helped the children to arrange the congregation in a sort of open square two or three deep, and to place a small table with five chairs in the centre. Then the children left; he extinguished the altar-lights, leaving only the dim glare of the red sanctuary lamp to make darkness visible, and the séance proper commenced.

There was considerably less of that plunging and kicking of the table which I find is comprehended under the title of physical manifestations. Our medium did not obtain those, and I was glad of it, for they are eminently unsatisfactory. The answers to questions came by means of minute raps, like the pecking of a bird, on the table; one of the sitters going through the alphabet, and the rap coming at the letter that was intended. There was nothing very remarkable, as far as I recollect; certainly nothing that even approached a test or might not have been communicated by any of those present. The first message that came was:—

"We are sent to tell you that God is love, and that we live."

There were little loving speeches addressed thus to

many of us, myself among the number, all of a strictly devotional character, and quite in keeping with the state of mind which might be supposed to be induced by the previous service: I was told indeed of direct writing, spirit-voices, faces and even forms, as being among the ordinary experiences of these séances, which had even obtained for it the name of the Miracle Circle; but I write strictly of what I saw myself: and to me the service was more marvellous than the séance itself.

On the next occasion when I was present the Communion was celebrated. The form used was an abridgment of the Church of England office, the Beatitudes being substituted for the Ten Commandments, as in some Unitarian Churches. It was claimed that the miraculous gifts of the first century had never died out, and that they were connected in the form of magnetic healing, with faithful reception of the consecrated—that is, they told us, the magnetized—elements. Several of those present averred that they were then and there cured of slight maladies, such as headaches, under which they laboured, and I had obviously no means of checking their assertions. In most cases, however, I was told the cure was gradual, and scarcely perceptible to any but the sufferers.

In the sermon that accompanied this service, I was surprised to hear the preacher distinctly claim to have revived the school of the sceptics—a name which I had always fancied hateful in spiritualistic ears. Taking his basis on the Reformation of the sixteenth century as an instance of destructive theology, the preacher said it was quite impossible henceforth to admit any dogmatic halting-places. Between the poles of Catholicism and Atheism there was no resource but Scepticism. This might be of an eclectic or simply an Epicurean character; and I may be wrong, but I thought the speaker evidently inclined somewhat to the latter, and that he was disposed to question authority in morals as well as belief, not without a penchant even for the extreme of Free Love or Elective Affinity.

A SPIRITUAL "ORGANIZATION."

There is a well-known and probably inevitable tendency on the part of all sets of opinions to organize themselves into systems, and eventually to become formulated into creeds and articles of faith. It is, no doubt, part of a general law pervading nature, and running up through the physical into the intellectual and spiritual spheres, bringing about at one time the proverbial "fortuitous concourse of atoms," which hardens the nebulæ into *terra firma*; at another stereotyping the crude notions of an individual or a small community into a regular, perhaps an established, religious "system." Such is the history of most, nay, of all "Faiths." First of all they live in the conceptions of one man, the Inspired or Illuminatus of his period; then disciples are made; the electric influence spreads with the strange contagion of sympathy from one to many, from many to more; and, the impetus once given, none can calculate the circumference; for the force is centrifugal, and may widen out to any area according to the force of the original bias and the opportunities for subsequent expansion.

This tendency is variously regarded by the

devotees of the Faith in question, and by its outside critics. While the former, led away by a transitory triumph, see in such culmination only the legitimate influence of their favourite dogmas, which are now to take the world by storm, the outside observer is accustomed to associate the period of prevalence and establishment with the beginning of decrepitude and decay. He points to history and says—"See how systems, like empires, havè risen to a climax and then toppled over: how they flourished while persecuted, but directly they became recognised and respectable, dwindled away!" They will even—but then these, of course, are Heterodox people—point to existing systems such as Wesleyanism, or even the Church at large, and say with Sir Christopher Wren's epitaph— "Si monumentum requiris, *circumspice!*"

Modern Spiritualism is just undergoing the throes of such a crisis in this year of grace 1874, twenty-six years from the time when, on the eve of All Fools' Day, the now historic Rochester Rappings were first heard in the Fox household. It has passed through all the infantile trials incidental to a nascent system —the moral measles and whooping-cough of communities—and now, feeling itself to have attained manly proportions, wishes to assume its *toga virilis* with all the ardour of young Hopeful, who pictures to himself the first dress-coat as the acme of existence. How little does that ambitious juvenile dream of the shawdowy frontier-line that separates the prime of life from senility; or would he not cling to his round jackets and aspire to perpetuate his knickerbockers, lest he developed prematurely (as it will always seem) into the "lean and slippered pantaloon?"

Emanating, then, most clearly from that Rochester homestead in the States, and still represented in Heterodox London by Mrs. Jencken, *née* Kate Fox, Spiritualism slowly but surely invaded these shores of the antique world. Mr. Home may be considered its St. Paul, for he was the apostle to whom is largely due the conversion of our Orbis Veteribus Notus. He has borne testimony before many of the crowned heads of Europe; and my own "experiences" of Spiritualism commenced from the fact of my being resident in Paris in the year 1857, and Mr. Home a nightly guest at the Tuileries. So it was that "circles" were formed. The Spiritual Institution of Mr. Burns was formed first at Camberwell, and then in the more central situation it now occupies at 15, Southampton Row. This has for years been the focal point of London Spiritualism; and only the more ambitious spirits even now feel they have outgrown the limits of that "Progressive Library." Then the Dialectical Society examined and reported upon the new creed. Fellows of the Royal Society fought about it in Quarterly Reviews and Journals of Science. Learned Serjeants of the Law wrote gravely of it; and here and there a clergyman, less timid or time-serving than his fellows, confessed there might be "something in it." So the influence spread, and is spreading; and so—wisely or unwisely—some of its professors have resolved to organize, and have chosen for themselves the lofty title of the "British National Association of Spiritualists," of whose platform more anon.

It is easy to see that such an organization, though possibly contemplating no rivalry with the existing "Institution," will certainly disintegrate the as yet United Happy Family. Far-seeing men, too, like Mr. William Howitt, have written deprecating the proposed organization on the grounds above-mentioned—viz., as being a possible precursor of decay; but the British Association is aspiring and ambitious, and will listen to no arguments from anxious friends. Probably before these pages see the light, that organization whose commencement they chronicle will be an accomplished fact.

Having been for so many years a careful examiner of the claims of Spiritualism, and a close attendant on all the meetings of the Dialectical Society during its examination there, I was honoured by the Provisional Council of the British Association of Spiritualists by being invited to a seat on their board. I did not feel able to avail myself of this privilege; but still was enabled to be present at one or two of their meetings while there was being waged what might be called the Battle of the Prospectuses. (One feels almost tempted to ignore declensions and write Prospect*i*, like the would-be classical lady who spoke of the omnib*i*!)

Two rival prospectuses had been put forward; one by Mr. Herbert Noyes, an Oxford graduate, and among the most devoted disciples of Spiritualism; another by a lady bearing the Charles Dickens-like name of Miss Kislingbury. Strange to say, the gentleman's document was long and diffuse, the lady's short and concise. Consequently the latter found favour with the British Association, and was perhaps, on that account, more fitted for general circulation; but Mr. Noyes's paper gives such an excellent idea of the present position, aims, and prospects of Modern Spiritualism, that I cannot forbear giving some excerpts from it at the end of this account.

When I accepted the invitation of the Provisional Council to be present at one of its sittings, I really thought I must have made a mistake; for, on repairing to the address specified, I found that it was one of the most palatial offices in the City of London. I must not, of course, give the faintest clue to its whereabouts; but it was with even more than my usual diffidence that I rang the bell and asked the janitor if "a meeting"—it was so I ambiguously phrased it—were taking place upstairs. It was all right; and he marshalled me into a resplendent office, where about a dozen gentlemen and two ladies were sitting round the largest circular table I ever saw. They might have been going in for a séance—I should have liked to see *that* table skip about!—but they were not. They were debating, paragraph by paragraph, Miss Kislingbury's very concise and practical Prospectus.

I will not relate how we sped slowly, word by word, through the two final paragraphs; how some gentlemen wanted to organize so fully as to start forthwith an Index Expurgatorius for excommunicating tricky Mediums; how Sensitives were to be "certificated" like cabmen; how, while one wanted a Spiritual Church to be included in the Association's Central Buildings, another felt that the new Faith had outgrown the necessities of Temples built with hands. There seemed every variety of religious and political opinion represented at that Eclectic Board; and it amused me to calculate the chances of their ever agreeing on the moral qualities of a Medium— or indeed on any other subject here or in the spheres!

Suffice it to say the "organizing" even of the short Prospectus took us three mortal hours, and they had had I do not know how many such sittings before my time. This was the form the document assumed whilst I was there; but the stiff-necked gentleman who went in for certificating Mediums gave notice that he should move resolutions next time calculated to re-model the whole affair. It struck me, however, that to quote this inceptive form of the shorter Prospectus, and Mr. Noyes', which was rejected solely on account of its dimensions, would be likely to give as good an idea as we could possibly get of the position of Modern Spiritualism in 1874.

I am, of course, unable to give names, or the faintest indication of personality; but let me state that those twelve men I saw round that voluminous mahogany were hard-headed practical men, well-to-do in their several professions, and the chairman, a grey-bearded gentleman, who went in at that Prospectus with as shrewd a business-like air as though he were prospecting a new company. There was no rhodomontade or nonsense. They were a practical dozen of men, met to embody principles in which they believed intensely, and which they thought it would serve the world to spread. This, then, was the document to which, so far, they were prepared to "set their hands and seals."

"DECLARATION OF PRINCIPLES AND PURPOSES.

"Spiritualism implies the recognition of an inner nature in man. It deals with facts concerning that inner nature, the existence of which has been the subject of speculation, dispute, and even of denial, amongst philosophers in all ages; and in particular, with certain manifestations of that inner nature which have been observed in persons of peculiar organizations, now called Mediums or Sensitives, and in ancient times, Prophets, Priests, and Seers.

"Spiritualism claims to have established on a firm

scientific basis the immortality of man, the permanence of his individuality, and the Open Communion, under suitable conditions, of the living with the so-called dead, and affords grounds for the belief in progressive spiritual states in new spheres of existence.

"Spiritualism furnishes the key to the better understanding of all religions, ancient and modern. It explains the philosophy of Inspiration, and supersedes the popular notion of the miraculous by the revelation of hitherto unrecognised laws.

"Spiritualism tends to abrogate exaggerated class distinctions; to reunite those who are now too often divided by seemingly conflicting material interests; to encourage the co-operation of men and women in many new spheres; and to uphold the freedom and rights of the individual, while maintaining as paramount the sanctity of family life.

"Finally, the general influence of Spiritualism on the individual is to inspire him with self-respect, with a love of justice and truth, with a reverence for Divine law, and with a sense of harmony between man, the universe, and God.

"The British National Association of Spiritualists is formed to unite spiritualists of every variety of opinion, for their mutual aid and benefit; to promote the study of Pneumatology and Psychology; to aid students and inquirers in their researches, by placing at their disposal the means of systematic investigation into the now recognised facts and phenomena, called

Spiritual or Psychic; to make known the positive results arrived at by careful scientific research; and to direct attention to the beneficial influence which those results are calculated to exercise upon social relationships and individual conduct. It is intended to include Spiritualists of every class, whether members of Local and Provincial Societies or not, and all inquirers into psychological and kindred phenomena.

"The Association, while cordially sympathizing with the teachings of Jesus Christ, will hold itself entirely aloof from all dogmatism or finalities, whether religious or philosophical, and will content itself with the establishment and elucidation of well-attested facts, as the only basis on which any true religion or philosophy can be built up.

"'The Association proposes, when circumstances permit, to establish a Central Institution, comprising a Hall, Lecture and Séance Rooms, also a Library for the use of Members, and for the benefit of all students of psychical and spiritual phenomena; to keep a register of Mediums or Psychics, with the view of affording facilities for investigation; and to promote co-operation and intercommunion between Spiritualists in all parts of the world.

"The Association, while aiming to unite the advantages of vigorous centralization with the benefits of independent local effort and local self-government, emphatically disclaims any right or desire to interfere with the action of Societies or Institutions already established. It is hoped that Local and Provincial Organizations will avail themselves of the powers afforded in its Rules by becoming affiliated with the 'British National Association,' and by appointing from their own body a member to represent them on the Council."

With reference to Mr. Noyes' prospectus, the *Spiritualist* (one of the organs of this denomination) says—

"Several of the members of the Council of the National Association drew up a prospectus each, and aftewards compared them. The one finally adopted originated with Miss Kislingbury, but some of Mr. Noyes' suggestions were incorporated with it, after which it was considerably revised by a committee. The prospectus suggested by Mr. T. Herbert Noyes, jun., B.A. (Oxon), was an elaborate document; it was not adopted, but is of interest, coming as it does from a highly-educated and intelligent gentleman, who has given much thought to the question, 'What work should a national organization undertake?' It touches upon many controversial subjects, and gives the opinions of Mr. Noyes as to the position which an organization should assume in respect thereto as follows:—

"I. The victories of civilization have been achieved by a judicious organization of the units of society, and the advantages of intelligent co-operation are now so universally acknowledged that it would be unpardonable for Spiritualists to ignore them.

"II. It has accordingly been determined to draw up articles of association upon the broadest possible basis, and invite the co-operation of all students of pneumatology and psychology—a numerous and flourishing minority, who may reasonably expect ere long to absorb the majority.

III. The first question for consideration was the choice of a style and title for the new Association, and after much deliberation it has been decided to call it, 'The British National Association of Spiritualists.'

"To obviate possible misconceptions, we proceed to define the meaning we attach to the terms selected.

"We have chosen the terms 'British National' to express our intention that all persons who for the time being are sojourners within the British dominions, shall be eligible as members, and having regard to the fact of the intimate association between *the spirit* and *the soul*, we have chosen the word *Spiritualist* with the intent that it should be taken to include all *Psychologists*, all students and investigators of facts and phenomena called *spiritual* or *psychical*, and that it shall not be taken to imply adhesion to any preconceived theory or any religious dogma whatsoever. We do not even intend that it shall exclude professed materialists who seek admission to our ranks.

"IV. The next question for consideration was the

definition of the functions of the Association, the aims and objects of its organization, and these we have now to enumerate.

"1. The first object of the Association is to secure the public and general recognition and intelligent appreciation of the marvellous facts and phenomena which first attracted public notice at Rochester in the United States, through the intervention of Miss Kate Fox, now Mrs. Jencken, and which have since been observed, with innumerable modifications and unexpected developments, by millions of credible witnesses in all parts of the world. Phenomena inexplicable by any previously recognised laws of nature, phenomena which have hitherto baffled the ingenuity of all critics who questioned their spiritual origin, phenomena which are daily occurring in our own family circles, and which now claim to extend the realm of nature and the reign of law to an invisible world, and bid fair to vanquish the scepticism of the votaries of science, as well as the prejudices of the religious world.

"2. The second object of the Association is to secure to all students and investigators the necessary facilities for systematic investigation and study—facilities which in the face of an adverse public opinion, due to our traditional prejudices and hereditary misconceptions, can only be secured by organized and energetic co-operation, and by the judicious management of a common purse.

"3. The third object of the Association is to study, formulate, and promulgate the new systems of metaphysical and moral philosophy and religious teaching, which would seem to be the legitimate outcome, and all sufficient justification of these same facts and phenomena, however trivial they may appear in their earlier manifestations to superficial observers.

"The achievement of these objects involves—

"1. The collection of records of such occurrences during the last twenty-five years, whether published or unpublished, and a diligent comparison of such records with the records of similar occurrences which have taken place in all ages and among all nations, but which have been misunderstood, misrepresented, and discredited, as being miraculous and outside of law, or assigned to superstitious and epidemic delusions.

"2. It involves the diligent investigation and verification of the occult sciences of the Middle Ages, and the much neglected science of Mesmerism, which are concerned with such phenomena, as well as the study of ancient religions and ancient mysteries, inasmuch as the experience of the past is useful for the elucidation of the present, and may itself be elucidated by the multitude of novel facts elicited by modern discoveries.

"3. It involves the collection, recording, and classification of contemporary testimony to the occurrence of similar phenomena in our homes, and the diligent scrutiny of multitudinous facts, collectively and individually on the part of the Association and its members.

"4. And inasmuch as these facts and phenomena are ascertained to take place only in the presence and by the intervention of certain exceptionally gifted persons, now called 'Mediums,' 'Sensitives,' and 'Clairvoyants,' but of old called 'Prophets,' 'Priests,' and 'Seers;' and inasmuch as their exceptional gifts have been proved to require cultivation and development under very subtle and delicate conditions, it involves much diligent labour in the discovery, cultivation, education, and classification of public and private Mediums, and, further, a diligent investigation of the conditions most favourable to the manifestation of the highest phenomena.

"5. And inasmuch as these phenomena are not only physical, but metaphysical, and have developed since the earlier manifestations into multitudinous phases which correspond to and even transcend the spiritual gifts enumerated in the New Testament, and throw new and unexpected light on the philosophy of inspiration and revelation, yielding cogent proof that there was no greater finality in the revelation of the Christian era than in the revelations of the Mosaic era—it involves an obligation to make these facts widely known, however unpalatable they may be to popular prejudices; it involves an obligation to publish the fact that if the world is unwilling to welcome unpalatable truths, it must be because it is unwilling to give up its malpractices—unwilling to welcome truths which will exhibit them in their true light, and prove it to be a wicked world; and it involves an obligation to proclaim that all who have the progress and prosperity of the world at heart, will do well to welcome Spiritualism.

"6. And, lastly, inasmuch as it has been found of great practical importance that séances should be held in rooms specially appropriated and preserved, like the chancels of our churches, from mixed influences, and that such conditions are at present difficult of attainment; and as, moreover, it has proved difficult to find even public lecture halls in suitable localities open to lecturers who do not belong to the reputed orthodox schools, and equally difficult to obtain free circulation for the literature of Spiritualism, it involves the founding of a Central Institution, comprising a public lecture hall, library, reading, and séance rooms, with all the machinery of a missionary organization in some central situation, as a model for similar institutions.

"Now, inasmuch as the world is now-a-days ready to receive truth, if convinced of it—willing to receive truth when it is found to be true—we think it is desirable to put before it the facts which we believe it will discover to be true. We think it will find that the mission of Spiritualism will be to introduce

Reforms into the political and social systems of the world, which will be the inauguration of a *New Dispensation*.

"We will, therefore, proceed to enumerate the missions of Spiritualism, as they appear to us to present themselves, under the influence of the teaching of the invisible world.

"THE MISSIONS OF SPIRITUALISM.

"1. To afford demonstration of the fact of the Immortality of the Soul, and so to arrest the materialistic tendencies of modern philosophies, and to disarm death of its terrors.

"2. To throw new light on the moral government of the visible universe by invisible agencies; to furnish fresh proofs of the perfections of the Almighty; and to dispel doubts of the efficacy of Prayer by disclosing its true philosophy.

"3. To supplement the ancient Revelations of the future state. To prove the unbroken continuity of conscious existence and personal identity in the mental condition of the departed, and their ability and inclination to open communications with those whom they have loved and left on earth.

"4. To disclose and promulgate the conditions and laws of such open communication, and to cause the experience of the most highly favoured few to be utilized for the benefit of the less highly favoured many.

" 5. To teach that the best preparation for our future state is a life of energy and activity, lived up to the highest physical, moral, and intellectual standard attainable in this world, by the harmonious development and adequate exercise of all the faculties with which each man is individually endowed, and that, while it is well to direct special attention to the cultivation of special aptitudes, none of the higher faculties can safely be left uncultivated.

" 6. To indicate and revive the time-honoured belief that the protection of *Guardian Angels* is still, and has ever been accorded to mankind, and to prove that these willing workers exert an occult influence even upon those who are wholly unconscious of their presence, and utterly ignore their agency; and that their special mission is to keep alive the still small voice of conscience, and flash bright thoughts into the head, and pure and holy aspirations into the heart, so long as their benign influence is not repelled by obstinate persistence in the paths of transgression. That they are, indeed, willing workers of all good works in the spirit world, ever ready to aid those who need their aid in all things needful for their temporal and eternal welfare.

" 7. To vindicate and revive the belief, as old as the days of Hesiod, that our Guardian Angels are generally the spirits of our departed fellow mortals, who, having once inhabited our earth, have their experience of the troubles of life to guide them in ministering to us.

"8. To rectify the current misconceptions of the powers of evil, and to prove to the world that the Prince of Darkness employs innumerable agencies, made ready to his hand by the rulers of the world in which we live; inasmuch as the hosts who do his work are the undeveloped Spirits who have passed unpurified from earth life into the spirit world, whence they gladly return to earth to gratify their own evil passions by inspiring men of like passions with themselves with evil thoughts and impure desires.

"9. To convince the world that the powers of evil will eventually be conquered by the invisible hosts of the Almighty, when the end of the present dispensation shall have come, but not till after the earth shall have been desolated by terrible wars, which, within the brief period of ten years from the present time, will have ceased for ever, if the world will but believe in the power of the angel world to deliver them from their invisible foes.

"10. To revive and place upon a rational basis the practice of praying for departed friends, by disclosing the fact that they often yearn for human sympathy, and are conscious of its being accorded them; and that if they have not yet risen to the happier spheres, and are still earth-bound spirits, messengers of mercy and love may be sent to aid them in answer to our petitions.

"11. To prove to the world that the state of the soul after its departure into spirit life is not fixed, final, and stationary, but a state of progressive and eternal development; not a state of rest and idleness, but a state of energy and activity, in which all its mental powers cultivated on earth will find suitable employment, and in which many other faculties now dormant will be developed—a state much more closely resembling our own than has heretofore been conceived. To show in short that the world has been heretofore left to look forward to rest in Heaven, as being the way in which it could best be taught to realize the soul's release from many of the physical sufferings of the earth-life which are intended for the purification of the spirit.

"12. To make clear to the world that the Day of Death is the Day of Judgment, and that the prevalent belief in the Resurrection of the body is due to a misconception of the fact of the resurrection of the Spiritual body, which is coincident with the death of the mortal body.

"13. To throw light on many most important physiological questions involved in the relations of the indwelling soul and spirit to the mortal body—to wit, the action of the mind upon the brain, and the action of the brain upon the nervous system.

"14. To discover and promote the development of

whatever faculties may be latent in human nature, and thereby to show that the unfolding of higher and nobler faculties is the ultimate destiny of every soul of man.

"15. To extend the domain of science to the realms of the invisible, the impalpable, and the imponderable, and to supersede the supernatural by proving that the occult mysteries of human nature, heretofore deemed beyond the reach of human intellect, if not forbidden to human research, are destined to be revealed to the truth-seeker, to the unspeakable advantage of humanity.

"16. To dissipate erroneous views of the distinction between Science and Religion, and to build up a new Church based on the identity of religious and secular knowledge.

"17. To winnow the wheat of truth from the chaff of theology, and reconcile antagonistic creeds by eliminating their errors, and making manifest the spiritual truths which underlie all systems of religious belief in the world.

"18. To encourage willing works of Love, Mercy, and Charity upon earth.

"19. To promulgate a sounder system of Political Economy calculated to remedy many crying social evils.

"20. To remedy the evils resulting from excessive irregularity in the distribution of Wealth under the present system of social and political economy which has made the rich too rich and the poor too poor.

"21. To sow the seeds of a general Reformation of Morals, and bring about the cure of moral and physical diseases in the way which nature would be found to prescribe when her occult laws come to be understood.

"22. To bring about a more rational observance of the Day of Rest and recreation by a more liberal application of the maxim that the Sabbath was made for man, not man for the Sabbath, a maxim which is opposed to the common practice of making it a fast day.

"23. To introduce a sounder system of Education by directing more special attention to the discovery and cultivation of the natural gifts of our children, and by encouraging the general teaching of the elements of physiological and psychic science in our elementary schools, seeing that an intelligent appreciation of these subjects is essential to the attainment of the highest physical, moral, and intellectual development.

"24. To vindicate, popularize, and perfect the much neglected but most important sciences of *Phrenology* and *Physiognomy*, and introduce them into our national schools and seminaries, with a view to the utilizing to the utmost of our educational resources, and to the great benefit that would accrue to society if the practical use of these sciences in dealing with their neighbours were understood by the people at large.

" 25. To suggest reforms in the principles of our Criminal Legislation, and in the practice of our penal establishments.

" 26. To reform the principles of our Lunacy Legislation and the practice of our lunatic asylums.

" 27. To bring about the liberation of many Sensitives and Mediums now wrongfully incarcerated in these asylums on account of their possessing faculties not comprehended by the Faculty, and who, if liberated, under judicious treatment, would prove to be some of the most useful members of society.

" 28. To inaugurate extensive Sanitary Reforms by enforcing the more general application of the principle that prevention is better than cure, and by suggesting radical improvements in the principles and practice of the healing art. Such improvements may consist in the introduction of more scientific methods of using resources provided by the beneficent action of the laws of the world of spirits, in the suggestions of novel applications of the use of changes of temperature, and of the uses of air, light, and darkness, in the disclosure of the use of many simple remedies at present unknown to the world, and of the efficient use of many hitherto misused drugs, and in the development of the remedial uses of electricity and magnetism, which, although of late introduced by a few enlightened practitioners, are still ignored by the Faculty at large.

"29. To suggest reforms in the principles upon which our Hospitals are conducted, and to bring their practice more into harmony with the laws which nature prescribes.

"30. To revive the ancient practice of *healing by imposition of hands*, and to build up as a science that beneficent art, as ancient as the world itself, which is known among us by the modern name of 'Mesmerism;' an art which is empirically practised all over the world under various names, but whose sphere of usefulness would be vastly enlarged, if the principles which lie at the root of the practice were made to yield their secrets to scientific research.

"31. To revive and popularize the ancient practice of *Cremation*, which is so preferable to burial, from a sanitary point of view, and which will be useful to make the world understand that the body will not rise again in the flesh, but in the spirit.

"32. To minister consolation to the bereaved, and prove that it would be more rational to mourn for the survivors.

"33. To suggest reforms in the principles of our Poor Law Legislation, and remedies for the terrible evils of our Workhouse system.

"34. To cause the rights of the Labouring Classes to a larger share of the produce of their labour to be conceded.

"35. To improve the condition of the Labouring Classes in this country in the matter of wages, in the matter of dwellings, in the matter of education, and in the matter of well-doing in the world; and especially to ameliorate the condition of the workers in factories, mills, mines, and mineral workshops and manufactories dealing with poisonous materials, who sacrifice their health for hire, and who will not help themselves; and those who labour in the seething workshops of private tradesmen who will not help their workpeople. We are not blind to the fact that the attention of the Legislature has of late been directed to these crying evils; but we know that Legislation has been powerless to eradicate them, and we believe that it will continue to be powerless until the true principles of action come to be better understood; and these principles we believe it to be the mission of Spiritualism to inculcate.

"36. To raise the standard of humanity, and improve the physical and mental conditions of future generations, by directing attention to many questions relating to *Marriage*, and the psychological influences affecting unborn babes which have been so grievously overlooked, to the great detriment of the human race; and especially effects resulting from marriages contracted from mercenary motives, and from the irregularities incidental to the more or less nominal celibacy of so large a percentage of the population.

"37. To cause the Rights of Woman to be recognised to the full.

"38. To cause the Wrongs of Woman to be redressed to the full.

"39. To open the Churches of England to the free use of the laity for the secular instruction of the people on week days and Sundays, after the brilliant example recently set by the Dean of Westminster, and to show that all truth, all knowledge, and all wisdom may fitly be taught therein without profanation from the pulpits hitherto monopolized by the clergy, but hereafter destined for the free use of faithful Mediums.

"40. To inaugurate a universal Missionary work with a view to make the world wiser and more willing to render efficient help to the poor, the weak, and the afflicted, wherever they are to be found, and generally to do the work of the Spirit-world in amending the evils of the world in which we live.

"41. To teach that the last will be the first in the Kingdom of Heaven, if the last is the most deserving in the world of spirits, and has been the most deserving in the earth-life; and that the first in earthly honours will be the last in spirit-life if he have won no higher place by his own merits.

"42. And generally to enlighten the world in all matters in which the occult influence of Spiritual agency has been heretofore ignored. . . . .

"Having thus enumerated some of the many missions which modern Spiritualism seems destined to fulfil, it becomes our duty to consider by what practical measures this Association may best improve the suggestions, and second the philanthropic aims of the invisible world.

"It has been decided that the corporate affairs of the Association shall be committed to a large and liberal representative Council, who trust that their initiative will be cordially seconded by the energetic co-operation of a very numerous body of members, working collectively and individually in their several spheres.

"It has been decided that the gates of membership shall be thrown open to all honest students and applicants who are able and willing to contribute as a minimum the small annual subscription of 5s.

"But inasmuch as a large expenditure must be incurred efficiently to further the multitudinous objects which have been indicated, it is hoped that special subscriptions and donations will be offered by those whose means enable them more liberally to promote the laudable and philanthropic work which is contemplated.

"It is proposed to establish, as soon as possible, in the most central situation that can be procured in the metropolis, an Institution comprising a public Hall and Lecture rooms, Reading-room, Library, and Séance rooms, where discourses may be delivered and séances held on week-days and Sundays; an institution which shall not only be a focus of radiation and attraction for all inquirers, worthy of the

Spiritualists of England, but also serve as a model for local affiliated institutions which it is hoped will ere long be found not only in all the different districts of the metropolis, but in all centres of population in the United Kingdom.

"It is proposed to found in connexion with this Institution, and so soon as funds will permit, a College of Mediums, at which all Psychics, Sensitives, Clairvoyants, and Mediums may be instructed how best to discover, cultivate, and develop their latent gifts; a College calculated to offer opportunities for the more systematic study of the various phenomena than can now be obtained, and special facilities for the study of the occult sciences in general.

"It is proposed that diplomas shall be granted by this College to all such Mediums and Sensitives, whether trained and developed within its walls or not, as are able to satisfy the Association of the genuine character of their gifts and their own trustworthiness, after undergoing such tests as may be deemed conclusive by the Council, and that diplomas shall also be issued to lecturers on Phrenology, Physiognomy, Mesmerism, Psychology, Pneumatology, and other occult Sciences, who are found qualified to undertake the missionary labours of the Association.

"It is proposed that registers and records shall be kept of all such Mediums, Sensitives, and Clairvoyants, and their specialties, for the use of individual members and affiliated Societies, and also registers of all important facts and phenomena communicated to the Society by its members and correspondents which can be authenticated to the satisfaction of the Council, and that the due authentication of all such recorded facts be the special function of a standing judicial committee of the Council. It is further proposed that in connexion with the Institution and the College of Mediums there shall be established a Mesmeric Hospital and a School of Mesmerism, in which that important branch of the healing art may be studied, practised, and developed into a systematic Science, and in which gratuitous treatment may be provided for the poor by the most gifted healers.

"It is proposed that the library of the Association shall be stocked with all the ancient and modern works on pneumatology, psychology, mesmerism, phrenology, physiognomy, and the kindred sciences, which can be collected, and rendered accessible to all members under the most liberal regulations compatible with security.

"It is proposed that public Services, Lectures, and Séances be held on week-days and Sundays, at the central Institution, so soon as it is possible to found one, and that in the meanwhile the Council shall do their best to further the objects of the Association, by promoting publicity and organizing lectures and public meetings in churches, chapels, halls, and lecture rooms in town and country, wherever and whenever it is practicable, but above all that they should direct their attention to the discovery and development of Mediums and Psychics willing to devote their gifts to the service of the Association and its missionary labours in the cause of truth ; and that steps be taken to make due provision to preserve all approved workers from the temptations of the necessitous. But inasmuch as the extent to which these operations can be undertaken must be regulated by the condition of the funds at the command of the Council, and their execution will involve grave consideration of innumerable questions of detail which will arise from time to time, it will be desirable that the work of progressive organization of the several departments should be remitted to standing committees of the council, who should report from time to time, and whose reports, when discussed and approved, should be duly circulated among the members in the journals of the Association and the quarterly reports of the Council.

"Meanwhile it is proposed that immediate steps shall be taken to raise the funds requisite for the establishment of this central Institution by co-operative action, under the provisions of the Limited Liability Acts, upon a plan in which all Spiritualists, Psychologists, and Students of humanity in the United Kingdom may be invited to assist according to their inclination; and of which it is intended to embody the details in a paper which will be circulated with the present manifesto."

From this it would appear that the method of the Spiritualists is something like a combination of pure Positivism with unlimited Scepticism. Much as they mislike that word in its loose colloquial sense, it really does, in its etymological acceptance, clearly express their tenets. They rest on the demonstrations of science—a science, however, which does not illogically stop short at the physical or intellectual, ignoring the spiritual portion of man's being, but applies its rigorous analysis to the domain of revelation hitherto disposed of in the wide category of the supernatural. Spiritualism has no such word as Supernatural. It substitutes the certainly less objectionable term supra-sensual—for who shall presume to define the limits of nature? It is quite impossible to set superciliously aside a system which has the support of such scientific men as Mr. Crookes, F.R.S., and Mr. Cromwell Varley, the former of whom has, while these sheets were passing through the press, declared his positive conviction, based on scientific experiment and the evidence of his senses, that the hitherto suspected Spirit Forms are no result of trickery, but a legitimate case of Double.

AN INSPIRATIONAL SPEAKER.

ONE of the most recent developments of that Protean thing called Modern Spiritualism is in the direction of Inspirational Speaking by gifted ladies. The Sibyls are generally, though not always feminine; and indulge in the very tallest of tall talk by the hour together under the guidance of possessing spirits. I once heard a plain-spoken old gentleman, the late Professor Donovan, say in public and in-presence of such a speaker, he really did not think much of this particular kind of manifestation, " because," he added, "it requires no ghost to come from the dead " *to make a lady talk !*" That was in reference to Mrs. Emma Hardinge, who was, I believe, the first Inspirational Speaker we had in England. She came to London in 1866, and when I was taken by Mr. Benjamin Coleman to hear her at the Beethoven Rooms, I at once recognised her, and remembered her name, as an actress at the Adelphi Theatre in the year 1850—51. Strangely enough—and it struck me as a great testimony to the new powers of Mrs. Hardinge—I recollected her as a then young actress who used to play in a farce called " My Precious Betsy," with Wright and Mrs. Frank Matthews; and the two veteran players took a delight in "gagging" and throwing out the young actress, who could not wander one degree from her part without floundering. Mrs. Frank Matthews remembered the circumstance distinctly; and agreed with me that about the last person she would ever have expected to see come out as a public speaker was Emma Hardinge! The reigning favourite at present in London is Mrs. Cora Tappan, who was better known as a medium in America by her maiden name of Cora Hatch. She came out with considerable *éclat* at St. George's Hall, after which she drifted to Weston's Music Hall in Holborn, in which slightly incongruous locality she set up her "Spiritual Church." Now she has abandoned the ecclesiastical title, and hangs out at Cleveland Hall, somewhere down a slum by Fitzroy Square. *Facilis descensus!*

It was in this locality I heard her a few Sundays since, after much inquiry on the part of my enterprising cabman, who thought he could find out the place, but could not. Our lengthened wanderings made us late; and by the time we had paid our shillings at the entrance Mrs. Tappan had begun· to pray, and the door was shut.

In a little time it was re-opened, so that the liturgical exercises must have been brief, and we were admitted into an unmitigated Dancing Academy, where a fair congregation was gathered, and at the farther end Mrs. Tappan was mounted on a platform extemporized from refreshment tables, and accompanied by an old gentleman in a chair, before whom was a table with a conventional water bottle which had seen better days, and a big Bible.

Mrs. Tappan was dressed neatly in black, with a profusion of golden hair—very golden indeed, falling in studied negligence over her shoulders. She had a tasteful bunch of flowers on her head, and another on her bosom. She is a fine woman, above the middle height, and decidedly good-looking. When we entered she was sitting in a plain Windsor chair, holding her head as though she had the toothache, but presumably in converse with the invisibles. The elderly gentleman read a few verses from 1 Corinthians xv., and we sang, first an anthem and then a hymn; after which Mrs. Tappan rose, and in a clear silvery voice, and strain of unbroken eloquence, delivered her Inspirational Address, as follows:—

"We propose this evening to give you some of the truths concerning the influences of the present life upon the future, and what condition the spirit shall occupy in reference to that future life. The passage which has been read from Paul, were we to subject it to the scrutiny that is usually given to secular writings, would not bear the test of strict logical criticism, inasmuch as it conveys within itself a seeming contradiction. This difficulty may be overcome by suggesting another word for the word 'it;' since it leaves the mind of the reader in somewhat of a doubt as to what 'is sown in weakness' and what 'raised in power.' In one instance he says it shall 'put on corruption;' 'it is sown a natural body; it is raised a spiritual body;' and in the next sentence, 'There is a natural body, and there is a spiritual body.' Now, if the same body is first a natural and then a spiritual body, why does he say there are two bodies—the natural body and the spiritual one?

"Upon this one chapter hangs largely the foundation for the belief in the resurrection of the material body; but we think no careful student, no one who reads it with an eye to the spiritual meaning, can for one moment determine that that which he refers to as being the part resurrected can apply to the physical body. We do not think there is the slightest shadow of foundation, except ambiguity in the use of the word 'it.' But this may be the fault of the interpreter. It may be that one word meaning the substance of man himself—the soul or spirit—is here referred to; and that this single syllable entirely perverts the meaning of the original writer. Most assuredly we must take into account the fact that Paul's writings were not all of them the teachings of Jesus; that he afterwards introduced and incorporated many of his own previous scholastic views; and with the exception of the general phases of the Christian teachings, Paul's doctrines were disputed among the early Christians; and the followers of Apollos and Cephas did not accept many of Paul's interpretations and his references to the present and future life. But whatever credit and whatever authority may be given to a singularly gifted, zealous, and studious apostle should be given to the writings of Paul. However, the question now promises a more speedy solution from the fact that it is not only impossible, but is confessedly at variance with the existing laws of nature to suppose that the whole mass of mankind shall be raised physically from their graves. We doubt even if the most tenacious adherent to the letter of these epistles believes it in reality. The earth itself does not contain substance enough to fashion material bodies for the entire human family that have lived upon it. The component parts of many human bodies in existence to-day have been parts of other bodies that existed ages ago ; and it would be a singular position in the laws of nature and anatomy to determine in what particular body an atom should take its place when it has now occupied many bodies before. But the spiritual significance of this discussion is apparent, and so apparent and plain that he who runs may read. Yet many there are who refuse to read with the eye of the spirit, and only interpret literally that which should be interpreted with the spiritual significance.

"The resurrection of Christ is referred to as authoritative with reference to the physical resurrection. But it must be remembered that the record is a little dubious in this account. When it is said that he lay in the sepulchre three days, and when it is said that previous to his death he said to the thief on the cross by his side, 'This day shalt thou be in Paradise,' where, during the three days he was immured in the sepulchre, was he? The tradition is that he visited the spirits in prison, and when he arose he requested those who saw him not to touch him, that he had not yet ascended to his Father. Now, either he did not know that he would ascend, and so could not make promises, or he had gone in spirit to Paradise to unseal the spirits in prison, and so afterwards returned to his material body—to his disciples in the material body. All these points of your belief it remains for the theological student to clear up; our own opinion being that the spiritual body was not sufficiently strong to undergo the contact of those who were about him, and that he appeared to them in a form resembling his own physical body. There is another point often discussed among theologians, but one with which we have very little to do, and that is as to the actual time when this resurrection shall take place. Those who believe in a final and entire resurrection contend that the dead yet sleep in their graves, and that this resurrection shall come at one time with the sounding of the trump referred to by Paul. But where were Moses and Elias who appeared on the Mount of Transfiguration? If they were resurrected from their graves in anticipation of this last day, it shows a singular partiality in the Divine Mind to allow them to rise from their graves, and leave other prophets slumbering until the trump shall sound. Again, he who appeared to John upon the Isle of Patmos declared himself to be an angel, and not God, as John believed. If the spirits can thus be raised without their physical bodies, and appear to man, does it not appear absurd that they should require, after many hundreds of years, this physical body again, if they can leave the grave and hold converse with mortals, and have taken on the clothing of the spirit?

"But the purpose of our remarks to-night applies to a more spiritual, and we trust a more interesting, subject than this. It is concerning the actual condition of spiritual life, and the effect which material organization has specifically upon that condition hereafter. Undoubtedly modern Spiritualism has revealed the fact to all who have come within the knowledge of its philosophy, that the communion with spirits proves not only their existence, not only that they inhabit a world real and tangible, but that their condition in that world is largely determined by the knowledge, the occupation, the thoughts that are held in this life, and that the wisdom and philosophy which can give to humanity a tangible and distinct revelation concerning the effects that this life and its thoughts have upon the next will do much to destroy the ancient fear of death—that death which Paul refers to as being sin. It is undoubtedly true that the existence of ignorance in the world concerning the elements, the primal laws of spiritual being, accounts not only for the crimes that are in existence, but for many of those weaknesses, faults, and foibles that would otherwise be removed.

"One of the most interesting inquiries concerning the future state connects itself, not only with those that are endowed with usual intelligence, gifted with the gifts of mind and the graces of the spirit, not only with those who, ordinarily good, are well qualified to enter another state of existence; but the question naturally arises, 'What becomes of those who are idiotic? those afflicted with madness? those who have moral obliquity from the hour of birth? those who commit crime seemingly for the love of crime? And what effect does idiocy, madness, moral obliquity have upon the spirit itself?' A most interesting and serious inquiry, since the perfections and imperfections of human life are all equally divided on an average; and since where an instance occurs of absolute aggressive evil or of an unaccountable malady, they form the subject of the study of the most enlightened men on the earth.

"We have said in previous discourses that the condition of the average man in the future life is in the beginning just what it is here; that you begin your new state of existence where you left off here; and you only leave behind you those tastes and appetites that are purely material, without leaving behind any of the immediate consequences of those material tastes or appetites. Now in the case of idiocy, many persons who have believed in immortality for the most of mankind have rejected immortality for those unfortunate beings. That might be extended to madness, when the human mind possesses no control over its thoughts or actions; it might also be extended to those who have only intellect without spiritual nature; and so in the general result we should only get a small minority of beings adapted to immortal life. If intelligence is to constitute the test, then who would venture to draw the line? For the beasts termed brutes (though many men being much less intelligent are far more brutal than they) might claim, with more propriety, admission to the immortal existence than those who abuse them.

"But it is not a question of this kind. The germ of spiritual existence belongs to all human beings, or it is doubtful for all. Everything wearing the human form has either the germ of immortal life, or there is no immortality; and that condition of future life which will unravel the mysterious and painful results of the violation of law in material life will go far to prevent that violation, and make it possible that immortal souls shall exist in fitting habitations hereafter. We claim that every being wearing the human form possesses an immortal spirit, that the spiritual life animates, pervades that form, or it could not exist; that the breath of the living soul that descended upon the first man, as recorded, descends upon every child that lives in the world, and that idiocy is only an obscuring of that intelligence from outward view, while the soul itself is immured in a prison.

"Dr. Howe, of Boston, a most distinguished physician and naturalist, says that there is as much difference between the cultivated idiot and one who is uncultivated as there is between an ordinary person of education and one who is uncultured. In the asylum for idiots established in that city, many hundreds who were supposed to have no intelligence whatever have been reclaimed from that abject state of ignorance to one of average knowledge by various processes. With some it is the intonations of music that fall upon the poor benighted intelligence in some captivating strain, and gradually they learn to read by musical sounds. With others it is a striking array of brilliant colours; and while the idiot in that direction could not learn to read the ordinary printed letter in black and white, if it is printed in yellow, or red, or green, or blue, the idiot will learn to read. This goes still further; and oftentimes sentiments of the deepest and profoundest kind, convictions, knowledge, are developed in that way, until what was supposed to be a human being lacking intelligence is made a useful member of society. You do not think deaf persons devoid of intelligence, and he that is blind is naturally the subject of your compassion. That which you term idiocy is but mental blindness—but the defects of organization, the result probably of antenatal influences that it would be well for you to understand and avoid. Those laws are within the range of human study and human comprehension. You immure the soul in the prison-house called the body, and there is oftentimes no release from that but death. The uncultivated idiot enters the spiritual world as the babe enters this life, with no experience, no intelligence, and it becomes a question of serious import concerning human physiology and anthropology whether you will allow beings to be born into this world that will give no experience to the spirit, and allow it to be transported to spiritual existence without the experience that human life was intended to give.

"If this be true of those who are so unfortunate as to be idiots, why not also true of the hundreds of thousands of infants who are sent prematurely from this world to the next, with no hour of earthly existence, with no hour of sunshine, but hurried on like pale overblown flowers that blossom in the shade of the wall or in the cold barrenness of the cellar, with nothing of the influence and strength of earthly life to give them the thought, the aspirations, the objects of being? Mankind are guilty of all this. The murder of innocent children lies at your doors and hearthstones; and thousands go out from the slums of your cities, from the halls and palaces of pleasure, daily and hourly, who have breathed no breath of earthly life. Idiots in spiritual existence! transported before they have taken root on earth; gathered there by scores; and unto these do the angels minister.

"You think it a great deprivation if your children in the flower, the maturity and bloom of early youth, are taken from you. But rather rejoice for those than for the young buds—the very fledglings that go out from your midst, ere they have plumed their wings for flight. Oh, you will meet them face to face in spiritual life, and they will look almost reprovingly upon you; for the experience which nature intended has been denied them, and they must ever learn in other ways than through the laws and forms of earthly life.

"Madness is in itself a disease of the mind. The madness that has once taken absolute possession of the human mind is almost invariably the result of disease, disorganization, the lack of physical knowledge. But there is no greater madness in the world than the fascination of pleasures, the allurement to crimes of that form of civilized life and that form of enlightened society that permits the souls of infants to go from earthly life ere they have tasted the experience intended by the Infinite. There is not a subject of greater import; there is nothing that you should learn more thoroughly and fully than to keep people here in earthly life, until they have achieved the experience of earthly existence. 'There are compensations for this,' you say; 'they are removed from temptation and crime.' But who is strong unless he learn to overcome temptation? and who is great unless he learn to battle with the realities of life? It is true they are removed to the care of loving hands, and that spiritual existence provides for growth in knowledge and education; but there is no knowledge like experience, no knowledge equal to that which comes to every individual from the *secret race* of their souls and actual contact with the living realities of life.

"Many are sent out thus, and they blossom like pale primroses along the hedgerows of immortal life, where the gardeners of God, who are the angels, culture them carefully; but they cannot become the stately trees, nor can they reach the height of blossom of the gorgeous rose, that hath reached the full fruition of life upon earth. It is a portion of your punishment when you come to spirit-life that you meet the result of your ignorance there face to face. It is a portion of your punishment that you find there not only the results of your earthly ignorance—but all those failures, all those longings, and all those unfulfilled words and thoughts of your own natures. You find them there even like those premature buds that have failed to experience the full fruition of life; and that is a part of your future remorse. Besides that, the whole system of existence in earthly life has been heretofore intended to satisfy

present need and present necessity and convenience.
That which is acceptable has taken the place of
right; and men have been taught to love honesty
because it is the 'best policy,' not because honesty is
the best; to be good, because goodness prospers in
the end, not because goodness is the divine fruit of
the tree of life; to love virtue, in order to gain the
esteem of your fellow-men, not because virtue is
better than vice; and finally, the whole sentiment
has become morbidly inactive with reference to those
spiritual duties and the absolute necessity of keeping
thought and mind and aspiration pure, as well as
conduct and life.

"We have referred to insanity in connexion with
the future life. Undoubtedly mankind are all
measurably insane; that is, there is a lack of the
essential power which constitutes perfect reason. You
do not all go mad and slay one another. You are
not dangerous maniacs in your households and among
your fellow-beings; but you are liable to be unbalanced by passing emotions, by popular impulses
and enthusiasm, by manias for war or greatness or
ambition. So it finally comes to be a test as to
whether the human reason itself is not liable to the
perversion and temporary suspension that permanently
fills the lunatic asylum and causes your madhouses
to be peopled. Unquestionably there are hundreds
of persons even in lunatic asylums no more insane
than you are when angry, excited, or unbalanced.

Undoubtedly there is many a maniac that occupies a throne and makes war upon nations in a methodical way whom you would not imprison within the walls of a lunatic asylum, and yet his sole madness is to slay his fellow-man, and he is possessed of the sublime frenzy of human ambition which looks upon human life as only valuable when belonging to one. There are those within the limits and jurisdiction of asylums who have no other madness than imagining themselves to be kings and queens; and there are those deemed mad whose only failing is that they see and hold converse with beings of another world. Such madness as this would make great improvements in the world, since the presence of such a lunatic in every house would aid largely to check the present imperfections and ignorance concerning that future life.

"But supposing the mind to be really unbalanced—supposing that, while the lack of reason exists in the maniac, it generally is the result of physical imperfection, either of a slowly creeping disease that has its seat in the vital centres, or of some organic difficulty, the result of hereditary taint; in which case it is physical; in which case the release comes when the spirit is disenthralled; in which case the person is irresponsible in the moral sense; and in which case there must be an awakening in spiritual life that will reveal some of the difficulties surrounding earthly existence.

"For much of this insanity the existing order of society is responsible; since subjects often agitate the minds of persons that are forbidden to be discussed, and when burdened with pent-up thoughts the mind will inevitably become unbalanced. The man so imprisoned may have broken down by the weight of a single thought, which, if expressed, would have relieved the mind from that natural tension and strife. Be careful how you suppress intense thought upon any subject. Be careful how you ask its suppression in others. Be careful as mothers and friends to guard the thought that presses down the sensitive daughter or friend. Be sure you study this infirmity, and become as alarmed as you would for any physical symptoms. The diseases of the mind are oftentimes more prevalent than those of the body; and the subtle influence of the thought that cannot find expression is oftentimes far more dangerous than the suppression of circulation, or any undue quantity of oxygen taken into the system. Be sure you study these as a portion of your lives, and that you make free outlets and avenues for the expression of anxious thoughts, that you allow in your children the expression of ideas, even if they are not compatible with your usual teachings; and above all that you do not suppress those intuitions and tendings to spiritual expression. They have much to do with the existing stages of insanity in the world; for persons endued with sensitive, impressionable natures are in another atmosphere than that which ordinary people breathe, have different thoughts and are acted upon by different extraordinary intelligence; and if that expression is forbidden, if they may not tell the vision they see; if they have to repress, lest they come in contact with some preconceived notion or opinion; if forbidden to teach of the grounds that relate to the spiritual nature and futurity—then insanity is the result, and the untoward effect is realized instead of that which is beneficent and true and good.

"Many persons that in childhood are surrounded by angels, and imagine (as you term it) themselves watched over by guardian spirits, in middle life become tormented by demons, because the good spirits have been forced away—because you have forbidden them to enter, and told the child not to believe, but only to think it imagination. That imagination turned recoils upon itself, and the doorway that was open is shut, the benign influences have been replaced by unkind ones, and the angels that have been sent away have given place to spirits who are undeveloped, and the victim is sent to the madhouse. Be sure also in studying these things that you take into consideration the fact, the sublime fact, that this life is the seed-ground, the time for sowing and planting the spiritual truths, for the reception of spiritual ideas. Be sure that you consider well that that which belongs to your highest interests and to your loftiest thoughts in future life is that which you should cultivate and study most here, not only because it brings here most happiness, but because it is absolutely the only enduring thing, those matters that pertain exclusively to the body, serving simply as experience; that those things that pertain exclusively to the body serve only as the means whereby the spirit has to gain knowledge of material laws; while that which is abiding, permanent, is the spiritual nature itself—the soul of man—the spirit that anon shall put on the spiritual body and wear the garment of incorruption.

"You have places well-nigh innumerable established for all kinds of physical maladies, and even idiocy and madness have received the kindest care of *materia medica;* but the more searching physician is needed in the soul—he that understands the spiritual nature and that can unite with the healing of the body the healing also of the mind; he that can minister not only to the disease of the body, but that knows the remedy for the spiritual disease. Find such an one, and you have found out the one that will disenthral the world. A principle may do it—it is not a person. Knowledge may do it—it is not an individual. Make known to humanity the results of certain pernicious forms of life and certain fictitious practices; make known the results of violation upon the hereafter, and you supply the healing balm. In ninety-nine cases out of a hundred no man will voluntarily plunge into the fire: make it for human knowledge and human happiness that the results of earthly existence and the conditions of future life depend upon certain known laws and principles that are just as easily followed, and just as natural as the laws of life, and you go very far to disenthral the world from every sin. Because from the knowledge of that sin and its causes comes freedom from ignorance in the same way; and as ignorance is the parent of sin, it comes to be a fact in the world that you have only to present the truths that belong to the spiritual nature, and you have a panacea for the ills of spiritual life and material life.

"He who understands fully the laws of physical life, protects himself from cold, will not voluntarily breathe poisoned air, will not enter a place where he is liable to misfortune; and, understanding, guards well his body, and sees to it that no untoward diversion comes in. Show man spiritually that these are just as distinct and decisive laws; let it be known that these laws by being understood, aid in strengthening and developing the soul, and that whatsoever you do in violation of these laws renders the spiritual nature weak, and makes the spiritual nature absolutely unimportant, and you do much to disenthral the world. Then it becomes also true that the expression of these truths in the world and their dispersion in society constitutes the saving grace of man; for that which does not apply to man's practical life is not really a thing of any value to human society. The golden rule is set high, engraven upon all the arches of your sacred temples, set in a shrine snowy and white, and in the secret altars of your souls you believe in it implicitly; but when it comes to daily life, and to the application of it in your actions, then you hesitate and falter, and the average man and woman yield on the side of selfishness—the average man and woman fail to meet this high and exalted ideal. Whatever shall bring that ideal within your grasp, that shall make you know not only that the golden rule is right proverbially, but right practically. Think of this every hour when you hesitate between one act and another; that will save you. You are in doubt about a course of conduct, yet you know perfectly well the moral law and the commandment that applies to that action. But you feel yourselves specially extenuated; you draw for yourselves a fine line of demarcation; you make metaphysical exceptions in your own favour, and expect to escape the consequences, merely because you know what is right; but that is the chief reason why you will not be exempt; it is just the reason why, with all your struggling, you do not attain that high expression.

"If the golden rule is applicable for any man, at any time, upon any given occasion, it is to all men, at all times, and upon all occasions. If it be true you must abide by it; there is no exception to that rule; no business justifies it, no commerce with nations, no laws, and no society. If it be true also that you know each of those sophisms that you weave to protect your self-respect and your individuality as sophisms, and that when you stand face to face with your own spirit you know it to be so, the cobwebs, the flimsy excuses that are woven by society, whereby you adorn your outward understanding and make yourselves believe that you do the best under the circumstances—these fall in fragments to your feet, and you see the pitiable excuses in their naked barrenness, that you stand face to face with your own ignorance, and that the soul itself must reap the consequences.

"You would consider that man most foolish who, in defiance of a cough and certain symptoms of consumption, exposes himself to the night air, going out unprotected, and adding little by little to this disease until it undermines his health and destroys his existence. So in spiritual matters, it becomes a very easy matter to extend a line of demarcation, and say, This little here and that little there will answer. The only absolute way is that the spirit shall be protected by final and ultimate laws, and that those laws shall be fearlessly, constantly, unequivocally followed without regard to the consequences. These laws are so clear and so distinct, so well defined, and so well known in the world, that no man ever need hesitate. The right and the wrong—the doing of an act, from the kindness that you bestow on the beggar by the wayside to those subtle, moral, and intellectual speculations wherein you consider your brother man and humanity—are all as clearly and well defined as the problems of Euclid, or as the system of mathematics. Make this known, let it be certain that every spirit suffers correspondingly to the neglect of duty, and rejoices and is glad correspondingly to the fulfilment of duty, and you have the solution of the whole moral problems of the world.

"The pursuit of happiness—the actual individual need of man—the desire to attain the greatest and loftiest good, these come within the range of every one; and it comes to be a fact that these selfish wants and needs, these narrow pursuits, those individual problems of happiness, melt and fade before the grand systems of spiritual happiness, that cause a man to withdraw from all yielding to mere external that he may in reality build up the spiritual.

"As we have stated, you enter spirit-life with all these imperfections and all these deformities upon you, and it becomes a question for mankind to have a perfect immortal existence instead of the physical temporal life that belongs to the material. You educate your young men to be statesmen, politicians, physicians, or clergymen. The average young man is not educated to any of these; but he must be a useful member to society. The nearer society cultivates these young men into exactly the resemblance of one another the better is society pleased. There are masses of minds ground through the same mill of classical education, and *belles lettres*, and legal argument. They come out precisely in the same mould, and the world feels that it is infinitely better when these highest types of legal, medical, theological, and literary gentlemen are in the world. Your daughters are all educated in the same mould; society requires certain forms of expression from them—they give them in obedience to society. The schools are founded upon this principle, and the nearer they resemble one another the better society is pleased.

"Your gardener, while cultivating similitudes in the types of daisies and roses, nevertheless encourages variety, and you consider that horticulturist the most successful who produces the highest individual types of each form of plant. That society will be the best, and that spiritual culture and material culture the finest, that shall make room in the world for the highest cultivation of each individual gift; not that there shall be so many good citizens merely, but that each citizen shall be an individual; not that there shall be so many good lawyers, and that each one shall possess his particular gift and qualification, and be the highest type of his kind; but that those individual attributes that make up the individual soul shall be allowed room to grow, and not that each individual shall be forced into the mould of artificial life. In spiritual life these all change. The similitudes that exist in societies of spirits are natural similitudes, because of some common grand attraction. But the highest attention is given to the individual growth of every individual soul. You are not received into spiritual existence as so many lawyers, doctors, and theologians; but you are each received as individuals, with the merit of immortal life peculiarly and distinctly your own, and with the advantage that eternity is large enough to allow of the culture of every individual quality that requires culture in spirit-life.

"Repression is the difficulty in mortal education; with spirits it is expression. Subjecting the intellect to the authority and dictates of another mind is the rule here; allowing that intellect the fullest growth is the rule in spirit. Making every child of earth a prototype of some other child is your practice; allowing every child of the spirit to become distinctly and absolutely itself, each working out that special individual experience and that special brightness that belongs to its ideal and individual being, is the practice with us. 'One star differeth from another in glory,' says Paul; every star has its appointed place, and every spirit is just as important in the spiritual firmament as every other one. The lowest of those whom you despise on earth is gathered into the gardens of Paradise and is one of the chiefest; the least of those souls that, almost without a murmur, go out from your midst, is endowed with some special individual attribute and quality; and those of you who imagine yourselves in the humblest position in life, and who are accustomed to look upon the great and wise and good as your superiors, you each have also as great a possession as the greatest. Among those whose names are enrolled upon the pages of history, and who have traced their work's record in shining deeds for their fellow-men; among those that have been the leaders of nations and societies, who have given to humanity some precious gift, and have adorned the world with the fruits of their genius; among those shining stars that rise above the horizon in human life, and seem to shape the destiny of nations by their calmness and grandeur—every human being is destined to occupy a place. Not one but is possessed of equal grandeur; not one but is endowed with as splendid attributes; not one but shall rise and shine even as the greatest have done. And those we have referred to, most unfortunate of earthly beings, whom you are accustomed to look upon with the greatest compassion, and for whom, perhaps, your pitying prayers and external professions avail little— these also are counted in the unnumbered hosts of spiritual beings as equal to the others; and these constitute some of the shining ones whose spiritual life shall be traced even as the stars are in their courses, even as the worlds are that decorate space.

"Chiefly let us remind you again of those little ones of whom Christ said, 'Of such is the kingdom of heaven.' Bear in mind that the earth is the nursery of souls; bear in mind that those souls that have not gained knowledge, and reaped the results of earthly experience, must go out and gain that knowledge under other conditions than those nature has provided.

See to it, that they go not to untimely graves; see to it, that they are not hurried and transplanted too soon to the bowers of eternal life; see to it, that those important laws of nature that become divine when they concern the welfare of the human spirit are no longer evaded; see to it, that you shape your lives, and become possessed of this knowledge, that the earth itself shall be a paradise, and that you here behold all the conditions of spiritual life."

Perhaps, however, some of the earlier discourses are more illustrative of the impromptu character of Mrs. Tappan's speaking. From these I select the one bearing the title:—

What Great Teacher has produced the most Potent Effect upon Society, and Why?

This Oration was delivered in St. George's Hall, on Sunday evening, September 28th, 1873. Before Mrs. Tappan entered the hall, the Chairman, Mr. Thomas Slater, the gentleman mentioned above, stated that, agreeably to announcement, she would speak on a subject selected by the audience, and that a committee should be chosen for that purpose. Drs. Sexton and Clark (Spiritualists) and Messrs. Watt, Goalen, and Cooper (non-Spiritualists) were accordingly duly elected to prepare a subject on which Mrs. Tappan should speak. During the early part of the service the committee retired and, on returning, Dr. Sexton announced that the question proposed by a non-Spiritualist and decided upon was that given on the previous page. A hymn having been sung, Mrs. Tappan proceeded with her address, having previously delivered the following characteristic

INVOCATION.

"Our Father, which art in heaven, infinite Spirit of love and of life, thou divine and supreme source of all intelligence, we praise Thee. Thy children would lay upon the altar of thy love their offerings of devotion. Some come to Thee laden with worldly cares, bowed down and oppressed with the manifold tumults of outward life. O, let them turn within and behold that, howsoever vast may be thy material workings, thy Spirit is infinite, and the treasures of knowledge are vast and boundless! Some may come to Thee laden with sorrow, mourning for the dead, and seeing no light above the tomb. O, above the grave, beyond the pall, may they behold the brightening glory of immortal life! may they see their loved ones in light and beauty around! Some come laden with joy, and these lay their offerings upon thy shrine, as doth the sun lay his full rich offerings upon the shrine of the morning, shedding radiance within upon the spiritual loveliness that gives light and kindles a flame of living beauty. But, whatsoever offerings thy children bring, Thou, infinite Spirit, wilt receive them. Thou alone dost understand the secrets of the human heart; Thou alone hast provided for its needs; and thy soul is in our midst, even though the clouds of materialism hide thy wondrous face. O living Love! O surpassing Spirit, glorious and full of all loveliness! let our words be of truth; let our minds be awakened to understand; let our spirits strive to know Thee, and then we shall have all knowledge. To thy name, O loving Father, will thy children for ever sing praise; and unto Thee must we for ever bring all our offerings of love."

DISCOURSE.

"*What Great Teacher has produced the most Potent Effect upon Society, and Why?*"

"We believe we state the subject correctly. Undoubtedly your committee do not expect us to go back into those ages of human history the records of which are lost, since existing society cannot be affected by those periods of civilization that are either wholly obscured in darkness, or have only just emerged from their obscurity through the investigating hand of modern science. Past ages, of which we know nothing except through the investigations of modern scientists, cannot have had much influence on the present condition of human society. But in what consists human society? It is customary to believe among Christian nations so-called that the enlightened portion of the earth's surface—that is, the most civilized of the nations of the earth—consists of those that have adopted and believe in what is termed the Christian religion. A large proportion of the earth's inhabitants do not accept, have not adopted, and are entirely ignorant of the enlightenment and civilization accompanying Christianity.

"The first influence, or the most remote influence of which history gives us any account, is the civilization that existed amongst the ancient Egyptians, although the Chinese claim still greater antiquity. But we must determine that the highest point of civilization in ancient times was reached among the Egyptians. Their worship, however, differed essentially from that of the modern worshipper. The veiled Osiris—the mysterious god, who had no external representation, but who was hidden behind his works—we may presume, represented the spirit of the universe, or creation. Isis, the mother Earth, was supposed to be the revelation of deity, or the immediate intercessor between Osiris and his children. The Egyptians, however, were not satisfied with this simple form of worship, but framed images of created things and established ceremonials. Amongst their various objects of worship was Apis, or the sacred ox. Then there was the worship of the bird Ibis, and of other beasts and reptiles, all of which were supposed to represent deity. The serpent amongst the Egyptians symbolized wisdom; not, as amongst you, evil. And every form in nature which the Egyptians worshipped was supposed to contain some element of deity. But the whole of this system of religion has been lost to the world, owing to the destruction of the Alexandrian library. The more subtle element of it, however, had already been lost—namely, the spiritual meaning of these forms; for, of a certainty, no nation ever possessed a form of religion that did not originate in some spiritual inspiration in the beginning, and however material the commencement, the first inception of their worship was from the Divine mind. Among the nations of the East, embracing India and China, of all the forms of worship—excepting the Mahomedan, which has latterly extended widely over the Eastern world—the most prominent are the Brahmin and the Buddhist. The Brahmin is an ideal worship. Its ideas of divinity are inverse from the senses. All forms of speculative spiritual theories, every abstract thought of divinity, rests with the Brahmin. He has no sympathy with the senses, although his system has its expressions; he dwells in the realm of transcendentalism. Brahma is concealed and veiled, but is represented by the three great powers or principles of nature. These principles are the Past, the Present, and the Future—the Creator, the Preserver, and the Destroyer of the universe. In these guises or forms sometimes he worships the past, sometimes bows in homage to the present, and sometimes wanders far into the regions of the future. The Buddhist, on the contrary, believes in an outward expression of divinity, wherein God, at certain and stated periods of time, manifests himself through Buddha, comes to the earth, and teaches the children of men. Buddhas have been numerous, and the last was about 200 or 300 years before the Christian era. This Buddha is supposed to come, at certain stated intervals, as the representative of the Divine mind.

"In the teachings of Buddha great prominence is given to the external forms of worship and practical charity and kindliness to our fellow-men. The Buddhist, contrary to the Brahmin, believes in the practical expression of religion, that human life should be governed by it, and that it should form its diviner part. We have the worshippers in the far East of various material elements, such as fire, air, and water; and, indeed, the Persian fire-worshippers form no small part of the wonderful systems of religion which hold sway in the world. The Indians, as you know, have their bibles, such as their Vedas and other sacred books. Zoroaster developed the principles of the religion of the ancient Persians in the Zend-Avesta, and many of its teachings compare favourably with those of more recent books, and in fact are the origin of the teachings of more modern religions. Among the Chinese the sacred books consist of the writings of Confucius. He represents the more modern and more concentrated thought of their ancient religions. The teachings of Confucius embrace the inspiration, and were the reproduction of the philosophy of ancient times, when the seers and prophets were truly inspired;

he represents the embodiment and handing down to posterity of the inspirations of all previous ages. Thus there have been at all times, outside the realm of inspiration of ancient days, certain leading minds which almost take the position of seers and prophets. The works of Confucius exhibit so perfect a code of spiritual ethics, as to constitute it one of the systems of the present day; and yet they are but the embodiment of the thoughts of the most inspired minds of his and previous times. For remember, all inspired works of Deity are not comprised in the so-called bibles of nations; and there have been prophets and sages reared up outside of established churches, and their inspirations have ever redounded to the benefit of humanity. The religion and theology of all nations represent the highest thought of their inspired writers united. Unquestionably the Bible of the Hebrew nation, said to be the progenitor of the Christian religion, is the embodiment or compendium of the writings of the Hebrew prophets and seers. But there have been superior minds, as we have said, like Socrates, Confucius, and Aristotle, who have concentrated and embodied the teachings of inspired men; and these concentrations, afterwards disentombed, have been found to bear the most searching light and criticism of inspired thought. The Hebrews were especially an inspired race. Hence we know they held their first communings with the Spirit of Jehovah—Je·ho·vah meaning Spirit of the Past, the

Present, and the Future—the one God, than whom there was no other, and before whom all other gods must bow. This was in contradistinction to the many gods of the other Eastern nations, while the Hebraic nation in their original simplicity believed but in the one Divine Godhead. Their seers and prophets looked forward to a time on the earth when Jehovah should manifest himself in person, and come to rule on the earth as their king. Consequently all the songs of praise, the prophecies, and inspirations of the Old Testament deplored the materialism of the age in which the writers lived, and looked forward to the great day when the very Spirit of God should dwell in the midst of the nations of the earth. This Hebrew nation, however, was rather exclusive; and if Deity had never spoken to the earth before, nor in any other manner, he surely has not spoken according to the Hebrews since; for, although they expected a Messiah, and looked forward to his coming, when at last it was supposed he had come, the Hebrews would not accept him, and they are yet waiting for their king who shall restore them to the New Jerusalem; and so firm is this conviction that they have preserved their temples and their ancient customs, and around their shrines gather only the children of the downcast nation of Israel. Spread abroad throughout the countries of the earth, they are building up material prosperity, awaiting their Saviour who is yet to come, as they contend.

"Meanwhile there came a voice in the East, simple like that of a child. There dawned a star, there beamed a day, and the wise men saw that the Christ they had so long expected had come. Now it does not matter, in our opinion, whether, as the infidel believes, this birth of Jesus is a tradition, or whether, as the Christian believes, it is a reality; the influence of that supposed birth upon the world is precisely the same—and whether you take it from the standpoint of the secularist or the standpoint of the religionist, it does not matter. The point we have to consider is, what effect this theory has had upon the world. Born in obscurity, raised in humbleness, and at last promulgated throughout the most advanced and civilized nations of the earth!—what effect has this had upon humanity? The religions of preceding ages—all religions antecedent to this of Jesus—accepted and believed in material worship. Temples were built, places were set apart, symbols of the Godhead were formed, and every religion became an idolatry on the face of the earth. The Spirit of God departed from the Egyptian, from the Brahmin, from the Buddhist, from the Persian form of worship, because they came to construct idols of wood and stone, and to build magnificent temples wherein no spirit could be found. Even the Hebrews because of their materialism were banished from their sacred Jerusalem, and their gorgeous temple was overthrown because they would not listen to the voice of the

Spirit. Christ's lesson from first to last, then and now, whether in the words recorded, or in the influences left upon his immediate disciples, was this: Past religions have believed that there were intermediate gods, and that the Most High God was entirely out of the reach of mortals. Christ taught that between the human soul and the Father there is no intercessor but love; and the divinest feature of his teaching was that it left the individual in the hands of deity, instead of in the hands of an outside god who might or might not listen to prayer. More than this, instead of offerings of bloodshed and burnt-offerings and sacrifices, he taught that the only offerings were those of the human spirit, that the only sacrifice was the sacrifice of the senses, and that to the spiritually-minded there is no need of an intercessor, for God is there and will listen. Could anything be more at variance with the materialism of the past than this? Could anything be more surprising to the existing forms of worship then upon the earth than this simple teacher, without retinue, without shrine or altar or priests, rising up in the midst of his fellow-people and declaring that God is not in any shrine or temple, but in the human heart alone? It was the advent of the Spirit as against matter, of the spiritual nature of man as against the material nature, the advent of the true form of worship as against idolatry; and, whatsoever man may have done in the name of Christianity and religion, the teachings of

Christ remain the same—clear, transparent, everlasting protests against all outward forms and ceremonies that are not born of the living spirit of inspiration. Christ's life and example represent the possibility of man as a teacher, as an elder brother. Why, the Roman Catholic Church even claims that he represents that to which all may become heirs by their spiritual gifts; and this may be said of the Roman Catholic Church, in spite of its idolatry, temples, and ceremonials, that it invariably preserves the spiritual gifts wherever they are authenticated, and places them upon the records of the Church as instances that the spirit is still alive, however much the matter that surrounds them may kill the spirit. But it is recorded that Christ taught that those who believed should perform even greater things than he had done. He gave his disciples the gifts of the Spirit—the gift of tongues, of prophecy, of the interpretation of tongues, and of healing. All these gifts he gave, and his disciples became possessed of them. May we ask where they are now? And do the believing possess the Spirit as they ought? Christ's teachings were those of lovingkindness and direct and perfect charity, that casts out all complaining and bitterness, and brings humanity closer and closer to the Father in the bonds of love.

"We do not criticise the Christian world to-day; we do not criticise the warfare, the bloodshed, and crimes that are incident to humanity. In spite of these the truth is abroad, and notwithstanding these the spirit of Christ is struggling in your midst to-day. It has been said that Christianity has been the cause of more bloodshed than all other religions put together. What can you say of Mahomedanism, that, with the sword in the one hand and the Koran in the other, devastates the whole of the empires of the East? Knocking at the doors of established customs and of ancient religions, it demanded instant acceptance or death. Mahomedanism had some inception of religion, but when its promulgation is accompanied by devastation and ruin, we can have no word for it but condemnation. But these nations have sunk into degradation, while the ancient religions have been quenched. It is true war has followed in the wake of Christianity; but it is not true that this is attributable to the spirit of Christianity. If men make war upon their fellow-men, shall we blame that religion which advocates love and human-kindness? Rather say that it is the undeveloped state of mankind; that, notwithstanding this light, human selfishness, cupidity, and ignorance seek to make a cloak and shield of religion to slay mankind. Shall we say that it is Christianity that has brought about all the revolutions of the last eighteen hundred years? War was known before. Cupidity and ignorance prevail; and if under the guise of religion man slays his brother, it is not because of religion, but in spite of it that he does so. Christ's teachings in their simplicity would lead only to peace. Christ's Sermon on the Mount, whatever sermons may be spoken or written, will never be transcended; it remains the one shining utterance on the page of all history that reconciles man to the Infinite. Christ's commandment—'A new commandment I give unto you, that ye love one another'—transcends the whole of the Mosaic law, since it brings humanity into close brotherhood, and makes them one with the Father. Christ's prayer to the Deity, recognising the Father, 'our Father,' makes every child of the earth one with the Infinite, and establishes the bond between humanity and God. Immortality, that was before a vague hope, an uncertain speculation that had no share and part in the ancient religions, except in some form of transmigration, re-incarnation, or some other method, was made clear and plain; and instead of mysticism and fable, it was brought to the understanding of every one. 'In my Father's house are many mansions; I go to prepare a place for you,' says Jesus to His loving followers. What more could you have of the future state?

"Then, when predicting his final change, he saw the glory of the life which should eventually follow; and when he said he should come again, it was literally fulfilled in his presenting himself to his disciples; and when he said, "If I go away, I will send you a comforter, even the Spirit of Truth,' has it not been proven that all who seek find it? We say nothing as to the different interpretations of Christ's teachings; we say nothing of the various creeds and theologies that have been built upon them, though all have their uses; we make no war with them even though they war with one another; but we say that if the foundation of the Christian religion be Christ's teaching, and the foundation of Christian society Christ's example, the world can never possess a higher standard; for it is better, if we fall short of the mark, aiming high, than if we only aim at the rocks beneath our feet. The golden rule should be inscribed on every altar and shrine, so that every one who strives therefor may have the consciousness of striving; and Jesus taught that those who strive, even though they fail, have some of the rewards of the spirit of God's love. We know that there is a very strong argument against the originality of Christ's teachings, and that materialists and infidels have searched history and found a parallel between the teachings of Christianity and those of other religions; that there was something similar in the writings of Confucius, and that other teachers taught the golden rule—but Christ was the first teacher who embodied his teachings in the loving works of his life and hands—Christ was the first teacher to awaken the consciousness that spirit is superior to matter, and that the soul transcends the casket in which God has placed it.

"And we know of nothing better to-day than in the fulness of the human understanding to know that these lessons, however perverted and abused among men, form the chief aim and inspiration of the loftiest minds in human society. Even when they do not know it, and when materialism enthralls the senses, the unconscious leaning is towards that high standard of moral excellence and spiritual worship; and though they are humble in thought, they shun the more external forms of creed and ceremonial, and seek this true and living spirit within it. The greatest thought of the Christian world is for the peace and advancement of humanity. Whatever kings may do, or selfish demagogues may demand, we know that Church and State are alike united with the greatest and highest powers of the earth to bring about 'peace on earth and goodwill to men;' that the British nation as a government has set its face towards the 'golden rule,' in striving towards that arbitrament that shall cause the sword to be set aside and the understanding of humanity to be used in its stead. When such a thought is in the minds of your rulers, we certainly do not despair; and when the greatest minds, moved by the impetus of human fellowship and love, look kindly and joyously towards the era when goodwill shall prevail, and when the nations of the earth shall be gathered together beneath the eye of God, and when human governments shall try the mild sway of the Christian, we cannot condemn, but on the contrary say that spirit is abroad in all the lands; that it forms the basis and foundation upon which the superstructure of human society is built; that the spirit will kill the letter as the letter has sometimes killed the spirit, is unquestionably true; and that in an age not far distant, without the eye of prophecy, the religionist and statesman can say there will be an entire end of wars and bloodshed and governments of force, and that the supreme law of all the land will be this law of peace. No other teaching could have wrought this work. It matters not, as we say, whether it be a clever creation of the early teachers of the Christian Church, or whether, as we believe, Christ was indeed an inspired teacher. It matters not: the influence upon society is still the same, and the great culmination of moral and spiritual thought was in the birth and life and teachings of Jesus of Nazareth."

Having finished her discourse, the lecturess offered to answer any question by the committee bearing upon the subject treated. Mr. Cooper rose, and, in the name of the committee, thanked Mrs. Tappan for her eloquent address, and said he only spoke the sentiments of all when he said they had all been delighted with what they had heard. He only wished such a sermon might be heard every Sunday in all the churches of the metropolis. Mrs. Tappan then offering to answer any question put to her by the audience, a gentleman asked, "Do you regard Christ as really God, or merely as a human teacher?"

To which the lectureress answered, "We were not asked for our theological views; we were only requested to state what great teacher had had the greatest influence on human society." Another gentleman considered the speaker had not fully answered the question embodied in the subject of the discourse. She had shown that Christ had had the greatest influence on human society, but had not pointed out why. He should have expected, and no doubt the gentleman who had asked the last question had expected, the answer—Because he was God. Mrs. Tappan replied that "For ourselves, we believe that all truth is of God, and Christ embodied in his form as much of deity as the truth he expressed; that he was the Son of God, and that he represented the possible of man, inasmuch as he promised the same gifts to others that he himself possessed. But we certainly decline entering into any discussion upon the creed of the Trinitarian or Unitarian, or any form of theological controversy. Christ's words when he says: 'I and my Father are one,' did not mean he was God; if he and his Father were one, it simply signified they were one in spirit; and the promise given to earth's children, the same as to Christ, is, that Christ could not have been a greater embodiment of deity than the divine and perfect humanity he represented." Another gentleman having understood the speaker to eulogize the connexion of Church and State, the answer was given: "We do not eulogize the connexion of Church and State unless the Church and State are so reformed as to have neither Church nor State." And to a further remark: "We believe all churches and religions should have free action in every land beneath the sun." A gentleman in the gallery, while speaking in high terms of the discourse as a whole, questioned the speaker's conclusions with reference to Buddhism. If she meant that Christ's teaching had exercised the greatest influence on Christian society, then he granted she was right; but if she meant human society, or the human race as a whole, then he begged to differ with her, for there were from three to four hundred millions of the human race who were believers in Buddhism, while only a small minority were Christians. Then again, he believed the speaker had been wrong in her estimate of Buddhism, in representing its central doctrine as the periodical incarnation of deity; the researches of modern science had led men to doubt very much whether the whole system was not an atheism. In her reply, Mrs. Tappan said that numbers were no criterion of excellence; it had been indicated that the Christian portion of the world was in a minority, yet in human society the Christian portion represented the most advanced state of modern civilization. It had been said that human society might fairly be called that portion of the human race which was in the most advanced state of enlightenment, and that portion was represented by the Christian nations. With reference to the second point, they must be allowed to have their opinion. They did not claim infallibility, and were open to conviction; they had been asked to give their opinion, and had given it.

The following particulars, too, relative to the spread of the belief, are extracted from one of the most widely circulated of its tracts :—

"Another fact, comparatively unknown, is that an important literature of the subject exists. For many years the subject has received the attention of able and courageous men, and many valuable works have appeared in relation to it. We may name the following:—'The Two Worlds: the Natural and the Spiritual; their Intimate Connexion and Relation, illustrated by Examples and Testimonies, Ancient and Modern;' by Thomas Brevior. 'The History of the Supernatural in all Ages and Nations;' by William Howitt; 2 vols. 'Footfalls on the Boundary of Another World; with Narrative Illustrations;' by Robert Dale Owen. 'Planchette; or, the Despair of Science;' by Epes Sargent. 'Modern American Spiritualism: a Twenty Years' Record of the Communion between Earth and the World of Spirits;' by Emma Hardinge. 'The Debatable Land;' by Robert Dale Owen. 'Outlines of Ten Years' Investigation of Spiritualism;' by T. P. Barkas. 'Hints for the Evidences of Spiritualism;' by M.P. 'Spiritualism: a Narrative, with a Discussion;' by Patrick B. Alexander, M.A., Edinburgh, Author of 'Mill and Carlyle,' &c. 'Experimental Investigations of Psychic Force;' by William Crookes, F.R.S., &c. 'The Report of the London Dialectical Society's Committee on Spiritualism.' 'Concerning Spiritualism;' by Gerald Massey. 'Nature's Secrets; or, Psychometric Researches;' by William Denton. 'Glimpses of the Supernatural;' by Adin Ballou. 'Spiritual Experiences;' by Robert Cooper. 'The Night Side of Nature;' by Mrs. Crowe. 'Spiritualism: its Facts and Phases; Illustrated with Personal Experiences;' by J. H. Powell. 'The Confessions of a Truth-seeker: a Narrative of Personal Investigations into the Facts and Philosophy of Spirit-Intercourse.' 'Scepticism and Spiritualism: the Experiences of a Sceptic;' by the Authoress of 'Aurelia.' 'Is it True? Intercommunication between the Living and the (so-called) Dead;' by a Working Man. 'Plain Guide to Spiritualism;' by Uriah Clark. 'Notes and Studies on the Philosophy of Animal Magnetism and Spiritualism;' by Dr. Ashburner. 'From Matter to Spirit: the Result of Ten Years' Experience in Manifestations;' by Mrs. De Morgan. 'The Magic Staff;' by A. J. Davis. 'Spiritualism;' by Judge Edmonds and Dr. Dexter. 'Supramundane Facts in the Life of Dr. Ferguson;' edited by Dr. T. L. Nichols. 'Experimental Investigations of the Spirit-Manifestations;' by Professor Hare. 'Incidents in my Life;' by D. D. Home. 'Spirit-Drawings;' by W. M. Wilkinson. 'The Scientific Aspect of the Supernatural;' by A. R. Wallace, F.Z.S. 'The Arcana of Spiritualism;' by Hudson Tuttle. Many of these works have had a great circulation, several of the volumes of A. J. Davis, the celebrated clairvoyant, attaining from ten to forty editions respectively.

"At the present time, in addition to these volumes, the periodical literature on the subject indicates a widespread interest in it. In the United States, the *Banner of Light* (Boston), a weekly paper, has been established for upwards of a dozen years, and enjoys a very large circulation. *The Religio-Philosophical Journal* (Chicago) is also a weekly paper, established some years ago, having an extensive circulation. *Britain's Journal of Spiritual Science* is a high-class quarterly, emanating from New York. In England we have the *Spiritual Magazine, Human Nature,* the *Christian Spiritualist* (monthly), the *Spiritualist* (bi-monthly), and the *Medium* (weekly). In the following countries Spiritualism is represented by forty-seven periodicals:—France, 3; Belgium, 3; Holland, 2; Denmark, 1; Russia, 1; Germany, 1; Austria, 3; Bohemia, 1; Spain, 15; Italy, 6; Greece, 1; Egypt, 1; Turkey, 1; Brazil, 2; Uruguay, 1; La Plata, 2; Peru, 1; Chili, 1; Mexico, 1. There was also one, until lately, in the Republic of Ecuador, but it has just been suppressed through the influence of the priests, as was also the case in Sicily. In all countries Spiritualism is regarded as the bulwark of religious freedom, spiritual enlightenment, and a higher morality; and hence it is equally opposed by the upholders of priestly dominion and those who are immersed in worldly pleasures and occupations.

"In the Australian colonies and in South Africa this work has taken deep root, though in the latter colonies no periodicals exist. In Melbourne the *Harbinger of Light* is published monthly, and a powerful local association exists. The *Echo* of Dunedin, New Zealand, advocates Spiritualism, and several other papers admit of its free discussion. Spiritualism is also making steady progress in India and the colonial possessions of various European countries.

"It is a notable fact, too, that many well-known men and women, with a good repute for learning, science, and sense, have been and are among the number of those who at least accept the 'facts,' whatever they make of them. We may name as 'believers'—the late President Lincoln; W. Lloyd Garrison; the poet Longfellow; Mrs. H. B. Stowe; Bayard Taylor; the late Dr. Kane, Arctic explorer; the late Rev. J. Pierpoint; Lord Lindsay; the late Lord Dunraven; Lord Adare; C. F. Varley, F.R.S.; the late Dr. Robert Chambers; Dr. Gully; Dr. J. G. Wilkinson; Dr. Ashburner; the late Dr. Elliotson; the late Professor De Morgan; H. G. Atkinson, F.G.S.; William and Mary Howitt; Mr. and Mrs. S. C. Hall; Gerald Massey; Dr. Sexton; the late W. M. Thackeray; the late Elizabeth Barrett Browning; Serjeant Cox; W. Crookes, F.R.S.; A. R. Wallace, F.Z.S., &c. &c.

"Amongst crowned heads Spiritualism has made many conquests. The late Prince Consort was deeply interested in clairvoyance. Mr. Home, the well-known medium, has visited the palace; and several members of the Royal Family are investigators. Mr. Home has also been a visitor at the Courts of St. Petersburg, Berlin, and Paris."

MODERN MYSTICISM.

CLOSELY connected with Modern Spiritualism—indeed so closely that some of us fail to detect the frontier line that separates the two—is the creed of Swedenborgianism. It is, I am aware, only by almost straining the somewhat elastic signification of my title that I am able to include the doctrines of the New Jerusalem Church in a work on "Heterodox London," and do it under protest, and simply for the sake of illustrating the larger subject; for—I do not say it offensively—Swedenborgianism certainly stands related to Spiritualism as the species to the genus. Swedenborgianism is the specific revelation of one particular seer, Emanuel Swedenborg, whom Emerson, in his " Representative Men," sets down as the Mystic *par excellence*, and whose utterances the more orthodox of the New Jerusalem Church deem final. They acknowledge the spiritual nature of the phenomena of Modern Spiritualism, but question their character. This point I have already elaborated with some care; and all I purpose to do in the present work is to describe very briefly the typical place of worship where these doctrines were represented at the period of writing my present work, and to add one or two of the most recent utterances from its chief exponent in London; more by way of pendant to what I have said above on the generic subject of Spiritualism than as going over again ground which I feel has been sufficiently covered already.

If we accept the impersonation of Emerson, above-mentioned, the New Jerusalem Church is the shrine and focus of modern mysticism. Under such an aspect, and not without reference to the present rather prominent claims of occult science to be heard in our midst, I determined to pay a visit one Sunday morning to the handsome chapel in the Mall, Kensington, formerly occupied by Mr. Offord, and recently handed over to Dr. Bayley, who removed thither from the New Jerusalem Church, in Argyle Square, King's Cross.

The Mall Chapel is a handsome and commodious building, and its fittings rich in the extreme. A finely draped altar bore, as is the custom in Swedenborgian places of worship, an open Bible, and was adorned with an exceedingly rich frontal, with the sacred monogram bordered with lilies of exquisite workmanship. Two pulpits stood within the chancel rails flanking the altar; and in one of these a young and— will he permit me to say it?—handsome man was reading the service. The other was occupied by Dr. Bayley himself, who took a large share of the prayers too. Each was habited in surplice and bands. A font stood in front of the altar rail; while over the Holy Table were the Ten Commandments and Christ's summary of Duty to God and Man. There was nothing in any of the arrangements to show that one was not in an "orthodox" Church of somewhat rich and complete adornments. The choir was a mixed one, and rendered the musical portions of the service effectively, to the accompaniment of an excellent organ well manipulated.

The service, which was one of a varied series of set forms arranged for the different Sundays of the month, opened with a prayer, culminating, as it were, in the Lord's Prayer. The Psalms were divided into portions for the year, and each bore above it Swedenborg's "Internal Sense." Two lessons were separated by an anthem—Elvey's "Arise, shine"—and succeeded by the Commandments with Kyrie. Another prayer followed; and then, after giving notice of Good Friday and Easter Sunday services, Dr. Bayley preached a sermon as follows:—

"'Now in the morning as he returned into the city he hungered. And when he saw a fig-tree in the way, he came to it, and found nothing thereon, but leaves only; and said to it, Let no fruit grow on thee henceforward for ever. And presently the fig-tree withered away.'— Matt. xxi. 18-19.

"This day being Palm Sunday has long been regarded as the appropriate time to commemorate the remarkable entry of our Lord into Jerusalem, in royal state, as described in the chapter before us. He fulfilled the prophecy of Zechariah, given five hundred years before. Jesus entered as the king of Jerusalem in its symbolic character, the Church. That prophecy is a very remarkable one. It runs, 'Rejoice greatly, O daughter of Zion, shout, O daughter of Jerusalem, thy King cometh. He is just, and having salvation, lowly, and riding upon an ass.'—Ch. ix. 9.

"The day of humiliation and gloom was at hand, but it was to be preceded by a day of exaltation and triumph. The Lord, before He suffered, was to be hailed as king. The disciples, the common people, and the children united to salute Him as the King of Zion. They went before to salute Him, and crowded around with branches in their hands and strewed them upon the way, praising God for all the mighty works that they had seen, and saying, 'Blessed be the King, that cometh in the name of the Lord: peace in heaven, and glory in the highest.' The full significance of this impressive procession will not be perceived unless we dwell a little upon the circumstances. The prophecy designates Jesus as the King of Zion. In every other place where the king of Zion is named in Zechariah, it is accompanied by words indicating the King Eternal. In the 14th chapter, v. 16, it is said 'The nations shall go up from year to year to worship the King, the Lord, or Jehovah of hosts.' And in the following verse, 'And it shall be, that whoso will not come up of all the families of the earth unto Jerusalem to worship the King, the Lord, or Jehovah of hosts, even upon them shall be no rain.' In verse nine of the same chapter, we find, 'And the Lord (Jehovah) shall be king over all the earth: in that day there shall be one Lord (Jehovah) and His name one.'

"The Lord Jesus then, in fulfilling this prophecy, was really intimating before His suffering that He was Jehovah in the flesh. Let us notice the incidents as set forth in this chapter, which preceded His last great entry into the corrupt and therefore self-doomed city.

"He sent two disciples into a village, over against Bethphage on the Mount Olives. Because He was omniscient He told them they would find an ass and her colt tied. They were to loose them and bring them to Him. Because He was the Great Proprietor of the Universe to whom all things belong, He was the Supreme Owner of these animals, and therefore He said, 'If any man say ought unto you, ye shall say the Lord hath need of them; and straightway he will send them.'

"These things were done. The Divine Saviour entered Jerusalem seated on the colt, accompanied by its mother, surrounded by His disciples and an exultant multitude, headed by children, singing 'Hosanna to the Son of David.' The whole city, we are told, was moved. The cry arose everywhere, Who is this? The answer given by the multitude was, This is Jesus of Nazareth of Galilee. But the Redeemer showed He was more than a prophet, greater than the temple, the Lord of the Sabbath.

"He visited the temple and found it, not the house of wisdom, prayer, and peace, but of traders. The desecrated sanctuary of God was turned into a den of thieves. Acting as the Divine Judge—and with the authority and majesty which he exerted whenever needed, and which over-awed alike the faithful and the faithless, which cowed evil spirits and calmed the sea—He cast out unresistingly all that bought and sold, overthrowing the tables of the money changers, and of them that sold doves. He then restored for a time the temple to its proper use. The blind and the lame came to him, and he healed them all.

"This reform, however, was not from within but from without, and therefore was but temporary. Jesus left the city again, and withdrew to Bethany.

"Interesting as these particulars are as acquainting us with the stirring events of the closing period of our Lord's life in the world, we shall derive far deeper and more profitable lessons if we regard them in their spiritual and symbolic character. The Jewish Church was corrupt, and drawing to its close. It was not wanting in knowledge, but it had systematically perverted what it knew. They loved darkness rather than light, because their deeds were evil. They had made the commandments of God of none effect by their traditions. The priests were like whited sepulchres, outwardly fair, but inwardly full of dead men's bones and all uncleanness. They had had their day, but it was rapidly drawing to a close. They had been visited, warned, admonished, invited. And now, for the last time, in the most impressive way, they were shown their duty, in the strongest yet in the tenderest manner. How often, said the Saviour, would I have gathered thy children as a hen gathered her brood under her wings, and ye would not. 'As he approached the city, He wept over it saying, If thou hadst known in this thy day the things belonging to thy peace; but now they are hid from thine eyes.'

"Such was their day. Every nation has its day, so has every individual. Time is to-day—the day of probation. Eternity is to-morrow. Alas! how sad it is when the day is evilly spent, as it was with Jerusalem, then is the to-morrow a period of condemnation and withering away.

"We shall understand still more vividly the spiritual lesson involved in the circumstances before us, arising out of their symbolic character.

"The fig-tree is an emblem of religion bearing fruit in daily life. The fig-tree was a fruit-tree, but not so valuable as the vine or the olive. It was not cultivated in oliveyards or vineyards, but grew on the way-side. Trees in Scripture are the emblems of truths in the mind. The cultivated soul is like a cultivated garden. There are truths of various kinds, as there are trees of various kinds. The truths of love, the slightest truths of religion, are represented by the olive. Hence, it is said, in Zechariah, there are two olive trees, the symbols of love to God and love to man, before the throne. Of the gentle influences which flow from these truths, the Psalmist speaks when he says, 'Thou hast anointed my head with oil, my cup runneth over.' The vine represents truths of faith, and its wine their power to comfort and cheer the soul. Hence, when the trees, in the parable in the ninth chapter of Judges, wished the vine to become their king, the vine said, 'Shall I leave my wine, that cheers both God and man, and go to be promoted over the trees?' God is cheered when man is made wise and happy. The fig-tree was also addressed and invited to be king, but replied, 'Should I forsake my sweetness, and my good fruit, and go to be promoted over the trees?' Kind deeds in daily life are very sweet. The fruits of integrity and genuine virtue are good fruits. Though not so showy as extraordinary talent, they are the solid bases of comfort, happiness, and progress in society. Jeremiah, in chapter 24, relates a vision he had of two baskets of figs. The good figs, he shows, represent the good and obedient people; and the bad, those who disobeyed the Lord, and became a curse and a reproach, wherever they might be.

"The fig-tree, bearing fruit, is the lowest type of a Christian life. It does not represent a Christian life from love, nor a Christian life from elevated and enlightened faith, but a Christian life from command, from obedience. That state of obedience is the last which remains when religion is declining with a man; or it is the first state, when religion is advancing with a man.

"Hence our Lord in one of His parables said, 'Behold these three years I come seeking fruit on this fig-tree, and find none; cut it down, why cumbereth it the ground?' And the cultivator answered, 'Lord, let it alone this year also, till I shall dig about it and dung it, and if it bear fruit, well; if not, then after that thou shalt cut it down.' No fruit on the fig-tree signifies no virtues in ordinary life. Where these persistently fail, a man does not belong to the Lord's Church at all. Why cumbereth he the ground? When the Lord is describing the rise of a new dispensation, after the end of a former one, meant by the end of the world, He says, 'Now learn a parable of the fig-tree: When his branch is yet tender, and putteth forth leaves, ye know that summer is nigh; so likewise ye, when ye shall see all these things, know that it is near, even at the doors.'

"When the young soul opens itself to the influences of religion, and is steady to the calls of virtue and duty, it is like the opening fig-tree. The branches are tender and put forth leaves. The sentiments are delicate and the thoughts are new, but a spring-time of the soul has begun and summer is nigh.

"A fig-tree all full of leaves, and no fruit, is like a soul all profession, and no real goodness.

"On the tree of human character you not unfrequently find a large growth of conversation, but no works of charity, piety, or integrity. They say, and do not. The apostle Paul terms such sounding brass and a tinkling cymbal. They are a fair show, but no reality. They have not the energetic sap which comes from earnest love. Divine love has yearned over them, and visited them from time to time, but there is no heartfelt response. They are selfish and cold. They have leaves, but no fruit.

> And they who only leaves can show,
> Still on the stock of nature grow.

"When such are in the Church of God, they are there only from mercenary motives. They are traffickers in the temple, mere moneychangers, or dealers in holy things for gain.

"There are many visitations made by the Lord in the conscience of a man, from time to time, and at last one more powerful exploration than ever before comes, and reveals the base and unworthy principles which are active in his heart, and for the time overawes and drives them out.

"If a man's religion, however, be pharisaical, and his heart selfish, no sooner is his terror over, and the restraint passed, than he comes out carping and cynical as before. Like the Scribes and Pharisees who heeded nothing of their own impieties, but were troubled at the children's joyous praise.

"From such a soul Jesus withdraws. He leaves their city. He retires within His own grace and mercy—represented by Jesus leaving the city and going to Bethany, whose name means the House of Grace.

"Their day ends; and what happens to them on the morrow or in eternity was represented by what is said in our text.

"Now, in the morning as He returneth into the city He hungered. There is a divine hunger, as well as a human one.

"I have meat to eat, said our Lord on one occasion, that ye know not of. I stand at the door and knock. If any man will open the door I will come in to him, and sup with him, and he with me.

"The Lord's desire for the salvation of his creatures, and conjunction with them, is His divine hunger. Spiritually minded men have such hunger in an inferior degree. Blessed are they who hunger and thirst after righteousness, for they shall be filled.

"It is this divine yearning for a man's real happiness that is expressed in the spiritual application of the words, He hungered.

"His coming to see the fig-tree, represents His exploration of the soul. He wishes to find fruit. Leaves are nothing in His sight, if they are not accompanied by fruit.

"But men who are like the fig-tree before us have

no fruit. By their fruits ye shall know them, our Lord said on another occasion, and by their want of fruits ye may know them.

"The fig-tree shows fruit before leaves. There were plenty of leaves, and ought to have been fruit. In Mark it is said the time of figs was not yet. But yet is not in the original. The meaning is there were no figs. But there ought to have been.

"In the eternal world, no knowledge, no religious thoughts, remain which have not been grounded in love, and embodied in works.

"If we come there without good works, all other talents wither away. Whenever you find judgment described in the Bible, it is a decision according to works. 'Unto him that hath shall be given, and he shall have abundance; and from him that hath not shall be taken away even that which he seemeth to have.' This is the divine and eternal law. No eloquence, no talent, no thoughts even, which have not been accompanied by goodness in the heart will remain. Charity remaineth, but shams and superficialities collapse and perish.

"It was to represent this, our Lord said to the fig-tree, let no fruit grow on thee henceforth for ever. And the fig-tree presently withered away.

"It was a striking and astounding spectacle to see this miracle performed. And no doubt the collapse of empty professors, of self-seeking and sanctimonious souls, will in the eternal world be as complete as that of the fig-tree. The same truth is often taught in the Word in other forms. When the man who had not a wedding garment was addressed by the King, in the Parable of the wedding feast, he was speechless. To the Church of Ephesus which had left its first love, the Lord said, 'I will come unto thee quickly, and will remove thy candlestick out of his place, except thou repent.' The same truth is implied in these various forms of speech. What is then that truth, dear brethren, to us? It is this, Let us become genuinely true and good—trees of righteousness, as the Prophet Isaiah says, branches of the planting of Jehovah. Let us beware of being trees of leaves only.

"The Lord visits us from time to time during our probation days! let us profit by His mercies. Let us plough our mental ground, and plant, and sun our mental trees until they bloom and bear the virtues of a holy life. Let us dread having a name that we live, though we are dead. Let us fear the to-morrow of an eternity that will find us with leaves only, for then the Righteous though loving Judge must say, 'Let no fruit grow on thee henceforward for ever.'

"But, on the contrary, let us realize the divine assurance, 'Those that be planted in the house of the Lord shall flourish in the Courts of our God. They shall still bring forth fruit in old age: they shall be fat and flourishing: to show that the Lord is upright: He is my rock, and there is no unrighteousness in Him.'"

Prefixed to the Service Book is a brief summary of the faith of the New Jerusalem Church, which is worth transcribing, as the principles of this religious body are little understood, and consequently often misrepresented :—

"That there is one eternal, self-existent God, who is infinite love and wisdom—the Creator and Sustainer of all things.

"In fulness of time, and for the redemption of man, He took upon Him human nature by birth of a virgin, and became 'God manifest in the flesh' in the person of Jesus Christ, in whom 'dwelleth all the fulness of the Godhead bodily.'

"The Lord Jesus Christ is the one only true object of Christian faith and worship; and in Him is centred the Divine Trinity of Father, Son, and Holy Spirit—the Divinity of the Father being the soul of the Son, and the Humanity of the Son being the body of the Father—so hence proceeds the Holy Spirit to regenerate and save mankind.

"The Lord became our Redeemer by subduing the infernal hosts and glorifying His Humanity, without which no man could have been saved, and by which all men are capable of being saved by belief in Him; such belief implying a faithful obedience to the divine laws as the means of receiving the gifts of salvation.

"The Sacred Scripture is the Word of God, and contains within its external or literal sense an internal or spiritual sense—being thus divine.

"On the death of the natural body, man rises again in a spiritual body; and, according to the quality of his life here, lives in happiness or misery hereafter.

"Now is the time of the Lord's second coming, not in person, but in the power and great glory of His Holy Word, to establish a new and permanent church, typified in the Revelation by the holy city, New Jerusalem, descending from God out of Heaven."

Perhaps, however, a more definite exposition still of the present position of the New Jerusalem Church may be gathered from the following extracts from "A Sermon for the Times: The second coming of Christ.—Christ is coming; but how?" by Dr. Bayley.

"'*He that hath my commandments, and keepeth them, he it is that loveth me; and he that loveth me shall be loved of my Father, and I will love him, and will manifest myself to him.*'—John xiv. 21.

"Christ is coming soon. The world is old, worn out and may quickly now be expected to end. The world is disjointed, corrupted, profligate, fraudulent, turbulent, immoral, and miserable; it is time it were judged and burnt up. The end of all things is at hand. It has been mistakenly placed in 1867, and at many other past periods. But it cannot be far off now. There were to be troubles, wars, and rumours of wars, and surely we live in very troublous and changing times. We do not know where we are going, or what it all means. Such are the remarks one occasionally hears or reads, and they are of a sufficiently startling character. Sometimes this sentiment takes a very curious form. There are religious persons who will not use the Lord's Prayer or let their children use it, because it contains the petition 'Thy kingdom come,' because they think it means that this glorious fabric of the universe will be destroyed, and leave not a wreck behind, when the kingdom of God shall come.

"I read in a newspaper the other day, that it was proposed by a minister who visited a small town in a county of Tennessee, America, that there should commence a Sunday school, in which the children might be instructed in the Bible, the good people of that town never having had such a thing as a Sunday school. The deacons, however, of a leading congregation of the place called the Hardshells, a species of Baptists, I believe, said, 'If these Sunday schools go on everywhere, the world will soon be full of the knowledge of the Lord, and then the end is to come, and the world will be destroyed. We dread this awful catastrophe in our day, we must stop this Sunday school.' And the Sunday school was stopped.

"On the contrary, there are numbers who maintain that the world is growing younger. Bad as it is, they believe the world is throwing off ignorance, superstition, selfish laws and selfish habits, enmities of people against people, and nation against nation.

Vice and crime and poverty are being struggled with as they have never been encountered before, and these feel assured that the day is coming, however distant, when—

> All crimes shall cease, and ancient fraud shall fail,
> Returning justice lift aloft her scale;
> Peace o'er the world her olive wand extend,
> And whiterobed innocence from heaven descend;
> No sigh, no murmur, the wide world shall hear,
> From every face He'll* wipe off every tear.

Those of this hopeful faith sing with Tennyson, and with all the poets, those prophets of the future—

> Ring out a slowly dying cause,
> And ancient forms of party strife;
> Ring in the nobler kinds of life,
> With sweeter manners, purer laws.
>
> Ring out the want, the care, the sin,
> The faithless coldness of the times;
> Ring out, ring out my mournful rhymes,
> But ring the fuller minstrel in.
>
> Ring out false pride in place and blood,
> The civic slander and the spite;
> Ring in the love of truth and right,
> Ring in the common love of good.
>
> Ring out old shapes of foul disease,
> Ring out the narrowing lust of gold,
> Ring out the thousand wars of old,
> Ring in the thousand years of peace.
>
> Ring in the valiant man, and free,
> The larger heart, the kindlier hand;
> Ring out the darkness of the land,
> Ring in the Christ that is to be.

"Such are the hopes throbbing in the bosoms of

---

* The Lord Jesus.

multitudes of thoughtful men now respecting the 'good time coming.' And certainly they are all warranted clearly by numerous places in Holy Writ, as I trust we shall see before this discourse is ended.

"Those who thus think have noticed that in Scripture the breaking up of the world means the change of a bad old system for a better. The end of the world means the 'end of a dispensation,' the end of one great system of thought and action (see 1 Cor. x. 11; Heb. ix. 26). . . . .

"A church with genuine God-given doctrines, having a priesthood devotedly pious, with pure hearts and enlightened minds, diligent in studying God's Word, and faithful in teaching it, will make a happy world. But when the Church, instead of leading men to struggle faithfully against their sins, excuses them, palliates them, invents methods by which people may imagine they can sin and take no harm, then it is bad for the world. Multitudes take advantage of a lax and dangerous doctrine, and suffer their passions or their lusts to go unchecked during a long life, soothing themselves with the delusion that a few pious thoughts and prayers, when nature is worn out, will make all right for heaven. So, selfish frauds arise and spread and multiply, until trade is altogether corrupted, and instead of the pleasures of honest dealing between upright men, there exists on every side, suspicion, trickery, and deceitful schemes of every kind, making life painful and difficult to multitudes who pray only to do their duty sincerely, and have a modest and temperate provision for their daily wants. . . . .

"The Church is, as it were, the heart of the world. When it is healthy, pure, and strong, holding up among men those grand principles of love, faith, justice, and judgment by which the Almighty enthrones Himself in the hearts of angels and of men, the pulsations of virtue flow freely, and carry health into all the ramifications of the social body, even to the very extremes. A nation having such a church becomes a wise and understanding people (Deut. iv. 6). But where a church is feeble, or, still worse, false, neglecting its high duties of holding up before men the laws of heaven as the guides of earth—suffering the young to grow up in ignorance, and permitting superstition to hold the place of enlightenment and good sense—weakly pandering to the pride of the powerful and passing by unnoticed the debasement of the poor—winking like some great owl in a bewilderment at every ray of new light, but securing a full share of the general plunder—the body of a nation will swarm with social evils. The whole state in such a condition of society is tainted by restlessness, uncertainty, private and public immorality tempered only by low motives, chronic convulsion, and general decay, until some stormy disaster comes, like the destruction of Jerusalem and the French Revolution. The once popular forms of religion have received severe blows during the last hundred years, and will continue to receive them, until the former heavens and the former earth have passed away, with all their corruptions, hypocrisies, and mummeries; and a religion true to God and true to man, a full development of the Word of God, a new heaven and a new earth, are established in their stead.

"Heaven and earth in scripture mean a church and a state of the world growing out of it. The church is the Lord's heaven upon earth. How plainly this will appear to the observant reader respecting the formation of the church when he regards the following language of the prophet:—'And I have put my words into thy mouth, and I have covered thee in the shadow of mine hand, that I may plant the heavens, and lay the foundations of the earth, and say unto Zion, thou art my people' (Isa. li. 16). No one could surely suppose that in consequence of the Lord putting His words into man's mouth, the starry heavens were planted, or the rocky foundations of the land were laid. The destruction of the church is equally represented as the reduction to chaos of HEAVEN AND EARTH by Jeremiah. 'For my people is foolish, they have not known me: they are sottish children, and they have none understanding: they are wise to do evil, but to do good they have no knowledge. I beheld the earth, and lo it was without form and void; and the heavens, and they had no light' (iv. 22-23). Here the vices and follies of the people are declared to have had the result of making the earth without form and void, and the heavens so that they had no light. But every intelligent reader will see that the language is only to be understood in a moral and spiritual sense. It refers to the church, its confusion, and the absence of spiritual light in it, owing to human traditions and human vices making the commandments of God of none effect. . . . .

"Let us now look at another class of passages— passages full of hope and consolation, but owing to the darkness which had been induced in the mind by the erroneous view respecting the end of the world, very much overlooked. These all speak of the latter days, as being a time of restoration, of universal light, love, purity, and peace, all flowing from a true knowledge of God in Christ, the Father in the Son. But how could such passages ever be fulfilled if the universe were to be burnt and pass away, leaving not a wreck behind?

"In Isaiah we read, and it is repeated in Micah, chap. iv., 'And it shall come to pass in the last days, that the mountain of the Lord's house shall be established in the top of the mountains, and shall be exalted above the hills, and all nations shall flow unto it. And many people shall go and say, Come ye, and let us go up to the mountain of the Lord, to the house of the God of Jacob: and He will teach us of His ways, and we will walk in His paths: for out of Zion shall go forth the law, and the Word of the Lord from

Jerusalem. And He shall judge among the nations, and shall rebuke many people; and they shall beat their swords into ploughshares, and their spears into pruning-hooks: nation shall not lift up sword against nation, neither shall they learn war any more. O house of Jacob, come ye, and let us walk in the light of the Lord!' (ii. 2-5). . . . .

"In the corruptions of the dark ages every condition and every occupation of life has been defiled and disfigured by selfishness—

> The trail of the serpent is over them all.

"Above all, the Lord is coming to sanctify the central work of domestic life, and imbue with His Spirit of Love and Wisdom the sacred ties of marriage. True religion and marriage go hand in hand together. Where marriage is lightly esteemed, religion is weak or worthless. When marriage is regarded as the focus of heaven's choicest blessings, and its best representative on earth, the nursery for angels, the centre, the safeguard, and jewel of human society, to be prepared for with sacred purity and guarded with holiest reverence, then will the world be purified in its sources of influence, and happiness, rich, deep, and pure, will irradiate every part. Government has been the trade of capricious and despicable tyrants, instead of the ennobling ministry of true kings of men: commerce, which is the friendly intercourse of mutual blessings, became the self-seeking gamble of men only anxious for sordid, and often fraudulent, gain. Christ does not yet reign at the dockyards; but He is coming, and, oh! what a clear-out of trickeries and treacheries must follow!

"Work has been despised and degraded. Labour, which is the use of man's God-given faculties, and which diffuses over the earth the myriad beauties and blessings which sustain, enrich, and decorate the world, has been deemed a curse. The rich and noble have been taught to glory in the dignity of having nothing to do. In the 'good time coming' it will not be so. Each man will be trained to rejoice in performing the work which God has prepared him to accomplish, and to do it in the best manner, as his best way of serving Him who is the Infinite Worker, and all whose works are done in truth. Our blessed Redeemer condescended to work as a carpenter, amongst other reasons to consecrate all labour by His example, and to teach all that happiness is to be sought not in selfish sloth, but in loving usefulness. O! let the laws and the spirit of our blessed Redeemer come into our workshops; let every youth who comes there come with a well-taught mind, trained by a previous sound education to delight in work—enough for comfort, enough for health, and enough for progress, but not debased by crushing toil, or withering, unhealthy conditions, and the Christian workman shall be Christ's man indeed. The hearts of the multitudes, which have been driven away from the religion of talk, of profession and of so-called FAITH ONLY, will come back to the Christ of loving-kindness. The Lord Jesus is coming again, and when He has come into the workshops, as the spirit of justice and love, there will be no oppression and no strikes; but mutual ministry among the employers and the employed will manifest that the Lord in very deed is Emanuel, GOD WITH US. Then will the promise of the latter-day glory be fulfilled—'O house of Jacob, come ye, let us WALK in the light of the Lord' (Isa. ii. 5). 'The nations of them that are saved SHALL WALK in the light of the holy city, and the kings of the earth do bring their glory and honour into it' (Rev. xxi. 24). . . . .

"There is no death to him who has conquered sin. His removal from earth is a departure to a higher life and a more perfect home. He who keepeth my saying, said the Redeemer, shall never see death (John viii. 51). Whosoever liveth and believeth in Me SHALL NEVER DIE (John xi. 26). The future life is a higher form of this, as the blossom is higher than the leaf, the butterfly than the caterpillar. He who is trained for heaven has already heaven in himself, already is in company with angels, and already is prepared for the golden sceptre of the messenger of heaven. He goes to heaven because heaven has come to him.

"Away, then, with those carnal dreams of a great parade in the outward sky. No outward trumpeters are wanted to make a clamour in the clouds. What we need is the still small voice of the Saviour God within; that comes like a dew from heaven to refresh and fertilize the wilderness of unregenerate souls, and make them blossom like the rose. 'The kingdom of God cometh not with observation' (outward show). Oh, when shall we learn the depth of that wonderful declaration—'Neither shall they say, Lo here! or, lo there! for the kingdom of God is within you' (Luke xvii. 20-21). Gaze not among the outward clouds expecting a coming of the Lord Jesus there. When you love Him, as our text says, He will manifest Himself to you. He is in all the wise arrangements of creation, but you will never see or feel Him there until you open your heart to receive Him as Christ in you the Hope of Glory (Col. i. 27).

"Let the Spirit of the Lord Jesus enter into all you do and say, let Him go forth with you into your farm, your counting-house, your warehouse, your manufactory, your workshop, your council-chamber, and your home, filling you with His Divine Love and Wisdom, and you will soon find the earth brighter about you.

"God's world is a glorious world, it only needs you to enter into God's idea of it. Be like-minded with angels, and you will soon find this world like heaven. You wish to enter heaven? Enter then. Heaven is here also when you let it enter you. There is nothing, my beloved brother and sister, wanting to the Lord's Second Coming, with all its splendour and happiness, but your heartfelt embrace of His Divine Will in all things. Come into His kingdom. 'The Spirit and the bride say, Come. And let him that heareth say, Come. And let him that is athirst come. And whosoever will, let him take of the water of life freely. Even so, come, Lord Jesus.'"

MR. BRADLAUGH *VERSUS* GOD.

The farther I pursue my subject, the more convinced do I become how unadvisable it is to act the part of ecclesiastical gentlemen of England and sit at home at ease, if we would rightly estimate the present state of religious thought in our midst. I am, of course, in my individual capacity, only taking London as typical of England; and I can assure my readers that the fertility and copiousness of my subject surprised, almost alarmed, me, though I had undergone some previous experiences in this way, and was prepared to find diversity where I had at first only expected uniformity. It is only thus, practically, by plunging beneath the surface, that one gets to realize the subdivisions of what we too often vaguely speak of as Free Thought or Infidelity, as if it were only one and not a hundred things.

Just, however, as I had on a previous occasion discovered that there were Plymouth Brethren and Plymouth Brethren—as I had found out that Judaism had its two schools of thought divided almost as strongly as Catholics and Protestants, so did I find, at an early stage of my present inquiry, that there were these three marked divisions to be realized, admitting in their turn, of copious subdivision: (1) descending, so to say, gradually from orthodoxy, Unitarianism in its manifold phases, differing from the Established Faith etymologically by the elimination of one dogma, but more generally by the excision of any Test, Creed, or Articles. (2) Theism, under varied aspects, from Christian Theism to Pure Theism; where, to speak again roughly, the whole idea of Mediator and much of Revelation was abandoned. And (3) Atheism, with its more advanced development of dogmatic Anti-Theism.

It would have been, of course, greatly to be desired that one should treat these matters in some definite serial order; but the detached mode of publication adopted for these papers precluded the possibility of that, while, at the same time, the work never assumed the proportions of a philosophical inquiry, but was content to aim at giving a series of pictures, more or less vivid, of religious life in London.

It will be inevitable that, wherever our subject is Atheism, especially in its more advanced phases, that picture shall resolve itself into a portrait of Mr. Bradlaugh, the drapings and adjuncts varying, but the man remaining the same. The influence of this one man in his department is simply prodigious, as any one can prove for himself who will only take the trouble to do what I have done; that is, not sit at home and read reports at second-hand, but, Sunday after Sunday, pass by the " customary hassock," as

Thomas Hood says, and follow Mr. Bradlaugh at the Hall of Science, or wherever else he may be found. Other forms of Free Thought have often many representatives; but at this most advanced outpost Mr. Bradlaugh is almost in sole command. There are one or two prominent men, whose names we shall have to mention by-and-bye, associated with him; but, as I have said, his influence is so pre-eminent that it is not only allowable but almost inevitable our picture-painting shall for awhile give place to portraiture.

I thought I could not do better, in laying down my first broad outlines of this portion of my subject, than to visit the Hall of Science, Old Street, St. Luke's, on a Sunday evening when Mr. Bradlaugh was to take as his subject the thoroughly distinctive one of the "Existence of God." We should, at all events, be sure to get at the root of the matter thus. The lecture was to take the special form of a reply to Francis E. Abbott, of the *Index*; but to me it was interesting only on its own merits; and accordingly I went to the Hall of Science, which is near the Aldersgate Street station of the Metropolitan Railway, about a quarter to seven on the Sunday evening in question. The lecture was to commence at seven.

Though I was a full quarter of an hour before time then, and fortified, moreover, by Mr. Bradlaugh's card to pass myself and friend to the reserved seats, I found that the vast area and galleries of the Hall of

Science were even then full, and I had great difficulty in struggling to a front seat, which soon ceased to be a front seat, for busy officials had to range forms in front again, thus destroying my fond hopes that I should have fair play for my somewhat extended legs. I was amazed, not only at the continuous stream of people which flowed into this building, paying, let us remember, their twopence and fourpence each, but also at their character. The large majority, perhaps, were of the tradesman and artisan class; but close by me, in the reserved seats, I had men-of-war's men in their naval costume, and real labourers and navvies in their working clothes; and I could not help asking myself the question, How is it Mr. Bradlaugh can get these people to pay fourpence and listen to an abstruse subject, while we cannot "compel them to come in?" Surely that problem is legitimately open to debate.

By the time the colossal head and shoulders of Mr. Bradlaugh—for he is a son of Anak—were seen struggling among the crowd, every inch of room for sitting or standing was occupied; and he had considerable difficulty in piloting his two daughters on to the lofty platform, where a few men were already seated on either side of his lecturing table. The applause was long and loud as he took his accustomed place on the left of the chairman; and when this subsided, that functionary passed at once to the business of the evening. First of all he gave notice that Mr.

Bradlaugh would open the new Democratic Club in that Hall on the following Saturday; that on a subsequent Tuesday he would expatiate on the Queen's Speech and the Premier's intentions; and finally—much to my delectation—that he would, previously to his lecture that evening, perform the ceremony of Naming an Infant. Then Mr. Bradlaugh rose—a tall, commanding figure, with a clean shaven face, and hair brushed back from his forehead; a quick, bright eye, and that massive appearance of the jaw which is so often seen in the habitual speaker. He first of all asked us if we who were sitting down would mind taking our hats off; those who were forced to stand could do as they found most convenient. Next he announced his intention of devoting the Sunday evenings of April to an examination of the volume issued by the Christian Evidence Society entitled "Historical Illustrations of the Old Testament," his general subject resolving itself into the inquiry, "Is the Bible true?" Then he stated that he had acceded to the wish of the parents that he should publicly name their child. He took the little crooning thing in his brawny arms, and said he did this, not in mockery, not in imitation of any religious bodies, but simply as a matter of public utility. The child must be known hereafter by a distinctive name; and he took it to be desirable that the name should be thus publicly bestowed. He here pronounced the name "Elizabeth," and, in handing the child back to its mother, kissing it as he did so, he took occasion to say that she at all events, could not consider his ministrations demoralizing since she entrusted her daughter thus to him. He did not ask the congregation to undertake a sponsorship, but he did ask them to bear witness to the ceremony, and hoped the child in after years would never have cause to regret her association with him.

He then went on to say that he had never, as an Atheist, concealed his views on the subject of the lecture. He stated them, not in bravado, but because he believed there was utility in his doing so. Some people said to him it was very well to criticise a book or a church, but why, they asked, should he unsettle men's minds? Why should we solve a problem in arithmetic? Why should we measure the area of an estate, or the distance between two towns? Why should we ascertain any truth at all? "Answer me that," he said, "and I will answer your question." Such was his very characteristic exordium.

Every truth, he proceeded, was useful, in its recognition and in its affirmation. There was no limit to human thought, and there should be no limit to the expression of those thoughts except honesty in their utterance. "Suppose that my theory were as false as I believe it to be true," he said, "it would be well that I should speak it out still. Unsettle men's minds! Surely that is a sign of weakness. Am I so strong that I can undo the knot which a million-clergy power has been so long tying? Either that must be intended as a great compliment to me, or must be a confession of weakness. I will presume it is a compliment to myself."

Then again others said, they could understand the demolition of the special God of the Koran or of the Buddhists, of the Persians or of the Hebrews; but the pure Theist said, What have you to say to us? It was to them he addressed himself on the present occasion. He would take Mr. Abbott and Professor F. W. Newman as his texts. (Alas! how impossible I had once thought it that anybody should take up his parable from the author of "Phases of Faith," as erring on the side of excess. Verily we live and learn in these progressive days!) Mr. Abbott spoke of a "God of Science;" and he generally found that every Theist assumed four-fifths of his positions, and turned a somersault over the other fifth. He meant a mental somersault, which differed from physical ones in this way, that in the latter you usually came to the ground, but in the former you often never came to earth at all, but remained in the clouds. He read a long passage from Mr. Abbott's article in the *Index* in support of this assertion; and I took occasion to look round and notice the gaze of that vast audience riveted on the lecturer. Truly, for good or ill, that man sways a vast power!

Those who owned this God of Science attributed to Him a magnificently successful plan. "I attribute just the reverse," said Mr. Bradlaugh. "If I could conceive an Infinite Mind, which I cannot," he proceeded, "I should say that the results are inadequate. The Infinite Mind contrived the teeth of the jack to eat minnows; but the same Infinite Mind devised the swiftness for the minnow to get out of the way of the jack. I shall be told it is blasphemy to say this; but is not the blasphemy rather on the other side? The vessel long owing puts into the port of New York, having encountered icebergs 1800 miles from land. Now, on the doctrine of Infinite Mind, were those icebergs planned to destroy the ship, which they did not, or only to frighten the people on board, which they did? Had He arranged those icebergs an eternity ago—and several eternities before that—or were they an effect on which He had not calculated?"

Then, again, there was Vesuvius. Was it a part of the plan that there should be no eruption for many years, and that the village of Torre del Greco should be built on the slopes; and then that the Creator, who had not worried the people with lava since the time when Pompeii was destroyed, should suddenly send down the fiery stream and destroy the villagers in the dead of night? This argument of the Universal Mind, he urged, proved too much. How could it be brought to bear on the hurricane and the earthquake? Creation to the Atheist was only change of conditions. If something came where nothing was before, who was there to create it? He protested against this question being regarded as a mere trick of words. It was meant to make those to whom he put it think.

Then he passed on to Professor Newman. This gentleman found Mr. Abbott's God too cold for him, and so wrote a letter to the *Index* called "The Two Theisms." A third might be added—namely, the Deism of the eighteenth century; but the two specially alluded to were (1) the Greek Theism, represented by Aristotle, which regarded God as the source of General Law, and might resolve him into a force—this was Mr. Abbott's doctrine, objected to by Professor Newman; and (2) Hebrew Theism, acknowledging God *plus* Providence. This latter Theism recognised the instinct of individual prayer. Said Mr. Bradlaugh, in his own positive way, "I deny it." Modern Science had proved that habits might be created and transmitted; and these, he urged, were often mistaken for instincts. He would examine the Prayer-Doctrine, not of the Bible or the Koran, but speaking as Atheist to Theist. Prayer was simply the appeal of the weak and ignorant for a result which they did not understand how it could be accomplished by other means. The "Greek Legions" (*sic*) prayed to Mars for success in battle. Tell me the difference, he said, between this and saying, "Our Father which art in Heaven, Give us this day our daily bread." If the sword arm of Horatius failed, Mars did not intervene to save. So, while we repeated " Our Father," men starved in Lancashire, if the work failed.

Sir John Lubbock, he went on to say, told us, in a book which he (Mr. Bradlaugh) had examined in that Hall, of certain tribes whose language contained no word representing prayer. They had no conception of it. " I," he said, " am the proof that it is not instinctive. I don't pray. Twenty-five or twenty-six years ago," he continued—and here Cleon's brazen voice sank to tones of the very tenderest pathos—" I as a young man *did* try to pray. I was suffering agony : and I prayed that some sign might be given me of my prayer being heard. None came ; and I doubted. I don't doubt now. I'm not a sceptic now. I know, and I disbelieve now ; mine is not a mind of doubt."

Then he would go into the reason of Prayer. " Why do you pray ?" he kept asking. If there were a Providential plan, you could not change the plan. If your prayer were part of the plan, it was useless to pray. But why did people pray ? To get something done for them ? On the supposition of the plan, all that was necessary would be done. It was an impeachment of the plan to try to modify it by prayer. The greater number of people, he thought, prayed without thinking why they prayed; but only fancy some twelve hundred millions of people in the world all praying for different things !

Multiply that by a few billions of worlds in the universe, and the idea became monstrous. The Christian Theist, in addition to this, believed in special salvation, and that the more he called, the quicker he should get it. Let them be sure, however, that, whether their God existed or not, the more they worked and the less they prayed, the safer they would be.

His own position was that of an Atheist. To him the word God represented nothing. He did not know what it meant. He did not know where, even in thought, to put God. Even if he could conceive Him, which he could not, the God so conceived could not be immutable. He was told of Providence, and he remarked how a high tide in the river destroyed the goods of a poor family which would have been saved if they had been rich enough to live one storey higher in the house. Or he thought of famine devastating large tracts of country. Now there should be no evil like this. Either God wanted to prevent such evil and couldn't, or else He deliberately planned it. "I am an Atheist," he added, in a bold apostrophe. "He must have planned *me!*" The vast assembly recognised the point, and applauded to the echo. "I am told this is immoral," he proceeded. "Nothing that is true is immoral. Show me that my doctrine is false, and you will compel me to abandon it. I do not say I shall be ready to concede the falsity. Prove me the falsity and I *must* abandon the position."

But it was asked, What would there be to hold men to the truth if you made them Atheists? What held them now? King William announced the slaughter of ten thousand men, and thanked God! "Go out," he added, "into the lanes around this Hall. The people don't believe in me. They have the name of God often enough on their lips. What good does it do them?

"What guide have I? If I had none, it would not make your Churches and Prayers true. It would only be the increase of my weakness, not of your strength. So far I haven't touched your Book. If you dare to put your Bible morality in evidence—do it."

It had been said that nothing had come of all this war of atheism against belief; but something had come. Freedom of thought had come. There was less cant—a good deal still, but less than formerly. It had come that men could not be burnt now for their opinions. Racks and *autos-da-fé* had disappeared. Education could not be shut out. Bruno and Shelley and Voltaire and Paine had done something; "though, remember," he said in conclusion, "we have only been able to talk for the last two hundred years. You have had thousands of years to deaden men's brains in." And so he sat down amid a perfect storm of applause.

A reply was invited, and it was stipulated by Mr. Bradlaugh that the same indulgence should be extended to opponents as to himself. They were strong and could afford to be generous. If they did not encourage discussion, they would get into the way of the "pulpit people."

One Mr. Jenkins, a feeble supporter of Christianity, passed most disadvantageously to the place Mr. Bradlaugh had occupied. He submitted that Sir John Lubbock's prayerless people were on a level with the brute beasts, and wound up a rambling oration by a verbal struggle with Mr. Bradlaugh, in which he had decidedly the worst. It was another case—of which I have seen only too many—where Christianity had to pray to be saved from its friends. I can quite understand that more harm would be done by Mr. Jenkins's weak defence than Mr. Bradlaugh's bold defiance; and I was really glad when Mr. Jenkins obeyed the forcible injunction of somebody in the audience to "shut up," though Mr. Bradlaugh and the Chairman protested strongly against the interruption. They were wise enough in their generation to see that Mr. Jenkins was playing into their hand.

Mr. Williams, who followed on the theistic side, was better; but still I cannot help thinking the Christian Evidence Society must be holding some stronger men in reserve. Why should not some of their *very* strongest dignitaries come down to the

Hall of Science and justify their title of "Doctors" —teachers—" of divinity?" Mr. Williams judiciously praised Mr. Bradlaugh's oration, which was too profound to be dealt with off-hand, and should be read and studied. Mr. Bradlaugh, however, was not to be thrown off his guard even by buttered sugar, and combated Mr. Williams's positions so severely that the method became dialectical or catechetical on a sudden. People tired of it then. They had come to " hear Bradlaugh," not to listen to discussion: but still Mr. Williams stood his ground manfully, and gained applause, when he wound up by saying that Atheism rested on a flimsy foundation, and urged his audience " in the name of common sense" to " prove all things.".

After a brief reply by Mr. Bradlaugh the meeting closed, and most of us went. Many remained, however, and broke up into little knots for discussion. There was a large sale in the room for Paine's works, for the *National Reformer* of the week, and notably for the following small pamphlet by Mr. Bradlaugh himself, " Is there a God ?" which sums up several of the arguments utilized on the occasion in question :—

"Is there a God?"

" Some of those who have heard me venture to examine the question of the existence of Deity *viva voce*, have desired to have my reasons for holding the Atheistic position briefly stated, and while I do not pretend to exhaust the subject in these few pages, I trust to say enough to provoke thought and inquiry. I do not say, 'There is no God,' and the scarcely polite rejoinder of those who quote the Psalmist cannot therefore be applied with justice towards myself. I have never yet heard living man give me a clear, coherent definition of the word 'God,' and I have never read any definition from either dead or living man expressing a definite and comprehensible idea of Deity. In fact, it has always appeared to me that men use that word rather to hide their ignorance than to express their knowledge.* Climatic conditions often, and diversity of human race always, govern and modify the meaning conveyed by the word. By 'God' one nation or sect expresses love—another, vengeance—another, good—another, wisdom—another, fire—another, water—another, air—another, earth—and some even confound their notion of Deity with that of devil. Elihu Palmer well observes: 'The Christian world worships three infinite Gods, and one omniscient devil.' I do not deny 'God,' because that word conveys to me no idea, and I cannot deny that which presents to me no distinct affirmation, and of which the would-be affirmer has no conception. I cannot war with a nonentity. If, however, God is affirmed to represent an existence which is distinct

---

* In Sir William Hamilton's Essay on Cousin, I find a note quoting M. Piesse on Kant, *in which the word God stands as the equivalent for a phase of the unknowable.*

from the existence of which I am a mode, and which it is alleged is not the *noumenon*, of which the word 'I' represents only a speciality of *phenomena*, then I deny 'God,' and affirm that it is impossible 'God' can be. That is, I affirm that there is one existence, and deny that there can be more than one. Atheists are sometimes content to say to their opponents, your 'proofs' are no proofs, your 'evidences' are failures, you do not, and cannot prove the existence of Deity. This ground may be safe, but the conduct of its occupier is not daring. The swordsman who always guarded and parried, but never ventured cut or thrust, might himself escape unwounded, but he would thus make but little progress towards victory over his opponent.

"It is well to show that the position of your antagonist is weak, but it is better to prove that you are strong.

"In a paper as limited as the present, it is necessary to be brief both in answer to opponents, and in the statement of my own opinions. This is rather intended as the challenging speech of a debate, not as a complete essay on the existence of Deity.

"There are two modes in which Theists endeavour to prove the existence of God, and each of these modes is in its turn denounced by Theistic writers—1st, the *à priori*; 2nd, the *à posteriori*. Of the former, Pearson, in his 'Prize Essay on Infidelity,' says: 'The *à priori* mode of reasoning is the ex-

clusive idol of many of the German logicians. . . . .
But in their hands this kind of reasoning has completely failed. It conducts the mind to no firm resting-place; it bewilders instead of elucidating our notions of God, of man, and the universe. It gives us no divine personal existence, and leaves us floating in a region of mere vague abstractions. Such reasonings are either altogether vain, or are not really what they profess to be. In our country the name of Dr. Clarke is chiefly associated with the *à priori* argument. . . . . Clarke himself found it necessary to stoop to the argument *à posteriori*, and thereby acknowledged the fallacy of attempting to reason exclusively *à priori*. . . . . The fate of Dr. Clarke's pretended demonstration, and the result, in so far as theology is concerned, of the transcendental reasoning of the continental philosophers, show the futility of attempting to rise up to the height of the great argument of the existence of God by the *à priori* method alone.'

"Of the latter, William Gillespie, in his 'Treatise on the Necessary Existence of Deity,' writes, that it 'can never make it appear that infinity belongs in any way to God.' It 'can only entitle us to infer the existence of a being of finite extension, for, by what rule in philosophy can we deduce from the existence of an object finite in extent (and nothing is plainer than that the marks of design which we can discover must be finite in their extent) the existence of a cause of infinity of extension? What, then, becomes of the omnipresence of the Deity, according to those who are content to rest satisfied from the reasoning of experience? . . . . It will be vain to talk of the Deity being present by his energy, although he may not be present by his substance, to the whole universe. For 'tis natural to ask not so much how it is proved that God is virtually present, though not substantially present, in every part of nature, as what can be meant by being everywhere present by mere energy?' This 'reasoning can no more make out that the Deity is omnipresent by his virtue, than that he is omnipresent as to his substance. . . . . And from the inaptitude of the reasoning under consideration to show that immensity, or omnipresence, belongs to God, it will be found to follow, directly and immediately, that his wisdom and power cannot be shown to be more than finite, and that he can never be proved to be a free agent. . . . . Omnipresence (let it be only by energy) is absolutely necessary in a being of infinity of wisdom. And therefore, "the design argument" is unable to evince that the Deity is in possession of this attribute. It likewise plainly follows, from the inaptitude of this argument to show that God is omnipresent, that thereby we cannot prove infinity of power to belong to him. For if the argument cannot make out that the being it discovers is everywhere present, how can it ever make out that He is everywhere powerful? By careful reflection, too, we may perceive that omnipotence of another kind than power which can exert itself in all places, requires the existence of immensity.' The design argument 'can never evince that God is a free agent. . . . . If we cannot prove the immensity or omnipresence of the Deity, we can for that reason never show that he is omniscient, that he is omnipotent, that he is entirely free. . . . . If the Deity cannot be proved to be of infinity in any given respect, it would be nothing less than absurd to suppose that he could be proved to be of infinity in any other respect.' It 'can do no more than prove that at the commencement of the phenomena which pass under its review, there existed a cause exactly sufficient to make the effects begin to be. That this cause existed from eternity, the reasonings from experience by no means show. Nay, for aught they make known, the designer himself may not have existed long before those marks of design which betoken his workmanship.' This reasoning 'cannot prove that the God whom it reveals has existed from all eternity, therefore, for anything it intimates, God may at some time cease to be, and the workmanship may have an existence when the workman hath fallen into annihilation. . . Such reasonings can never assure us of the unity of the Deity.' 'Whether there be one God or not, the argument from experience doth by no means make clear. It discovers marks of design in the phenomena of nature, and infers the existence of at least one intelligent substance sufficient to produce them. Further, however, it advances not our knowledge. Whether the cause of the phenomena be one God or many Gods, it pretends not to determine past all doubt. . . . . But did this designer create the matter in which the design appeared? Of this the argument cannot convince us, for it does no more than infer a designing cause from certain appearances, in the same way as we would infer from finding some well-contrived machine in a desert, that a human being had left it there. . . . . Now, because this reasoning cannot convince us of such a creation, it cannot convince us there is not a plurality of deities, or of the causes of things. . . . . If we cannot prove the eternity of God, it is not possible we can prove the unity of God. To say that, for anything we know to the contrary, he may have existed from all eternity, being much the same as saying that, for anything we know to the contrary, there may be another God or many Gods beside.' Sir W. Hamilton considered that the only valid arguments for the existence of a God, and for the immortality of the human soul, rest on the ground of man's moral nature.

"Dr. Lyman Beecher issued, some few years since, a series of lectures on Atheism, without merit or fairness, and which are here only alluded to as fairly illustrating a certain class of orthodox opposition. His statements of Atheistic opinions are monstrous perversions, and his answers are directed against the straw man built together by himself. The doctrine of 'almighty chance,' which Dr. Beecher attacks, is one which I never heard an educated Atheist teach, and the misrepresentation of Free-thought objects is so obvious, that it can only be effectual with those who have never freed themselves from the trammels which habit and fashion-faith bound upon them in their infancy, and which have strengthened with their growth. The Rev. J. Orr, in his 'Treatise on Theism,' says, 'All inquiry about chance is, however, impertinent in the present day. The idea is an infantine one, possible of entertainment only in the initial state of human knowledge. Chance is *not* the position relied upon by modern Atheism. And when, therefore, the Theist expends the artillery of his argument upon this broken-down and obsolete notion, he is intermeddling with the dead, and after accomplishing the destruction of the venerable fallacy, the modern Atheist will likely ask him to come down to the nineteenth century, and meet him there.'

"The only attempt at argument in Dr. Beecher's book is founded on the assumption—1st, That there is an existence called matter. 2nd, That there are certain effects perceivable which cannot result from matter. 3rd, That therefore there is a God the cause for these effects. Where are there any Materialists who accept Dr. Beecher's limitation of matter? It is a word I do not use myself.

"On the question of evil, Coleridge, in his 'Aids to Reflection,' says:—'1st, That evil must have had a beginning, since otherwise it must either be God, or a co-eternal and co-equal rival with God. 2nd, That it could not originate in God; for if so, it would at once be evil and not evil, or God would be at once God—that is, infinite goodness—and not God.' If God be infinite goodness, can evil exist at all? It is necessary above all that we should understand the meaning of each word we use. Some men talk as if their words were intended rather to conceal than to express their ideas. So far as this essay is concerned, I will endeavour to avoid this difficulty by explicitly defining each special word I use. Dugald Stewart, indeed, says, 'That there are many words used in philosophical discourse which do not admit of logical definition, is abundantly manifest. This is the case with all those words that signify things uncompounded, and consequently unsusceptible of analysis—a proposition, one should think, almost self-evident; and yet it is surprising how very generally it has been overlooked by philosophers.'

"The advantages, however, accruing from frequent definitions are very great; at the least they serve to explain what was meant by the persons using the word, whereas sometimes two men confuse each word by using words to which each attaches an opposite or a dissimilar value.

"Men will talk of 'First Cause,' and 'Intelligent

First Cause.' Do they know what they mean? I confess I do not, and from the manner in which they use the words, the most charitable conclusion is that they use them because others have done so, and for no worse or better reason. They talk of the 'Beauties of Creation,' and 'Works of the Great Creator.' If by creation is meant the origin of existence, then each utterance of the phrase is an absurdity. The human mind is utterly incapable of construing it in thought as possible that the complement of existence has either been increased or diminished. Man can neither conceive nothing becoming something, or something becoming nothing.

"DEFINITIONS.—1, By existence, or substance, I mean that which is in itself and is conceived *per se*— that is, the conception of which does not require the conception of anything else as antecedent to it. Whenever I use the words universe or matter, I use them in the same sense as representing the totality of existence. Existence can only be known in its modes, and these by their attributes. 2, By attribute, I understand that by which I cognize any mode of existence. Hardness, brightness, colour, life, form, &c., are attributes of conditioned existence. 3, By mode, I understand each cognized condition or accident of existence. 4, By eternity, I mean indefinite duration; that is, duration which is to me illimitable. 5, By infinity, I mean indefinite extension. The axioms, so far as I shall give them, are in the precise language of Spinoza. '1, Everything which is, is in itself, or in some other thing. 2, That which cannot be conceived through another *per aliud*, must be conceived *per se*. 3, From a given determinate cause, the effect necessarily follows; and *vice versâ*, if no determinate cause be given, no effect can follow. 4, The knowledge of an effect depends on a knowledge of the cause, and includes it. 5, Things that have nothing in common with each other, cannot be understood by means of each other—that is, the conception of one does not involve the conception of the other.'

" PROPOSITIONS.—Existence is prior to its modes. This follows from definitions 1 and 3, because modes of existence are conceived relatively and in dependence on existence, which is absolutely precedent in such conception. Existences having different attributes have nothing in common with each other. This is founded on definition 1. Existences having nothing in common with each other, cannot be the cause of, or affect one another. If they have nothing in common, they cannot be conceived by means of each other (*per* axiom 5), and they cannot be conceived as relating to each other, but must be conceived *per se* (*per* definition 1); and as (*per* axiom 4) the knowledge of an effect depends on the knowledge of the cause and includes it, it is impossible to conceive any existence as an effect, so long as you cannot conceive it in relation to any other existence. By 'cause' in the absolute, I mean 'existence.' In its popular or relative sense, I use 'cause' as an effect of some precedent causative influence, itself the cause of some consequent effect, as the means towards an end, in the accomplishment of which end it completes itself.

"What fact is there so certain that I may base all my reasonings upon it? My existence is this primary fact—this, to me, indubitable certainty. I am. This logic can neither prove nor disprove. The very nature of proof is to make a proposition more clear to the mind than it was before, and no amount of evidence can increase my conviction of the certainty of my own existence. I do not affirm that I am in existence, but I affirm that there is existence. This existence is either eternal, that is, unlimited in duration, that is, indefinite in duration; or else it had a beginning, that is, it has been created. If created, then such creation must be by some existence the same as itself, or by some existence differing from itself. But it cannot have been created by any existence the same as itself, because to imagine such, would be to conceive no more than a continuance of the same existence—there would be no discontinuity. 'But,' says S. T. Coleridge, 'where there is no discontinuity, there can be no origination.' And it cannot have been created by any existence differing from itself, because things which have nothing in common with one another, cannot be the cause of, or affect one another. Therefore this existence has not been created, that is, its duration is indefinite—that is, you cannot conceive a beginning—that is, it is eternal. This eternal existence is either infinite in extent, that is, is unlimited in extent, or it is finite, that is, limited. If limited, it must be limited by an existence the same as itself, or by an existence differing from itself. But the same arguments which applied to a limitation of duration, also apply to a limitation of extension. Therefore, this existence is unlimited in extent; that is, is infinite and eternal—that is, there is only one existence. It is at this point that Atheism separates from Pantheism. Pantheism demonstrates one existence, but affirms for it infinite attributes. Atheism denies that attributes can be infinite. Attributes are but the distinguishing characteristics of modes, and how can that be infinite which is only the quality of finity? Men do not talk of infinite hardness or of infinite softness; yet they talk of infinite intelligence. Intelligence is not an existence, and the word is without value unless it strictly comprehend, and is included in, that which is intelligent. The hardness of the diamond, the brilliancy of the burnished steel, have no existence apart from the diamond or the steel. I, in fact, affirm that there is only one existence, and that all we take cognizance of is mode, or attribute of mode, of that existence.

"I have carefully abstained from using the words 'matter' and 'spirit.' Dr. Priestley says:—'It has generally been supposed that there are *two distinct kinds of substance* in human nature, and they have been distinguished by the terms *matter*, and *spirit* or *mind*. The former of these has been said to be possessed of the property of *extension*—viz., of length, breadth, and thickness, and also of *solidity* or impenetrability, and consequently of a *vis inertiæ*; but it is said to be naturally destitute of all other powers whatever. The latter has of late been defined to be a substance entirely destitute of all extension, or relation to space, so as to have no property in common with matter; and therefore to be properly *immaterial*, but to be possessed of the powers of perception, intelligence, and self-motion. Matter is alleged to be that kind of substance of which our bodies are composed, whereas the principle of perception and thought belonging to us is said to reside in a spirit or immaterial principle, intimately united to the body; while higher orders of intelligent beings, and especially the *Divine Being*, are said to be purely immaterial. It is maintained that neither matter nor spirit (meaning by the latter the subject of sense and thought) correspond to the definitions above mentioned. For that matter is not that *inert* substance that it has been supposed to be; that powers of *attraction* or *repulsion* are necessary to its very being, and that no part of it appears to be *impenetrable* to other parts; I therefore define it to be a substance possessed of the property of extension, and powers of attraction or repulsion; and since it has never yet been asserted that the powers of *sensation* and *thought* are incompatible with these (*solidity* or *impenetrability*, and, consequently, a *vis inertiæ*, only having been thought to be repugnant to them), I therefore maintain that we have no reason to suppose that there are in man two substances so distinct from each other as have been represented. It is likewise maintained that the notion of two substances that have no common property, and yet are capable of intimate connexion and mutual action, is absurd.'

"I do not conceive *spirit* or *mind* as an existence. By the word *mind*, I simply express the totality of perception, observation, collection, and recollection of perceptions, reflection, and various other mental processes. Dugald Stewart, in his 'Essay on Locke,' says:—'We are conscious of sensation, thought, desire, volition, but we are not conscious of the existence of the mind itself.'

"It is urged that the idea of God is universal. This is not only not true, but I, in fact, deny that any coherent idea exists in connexion with the word 'God.' The chief object to which the emotions of any people were directed in ancient times became their God. When these emotions were combined with vague traditions, and a priesthood became interested in handing down the traditions, and increasing the emotions, then the object becoming sacred was hallowed and adored, and uncertain opinions formed the basis of a creed. Any prominent phenomenon in the universe, which was not understood, was personified, as were also the various passions and phases of humanity. These, in time, were preached as religious truths, and thus diverted the people from inquiry into the natural causes of phenomena, which they accounted for as ordained by God; and when famine or pestilence occurred, instead of endeavouring to remove its cause or using preventive measures against a recurrence of the evil, they sought to discover why the supernatural power was offended, and how it might be appeased, and ascribing to it their own passions and emotions, they offered prayers and sacrifices. These errors becoming institutions of the country, the people, prompted by their priests, regarded all those who endeavoured to overturn them by free and scientific thought and speech as blasphemers, and the Religion of each state has, therefore, always been opposed to the education of the people.

"Archbishop Whately, in his 'Elements of Rhetoric,' part 1, chap. ii., sect. 5, urges that 'those who represent God or Gods as malevolent, capricious, or subject to human passions and vices, are invariably to be found amongst those who are brutal and uncivilized.' We admit this, but ask is it not the fact that both the Old and New Testament teachings do represent God as malevolent, capricious, and subject to human passions and vices—that is, are not these Bible views of God relics of a brutal and uncivilized people?

"There is, of course, not room in a short essay like the present to say much upon the morality of Atheism, and it should therefore suffice to say, that truth and morality go hand in hand. That that is moral which tends to the permanent happiness of all. The continuance of falsehood never can result in permanent happiness; and therefore if Atheism be truthful, it must be moral; if it be against falsehood, it must tend to human happiness.

"Yet if quoting great names will have effect, Lord Bacon, who is often quoted against Atheism, also says: 'Atheism leaves a man to sense, to philosophy, to natural piety, to laws, to reputation, all of which may be guides to an outward moral virtue, *though religion were not;* but superstition dismounts all these, and erecteth an absolute monarchy in the mind of men; therefore Atheism never did perturb states, for it makes men wary of themselves, as looking no further; and we see the times inclined to Atheism—as the times of Augustus Cæsar—were civil times; but superstition has been the confusion of many states.' George Combe says: 'I have known men in whom the reasoning organs were amply developed and well cultivated, who assured me that they could not reach the conviction of the being of a God. I have known such men equal in point of integrity and practical benevolence to the most orthodox believers.' In the West Riding of Yorkshire, amongst the men themselves, a wealthy employer bore favourable testimony to the conduct and intelligence of Atheistic working men. Nay, even the fanatical Dr. Lyman Beecher is obliged to concede that Atheism made converts amongst 'females of education and refinement—females of respectable standing in society.'"

Outside in Old Street there were people distributing Christian tracts, and the Golden Lane Mission had got the words "God is Love" in gas jets above the door, to attract people *en route* to the Hall of Science. At the Beckford's Head public-house close by, an enterprising gentleman gave Shakspearian readings gratuitously every Sunday evening; but the Hall of Science was full and enthusiastic, and surely must present itself to the regards of the Christian Evidence Society as crying out, in the language of the Man of Macedonia, "Come over and help us!" One of the most extraordinary phenomena of this age is that, with an expensively officered society, Mr. Bradlaugh, who pluckily invites argument, should be left to the well-meant but puny efforts of Messrs. Jenkins and Williams.

THE LITERATURE OF INFIDELITY.

I was riding home in the Underground Railway after service on Ash Wednesday evening, when the talk fell on Lenten duties in general, and on subjects of Lent study and meditation in particular. We were several in party; and one proposed this, another that. The London Mission had ended the day before, and had set us all more or less thinking, when I resolved, under excellent advice, to take up as a definite study during Lent, God willing, the subject of Modern Unbelief, especially in London, where my own lot was cast. I had commenced the study, and indeed written about it elsewhere in a fragmentary and desultory way; but now I would try to make my study a systematic one. This much, at least, the Mission had taught us, that we could no longer afford to stand aloof from any form of sin, and say that it did not concern us. If Father Prescott gathered the *habituées* of the Argyll Rooms to listen to him in S. Peter's, Windmill Street; and Father Steele, of S. Thomas's, Regent Street, not content with doing the same, went out into the alleys and compelled them to come in, surely it was not competent for any Christian clergyman to say that his hands would be soiled by

L 2

contact with the refined infidelity of London; no longer, be it remembered, the coarse, vulgar type of a century since, but polished, argumentative, often tender and courteous; but on those very accounts surely the more insidious, surely the more imperatively demanding the very best attentions of those who would study the signs of the times.

I have often made my friends—good, timid, narrow-minded people—lift up their hands in blank dismay when I told them that I joined the London Dialectical Society, and sat patiently once a week during two years on their committee for the investigation of Modern Spiritualism. The motto of the Dialecticians is, that they accept nothing except as the conclusion of a logical argument. The tone taken in reference to Modern Spiritualism was this: That its miracles were better attested than those of the Bible, because they appealed to the evidence of the senses, and claimed something like demonstration; while the sacred miracles must be accepted on the written testimony of a Book, whose authenticity (so ran their Socratic logic) was very doubtful. I thought it was just as well to hear all they had to say—and they had a very great deal to say—on this and many other matters; and I am sincerely glad that I laid aside my clerical starch and joined their circle.

In the same way I proposed, during the Lent of 1874, to attend as many of the atheistical, infidel, and free-thinking meetings in London as I could, and also look in upon those republican gatherings which are always so closely associated therewith, as though the two commands "Fear God" and "Honour the king" had really a very close connexion one with the other. I, as an individual, resolved to do what the Christian Evidence Society had done in their corporate capacity, namely, to visit personally the headquarters of Unbelief in London, and gather what was to be heard and seen there. As a guide to my footsteps (for I was profoundly ignorant of the geography of Infidel London), I went to 17, Johnson's Court, Fleet Street, and bought the *National Reformer* of the current week. I passed to Mr. Truelove's, the publisher's, at 256, Holborn Bars, the office of the *Sunday League*, and invested sixpence in the *Secular Almanac*, turning in *en route* at a shop in the Strand to buy for a penny that which has been truly described as a "a most alarming sheet," the *Republican Herald*. Armed with these, I could, at all events, find my way about for awhile.

A mere description of these organs will perhaps give as good a general idea of the ramifications of London infidelity as we could desire. The *National Secular Almanac*, edited by Charles Bradlaugh and Austin Holyoake, gives, under the guise of an innocent calendar, a very complete account of the Secularist body and its principles, throwing in occasionally a lighter leaflet or two in the way of *bon-mots* which, from a religious point of view, would be considered decidedly profane. The book, in fact, is a clever organ of secular propagandism. I am not complaining of this. Respectable insurance offices issue "Year Books," covering, under a similar veil of light literature and an almanac, advertisements of their own claims on public attention. Mr. Lynes, the merchant-tailor of Shoreditch, issues from time to time a veritable magazine to which authors of established repute contribute, but whose pages are designed to promote the spread of Messrs. Lynes's "Kensington suits." Why should not Messrs. Bradlaugh and Holyoake do the same? They are intensely earnest, and verily believe that the promotion of their opinions would hasten the Millennium, which, being translated into secular language, means the "good time coming."

The volume consists of seventy pages, only one dozen of which are devoted to the almanac and kindred topics, such as eclipses, &c., and, even in the almanac, most of the days are described in their reference to some secular hero, as, for instance; "January 29. Thomas Paine, republican, born 1737." "February 16. George Odger polled 4382 votes for Southwark. 1870." " June 29. Jean Jacques Rousseau born 1712;" and so on. Then we merge at once into a " Retrospect of Secular Progress," and the kindred " Republican Movement." Mr. Francis Neale tells us " What Secularism is;" Mr. Austin Holyoake writes " In favour of Atheism;" Mr. Maccall describes " Pantheism" for us; and then follows more purely literary matter, occasionally breaking out in the form of poetry. Padding takes the shape of a verbatim report of the debate on International Arbitration, and the whole winds up with an ode which is too curious to be omitted :—

IMPROVED SECULAR NATIONAL ANTHEM—" SAVE OUR NATIVE LAND."

(DEDICATED TO ARTHUR TREVELYAN BY THE AUTHOR.)

TUNE—" *God Save the Queen.*"

O! save our Native Land!
Prosper fair Freedom's band—
 Prosper and bless;
Make them victorious,
Happy and glorious,
That long may reign over us
 Concord and Peace!

Friends of the People! rise,
Instruct our enemies—
 Make falsehood fall!
Confound bad politics,
Frustrate all knavish tricks,
On Justice our hopes we fix—
 Truth save us all!

Perish vile slavery,
Priestcraft and knavery—
 Hypocrisy cease!
In amity then we'll join,
Commerce and Art shall shine,
Knowledge and Truth divine
 Widely increase!

Champions of Freedom! stand
Firm in your native land!
 Thus flows the strain;

> Guarded by Truth and Light,
> Virtue and Honour bright,
> May Freedom and equal Right
> Triumphant reign!

Prior Hall, Northumberland,　　　　GEORGE SNOWBALL,
　May 20, 1830.　　　　　　　　　　　　*Tenant Farmer.*

Among the advertisements stitched up with the almanac is one of the "Secularist's Manual," which bears strange evidence to man's necessity for *some* ceremonies at the crises of his life. Among the contents we find "Secular Ceremonies.—The Naming of Infants; A Marriage Service; and a Burial Service," all by Austin Holyoake. Mr. Holyoake seems to stand in much the same relation to Secularism which Comte during the later portion of his life did to Positivism. He was its High Priest in everything but name.

The chief attraction in my eyes, however, was that the volume gave me the names of some twenty places in London where I could go and see Secularism at work, as I have done. Thirty-six provincial towns were deemed of sufficient importance to have their secularist institutions chronicled herein; and there was, moreover, a list added of three metropolitan and sixteen provincial republican clubs. A few of the London haunts were previously known to me, such as the "Hall of Science," the "Positive School," and "South Place Chapel;" but I learned for the first time of the "United Secularists' Propagandist Society," the "Eleusis Club," the "Minerva Club," the "Advanced Unitarian Church," and several others, which I set down for instant anatomization.

Then I proceeded to regale myself with my *National Reformer*, which I found well written and well edited, and with very unmistakable evidences throughout of the genius of Mr. Bradlaugh, who had just returned from his American tour. It would be the greatest mistake possible for Christians to depreciate their foe, or pretend to look down on Secularism. It is to correct this mistake—to give Christians some idea, at all events, of the dimensions of the system with which they venture to make war, that is among my chief objects in writing these papers. It is all very well for Orthodoxy to hold up its hands and say it is wicked to go among "these people;" but unless somebody goes among them, how are those Christian gentlemen who sit at home in ease to know anything at all of what "these people" are like?

There I learned, too, somewhat more in detail, the sort of entertainment provided on Sundays at the various places of meeting whose names I had as yet only seen chronicled. At the Hackney Secularist Association a debate had been opened on the "Justifiability of Suicide," an announcement being added that, on the following Sunday, the subject would be "What has Christianity done to benefit Mankind?" At the Advanced Unitarian Church and Theological Discussion Society "Sacrifices and Sacraments" were demolished. The Hall of Science devoted itself to the well-worn subject of Thomas Paine's Life, with an "ovation" to Mr. Bradlaugh, who had just returned from the United States; though many of the institutions had not got over the election fever, and were more given up to political than religious, or irreligious, matters.

I reserved the "alarming sheet" as my *bonne bouche* for the last; and well indeed the *Republican Herald* deserved such an honour. The quality of the spice with which their journal is flavoured may be inferred from the following extracts, which are curious and appropriate in this connexion as each emanating from clergymen of the Established Church :—

"The Established Church.

"My own experience of the Established Church, which has been varied and considerable, has irresistibly led me to the conclusion that this Church is dead, and must be buried. Indeed, I have been driven to the conviction that the whole state of Christendom, involving all the old orthodoxies, with the feelings, hopes, and conduct to which they are akin, are devoid of true spiritual life, and must, therefore, be put entirely away. As from the Established Church of England, which is identical in its fundamental doctrine with the Church of Rome, the voluntary Churches which go by the name of Christian, have in a great measure taken their cue, I shall, by laying bare the evil and benighted condition of the English ecclesiastical Establishment, at the same time be exhibiting the false and uncharitable character of the other so-called Christian sects in this and other countries.

"A Church, or dispensation, of spiritual life and light, like every other finite thing, has its rise, progress, culmination, and gradual decay, till it reaches its close, when it is succeeded by a new Church, or new spiritual state which is opened in those who are fitted to receive it. This was the case with the Jewish Church. This, too, is now the case with the first Christian Church. It was distinguished by attachment to the person of Jesus Christ, and by a life in accordance with His verbal directions. It flourished in the simple charity and mutual helpfulness of its members. In the face of earthly powers and persecutions it grew and multiplied, extending its sway solely by the power of good example and the simple truths which it taught. It had begun to decline when, in the beginning of the 4th century, it consented to become an instrument in the hands of the State. The process of degeneracy went on till its chief officer assumed the power of the keys, teaching that he had the prerogative of opening and closing heaven, and of dooming to eternal perdition those whom he denounced as the enemies of the loving God. Wars were undertaken in the name of religion, and the priesthood became the central corrupters of mankind. The Reformation, in the 16th century, exposed in some measure the wickedness of the Church, and, by dividing the priestly power, in some measure weakened it, but it did little if anything for the reformation of religion itself. The good which resulted was owing to the freedom which then became possible to minds of a certain temper, unwilling to yield implicitly to priestly authority. But the decay of the Church went on, and the first unmistakable indication of its death was presented by the French Revolution, when priests threw off the mask, declaring that for years they had been infidels, hardly able to preserve a decent solemnity of countenance during the celebration of the prescribed services, and the people revelled in the slaughter of their fellow men. In England, Catholics in power persecuted the Protestants, and Protestants, when they were able, persecuted the Catholics. The Puritans in the days of Cromwell persecuted the Episcopalians, and dealt so hardly by the Friends that George Fox predicted that God would overthrow the followers of Cromwell and bring back the Episcopalians into power, as the latter were less cruel than the former. The Puritans, who had their noses slit and their ears cut off by the Royalists, fleeing to America for a new home, there cut off the ears and slit the noses of Friends because they could not compel them to think as they themselves thought. Episcopalians and Presbyterians treated each other with equal barbarity. When that which had been intended as a blessing to mankind had evidently been converted into a curse, and when in England, as elsewhere, this corrupted and perverted religion was established and endowed by the State, as it still is, it is as clear as anything can be that the breath of life has departed from the Church.

"The division of the Godhead into three persons; the sufferings and death of the second person to appease the wrath and satisfy the offended justice of the first person, who, because of Adam's transgression, was supposed to have turned away His face in displeasure from His own children, and to have been minded to destroy or torment them for ever in hell; justification by faith alone in the sacrifice of Jesus Christ, as needed for the salvation of the sinner, is to reconcile God to him, which if he possessed, he would, quite irrespective of his own mental and practical character, be regarded by the Almighty as clothed with the perfect righteousness of Christ, and consequently meet for the Kingdom of Heaven—these, viz., tri-personalism, Divine vindictiveness and substitution, are the essentials of the Established Church, as they are of the Roman Church, and of all the old Christian denominations in the world. Now, to hide the immorality and hideousness of this doctrine from the eyes of the laity, it has been feigned and taught that good works as necessarily spring from this faith as good fruit is brought forth by a good tree. But as man cannot add to a Divinely finished work—as he cannot amend or supplement the free gift conferred by the grace or favour of God, as it is impossible for him to improve the work of the Holy Spirit, nay, should he even think of doing any good thing for the sake of God, or his own soul, or eternal life, he would, as the doctrine runs, by his blindness, presumption, or ingratitude, profane the work of Christ, and thus sin against God—it may be easily seen what is the character of these good works. Salvation according to orthodoxy, is secured without them; in respect to religion, they are, therefore, not good, they can, therefore, only be accounted good in securing worldly advantages; and it thus becomes indisputable that they never would have been mentioned at all in this connexion, but as a veil to screen from the public eye the real nature of justification by faith alone, which in reality justifies every description of injustice, thus blaspheming God and degrading man. These doctrines are the all in all of the fallen Church. If consistency were duly observed, nothing else would ever be preached as necessary to salvation. Besides these doctrines, which are sufficient to convict the Established Church of degradation and benightedness, there are other tenets which set all sober reason at defiance and are antagonistic to wise benevolence. Amongst these may be enumerated the doctrines of an almost omnipotent devil, who disputes with God for sovereignty over men's souls and has a delight in torturing the lost in hell, multitudes believing he will torture them there for ever; of death being a punishment inflicted by the Almighty upon every one for the disobedience of Adam; of the resurrection of the rejected body, no one knows when; all the departed beings in the meantime without eyes to see with, ears to hear with, hands to handle with, and feet to walk with; of the general judgment at the last day in this world, and then of the destruction by fire of the world itself. Besides all this, according to orthodoxy, only one profession is holy, one day in the week is the Lord's day, one house in a parish is God's house, one piece of ground only is holy ground, one set of services alone are services rendered to Almighty God, and one book only is the sacred Scripture. Viewing so much as unholy, with which nevertheless men have to do, it is not wonderful that the spirit of unholiness or injustice should be so prevalent even amongst those who are called Christians. One of the Articles of the Church of England teaches that it is lawful for Christian men at the commandment of the magistrate to wear weapons and serve in the wars. If this be not murderous teaching —in direct opposition to the true Christian teaching of forbearance, forgiveness, and charity; that charity which commands us to return good for evil, and so overcome evil by good, the only means by which it can ever be effectually overcome—language has no definite meaning, and the human understanding can never be a fair interpreter of words.

"Now, it has been stated that when an old state of

religious faith and life comes to an end, a new state is always raised up by Divine Providence, man's destiny in this world being discipline for a better. And beneath all the theological confusion observable within the Established Church, as well as beyond it, there is a seed of better things. The reform which underlies every other reform, and which is the source from which every other true reform springs, is religious reform. The best of the clergy, and the best and most thoughtful in all classes, are losing more and more their hold upon the old tenets. The sharp-headed artisans of our large towns are, in a great measure, too intelligent to believe in an angry God, a tri-personal Deity, salvation by substitution, and an endless hell. Yet we should come to a wrong conclusion if we thought or said they were all without religion. It is the New Church within them and others, the Church of genuine faith and love, faith in the will of the Good God as revealed in individual conscience, and practical love for all God's children, which has destroyed their faith in the old Church, and will compass the overthrow of the Established Church of England, and of all other worn out sectarian organizations. It is this new religious life, this new-born love of justice and true brotherhood, which is showing men more and more that the Established Church is simply a corrupt department of a corrupt State; that it is a political injustice to all Nonconformists; that it is a huge barrier to progress, and that for religion's sake, and the State's sake, it must be entirely swept away.

"Sometime ago a very celebrated member of the Cabinet asked me if I would not again resume my ministry in the Established Church. My reply was, 'No. If England were a truly religious country there could not be an Established Church in it.' He said, with a grave look, 'Well, that is my way of thinking.' The other day a brother clergyman put a similar question to me. The answer I gave was this—'If the Church were disestablished and the Act of Uniformity repealed, so that I could keep my conscience clear, then I should be very glad to minister again.' But such ministry would be that of the New Church; of service to God in service to mankind.

"In reality the Church and the State are inseparably and eternally one. The people in their spiritual capacity are the Church, and the same people in their political capacity are the State. The Church is the soul of which the State is the body. The Church is within and above the State, as the human soul is in and above the human body. The State derives its quality from the Church, as the body its quality from the soul. Then, as is the Church such must be the State. Were the Church pure and noble, the State would be pure and noble too. When the Church is of a mixed character, the State must have a mixed character. When the Church is dead, the State is dead also. It is only when there is no Church within to inspire, and mould, and lead the State, that the State sets up, endows, and controls an ecclesiasticism which it misnames the Church, and which it uses chiefly to school the people into obedience to the civil power, irrespective of its character. Accordingly we find clergymen, as a rule, the greatest aid and abettors of every cruel law and of every political abuse.

"I must beg the reader's kind indulgence for all the imperfections with which I am persuaded this article, as a literary production, must abound; for I am so hurried that I have not time to re-write, amend, or polish a single sentence. I present it as it is; only asking for it that earnest consideration which the subject undoubtedly demands, and that practical fidelity to the lesson it contains which is necessary for the removal of the Established Church and many cognate evils, and for the growth and development of that New Church of spiritual truth and goodness which is necessary to purify and bless the outward, social, and political life of mankind.

"WILLIAM HUME-ROTHERY.
"Merton Lodge, Tivoli, Cheltenham."

The second is poetical in shape :—

PIOUS MINSTRELSY.
BY A PROGRESSIVE PARSON.

OUR PATRON SAINTS.

Great Simon! It's not St. Peter I mean,
Nor Stylites, piously unclean,
But one who from Thames to Tagus,

Owns empire of a wider scope,
Object of every church's hope,
The cynosure of prelate and pope—
  Adored St. Simon Magus!

Come—to my impecunious self
Teach thy lessons of holy pelf;
  Nestorian or Pelagian—
Whatever be my heretical drift,
My bishop I know will give me shrift,
If I only study the law of thrift
  And turn out a Simon-Magian!

Oft have I sought a slice of fat
From my lord in apron and shovel-hat,
  When some swell, inside an all-rounder,
Has raised his voice my claim above,
Getting more for money than I for love,
Slipping as into his lavender glove,
  To my lord's ten thousand pounder.

That, as the ball commercial rolls,
Is the price of a London "cure of souls,"
  But, alas! I cannot try money;
While this more adventurous clerical gent
Knows the true episcopal bent
And borrowing money at sixty per cent.
  So shaves the edges of Simony.

Come to my aid, auriferous saint,
Bring me money to aid my plaint,
  Or a war unequal wage I;
Even in Sacred legends we're told
How livings of yore were bought and sold,
For were there not heaps of glittering gold
  In the gifts of adoring Magi?

Come Iscariot, lord of the money-bag,
Saint of the apostolic swag,
  Then, stretched beneath the *fagus*,
I may spend the rest of my pious days
Singing ever thy saintship's praise,
And studying all the pleasant ways
  Of thyself and St. Simon-Magus.

> High in episcopal regard,
> When death shall waft me to my reward
>   In swift celestial chariot,
> Up shall I soar to the asphodel wold,
> By the glassy sea with its sands of gold,
> And eternity spend in bliss untold
>   With Magus and Iscariot!

Perhaps this latter extract had more attraction for me, through my having just lost my curacy, after a six years' tenure, in consequence of the living having been sold!

To excuse is to accuse one's self, I repeat. I am quite sure that some persons will quote the old proverb, "Where ignorance is bliss, 'tis folly to be wise." But is ignorance *ever* bliss? Is it ever folly to be wise? These sheets are being sown broadcast on the metropolis. Is it any good to sit down and shut our eyes; and then, one of these days, helplessly wonder at the crop of tares? *Quieta non movere* has been too long our policy; and now we have to lay on missions, and employ all sorts of special machinery to combat influences we can no longer ignore. It is surely better to learn the strength of our opponents, and measure our own against it. And how can this be done without employing that disagreeable but most necessary instrumentality, a spy in the camp?

THE RITUAL OF INFIDELITY.

It has always struck me as the most marvellous concession, not only to man's need of religion, but of the necessity of outward forms to express that religion, when Comte, the founder of Positivism, in his later days, and after being saddened by sorrow, became a sort of high priest of his own system, and overlaid what was before the most unsymbolic creed with a culture more elaborate than the Roman itself. So too is it with that kindred system which really differs from Positivism only in name—Secularism. Since it foregoes everything in the shape of a creed, one would not expect to find anything like ritual attaching to it; in fact, I doubt not but that the title of this paper will seem at first to some persons to involve a contradiction of terms. It is not so, however; Secularism, though without a creed, has, illogically enough, a ritual. It differs, as might be expected, from all that we signify by the name as widely as Secularism itself differs from Christianity; and the diversity here is polar.

Adopting my plan—the fairness of which none can question—to let those whose opinions I am describing speak for themselves, I find Mr. Francis Neale thus portraying and defending Secularism:—

"Secularism may be briefly defined as the science of this life—the philosophy of the present existence. Secularism is a religion without superstition—a theology the divinity of which is humanity. It teaches a man how to live without dependence on a God, and how to die without the fear of a devil. It instructs him how to prosper without a Providence, how to live happily without a priest, how to be moral without a Bible, how to be useful without theological belief. It asserts the possibility of a Paradise without the necessity of an ascension, and thinks salvation attainable without the blood of the 'Lamb.'

"Secularism devotes itself to the present existence entirely, the improvement of which it is its mission to attempt. Should there be another existence, then it holds that he is the more fitted to enter upon it who has done his utmost to make the best of this.

"Secularism does not say there is not a future state, nor does it say there is. On this subject men have been long and hopelessly disagreed, and in the absence of conclusive evidence on either side, Secularism does not presume to dogmatize or decide. But Secularism points to the present existence, about which there can be no doubt, difference, or dispute, and asks its adherents to attend to this in preference to longing, waiting, watching, praying, and sighing for another, which, after all, may never come. Of this life we are certain; no one in his senses can dispute its reality, its significance, its importance. We know it, can feel it, can enjoy it, can appreciate it, with a keenness no logic, no sophistry, can dull or destroy. But of another life we are not so certain; at the best it is but a matter of probability, of faith, of hope, of belief."

It seems difficult to see how, on such grounds, there can be anything like a confederation or society of Secularists. Its very eclecticism seems to involve isolation. Such, however, is again not the case. Secularists are better than their principles, and have not forfeited altogether their character as social beings. Witness the following:—

"PRINCIPLES OF THE NATIONAL SECULAR SOCIETY.

"This Association declares (1) that the promotion of Human Improvement and Happiness is the highest duty.

"2. That the theological teachings of the world have been, and are, most powerfully obstructive of human improvement and happiness; human activity being guided and increased by a consciousness of the facts of existence; while it is misjudged and impeded in the most mischievous manner when the intellect is warped or prostrated by childish and absurd superstitions.

"3. That in order to promote effectually the improvement and happiness of mankind, every individual of the human family ought to be well placed and well instructed, and all who are of a suitable age ought to be usefully employed for their own and the general good.

" 4. That human improvement and happiness cannot be effectually promoted without civil and religious liberty; and that therefore it is the duty of every individual—a duty to be practically recognised by every member of this Association—to actively attack the barriers to equal freedom of thought and utterance for all upon political and theological subjects.

" The admission of members is in the discretion of the Executive, subject to appeal to a general meeting, and any lady or gentleman desiring to be admitted, must sign the form printed on the next page.

" The *National Reformer* is the recognised organ of the Society, and all advertisements, &c., of the Society appear therein.

" The chief place of meeting of the Society is at the New Hall of Science, a central position, where friends from the country will find a comfortable place at which they may obtain refreshments, and where they may have their letters sent.

" The members are either active or passive.

" The active list consists of those who do not object to the publication of their names as members of the National Secular Society. An active member's duty is to send, as often as possible, reliable reports to the President of the doings of the local clergy, of special events, sermons, lectures, or publications, affecting secular progress. He should also aid in the circulation of secular literature, and generally in the freethought propaganda of his neighbourhood. Where a local society exists, he ought to belong to it, whether or not it be a branch of this Society.

"The passive list consists of those whose position does not permit the publication of their names, or who do not feel able to do any active duty.

"*Form of Declaration.*

"'I declare that I am desirous of joining the National Secular Society, in order to promote the improvement and happiness of myself and my fellows. That I pledge myself to do my best, if admitted as a member, to co-operate with my fellow members to attain the objects of this Association.

    "'Name ....
    "'Address ....
    "'Occupation ....
    "'Active or Passive.' ....

"This Declaration, signed with the name and address of the candidate, being transmitted to the Secretary of the Association, Mr. DAVID K. FRASER, 17, Johnson's Court, Fleet Street, E.C., with Threepence for a Quarter's Subscription, a Card of Membership will be issued available for three months. Any further subscription is in the discretion and according to the means of the person joining.

"*Objects.*

" The Executive of the National Secular Society, finding that the power of the free-thought body in the State is specially recognised in connexion with the political and social changes now taking place, points out to its members and friends the following matters as deserving of their earnest and active attention :—

" 1. To obtain the repeal of the Blasphemy Laws as a special matter affecting its members.

" 2. The disestablishment and disendowment of the State Church, and the placing all religions and forms of speculative opinion on a perfect equality before the law.

" 3. Specially the improvement of the condition of the agricultural classes, whose terrible state of social degradation is at present a fatal barrier to the formation of a good state of society.

" 4. A change in the Land Laws, so as to break down the present system by which enormous estates are found in few hands, the many having no interest in the soil, and to secure for the agricultural labourer some share of the improvement in the land he cultivates.

" 5. The destruction of the present hereditary Chamber of Peers, and substitution of a Senate containing Life Members, elected for their fitness, and therewith the constitution of a National Party intended to wrest the governing power from a few Whig and Tory families.

"6. The investigation of the causes of poverty in all old countries, in order to see how far unequal distribution of wealth or more radical causes may operate. The discussion in connexion with this of the various schemes for social amelioration, and the ascertainment if possible of the laws governing the increase of population and produce, as affecting the rise and fall of wages."

We have heard a great deal at different times—very much more than most of us probably believed—about certain "Jesuitical" tricks on the part of a particular school of thought in the Church, and how those of one branch which was unpopular, "reserved" or disguised their opinions by remaining in another section which *was* popular. Secularists especially have always been prone to talk of "wolves in sheeps' clothing;" but if this distinction into "active and passive" members be not a piece of diplomacy, to enable men to conceal their opinions, we do not know what is.

But still, so far, we find no sign of sacerdotalism, save that which the infidel falsely attributes to the believer, and is here found to be adopting full-fledged himself; nor is there any symptom of ritual. Mr. Bradlaugh has not yet, as far as we know, constituted himself Pope, Archbishop, or Grand Llama of the

Secularists; but Mr. Austin Holyoake and Mr. Watts, it appears, have. In that which Mr. Gladstone is, rightly or wrongly, said to have called "a questionable book," namely, *The Secularists' Manual*, I find something like the Rituale Holyoakense or the Hierurgia Secularis. It concedes, like Comte, the fact that man cannot live without a worship of some kind; and that, grotesque as he may elect to make it, he must have that worship. Between Fetishism and Secularism it is only a question of degree, not of kind, when once the old moorings of Revelation are abandoned.

At those solemn crises in life whose records fill so strangely the first column in our giant paper, which read so prosy and unromantic there, but are so full of that deepest of all romance, reality, then it is that, as it were instinctively, man adopts a ceremony of some kind; and it cannot but be interesting to contrast the utterances of secularism with those of theology. Do not the former read cold and dead; reminding us, in the Apostle's own words, of the "body without the soul?" From the "questionable book" above mentioned I gather the following:—

"SECULAR CEREMONIES.

"I. *The Naming of Infants.*

"BY CHARLES WATTS.

"In publicly naming the infant now before us we recognise the parents' desire to identify their offspring with the Secular Party, which proclaims the necessity of unfettered thought during the formation of character. Diversity of organization precludes uniformity of belief; we do not, therefore, guarantee that in after life a child shall profess any particular class of opinions. But by keeping its mind free from theological creeds we enable it the better to acquire a more liberal education than is permitted by the conventional faith of the Church. During infancy the imagination frequently revels in the ideal; care should be taken, therefore, to protect the child as much as possible from the beguilements of superstition. For in the sunny days of childhood, when the heart leaps with joy, when innocence beams on the cheek, and hope sparkles in the eye—when the mind in its purest simplicity is unable to detect the snare, then the seeds are sown which in after years frequently bear unfortunate fruit. An opportunity should be given for the faculties to be fairly developed before the judgment is taxed with the mysteries and perplexities of theology. The true and the beautiful in nature should be placed before the young with a view of inspiring them with a desire to understand and appreciate the realities of life. Theological prejudice and religious bigotry prevent the realization of this object. Hence it is our duty to surround the child with influences that will enable him to avoid those evils.

" Viewing this emblem of innocence, we recognise

lineaments of love and simplicity, which are an index to the goodness of its nature. The germs of virtue are here awaiting judicious cultivation, that they may bud forth and ripen into moral fruit. Youth is impressible. The conduct of children in after life is generally a reflex of their earlier education. Encircle them with pure influences, place before them examples of integrity, foster the desire for excellence which is allied with human affections at the dawn of life, you will thereby open the avenues to the purest instincts of their nature, and knit a bond of union between them and their parents which all the turmoil of life and strife of the world will fail to sever. Seek to win the affections of children with love, not repel them with fear; inspire hope and joy, awaken not dread and despair. The infant mind is sensitive, and requires to be irradiated with smiles, not darkened with gloom. Parental indifference, harsh treatment, and cruel frowns produce stultified intellects and unpleasant dispositions; but kindness, care, and forbearance evoke intelligence and cheerfulness of conduct.

"We sincerely hope that in after life [here name the child] he [if the child be a girl, substitute the feminine gender] may have reason to rejoice in his fellowship with us. May the principles of Freethought enable him to brave successfully the battle of life. And as he sails o'er the billows of time, may experience increase his guiding power, that when arriving at maturity he shall have acquired sufficient knowledge to enable him to regulate aright his further career. And when the evening of his existence has arrived, may he obtain consolation from the reflection that his conduct has won the approval of the wise and the good, and that to the best of his ability he has been faithful to the mission of life.

ON THE BIRTH OF AN INFANT.

Joy to thy parents, O mayst thou be found;
Peace as a halo thy pathway surround;
Duly approving and prompting thy care,
Love in its fulness fulfilling its share.

Goodness attend thee wherever thou go,
Mercy defend from the shafts of its foe;
Virtue still proving thy waymark to be —
Nothing presuming through sweetness in thee.

Sweetness resembling the flow'rets of spring,
Nurtur'd by dewdrops fresh odours to bring;
Tear-drops of pity, of feeling, of soul,
Temper with prudence, their force to control.

Sunbeams of wisdom illumine thy day;
Chase the dull meteors of folly away;
Point, as the shade on the dial will move,
How the fleet moments of time to improve.

Knowledge engage thee its wonders to scan;
Teach thee the greatness, the weakness of man!
Show thee of life, how its dangers to pass,
Show thee thyself in humility's glass.

"II. *A Marriage Ceremony.*

"BY AUSTIN HOLYOAKE.

" We have met here to-day to perform the pleasing duty of celebrating the marriage of our two young friends, A. and B. They are entering upon a new mode of life, the paths of which may be strewn with roses, if love and mutual respect guard the way; or with thorns, if harshness and petulance are allowed to invade the domain of the affections.

"May health, happiness, and long life await them.

"Marriage is the most momentous event in the life of both man and woman. On it depends the happiness or misery of their future. Carefully then should the inducements be weighed that impel to so important a step, that the contracting parties may be sure that love, and love alone, has prompted them to the act. Any sordid or capricious motive will speedily bring its own punishment. It is the union of hearts, not hands, that constitutes a true marriage. But while the heart should be the prime mover, the head should take care of it, or the happiness of the married couple will be a matter of accident, where it should be the result of the most careful and enlightened judgment. Marriages of mere passion are as disastrous as those of avarice or ambition.

"Marital love is necessary to the perfection of life; and the love of children springing therefrom is the purest emotion known to humanity. In the domestic affections is to be found the highest happiness, and they who fail to cultivate them lose half the joys of existence.

"Our young friends who have now entered upon the married state, must not forget that it has its duties as well as its pleasures. New responsibilities will devolve upon them, and the fittest preparation they can make to enable them to properly meet them, will be to so order their own lives that their minds may be free from the bickerings and irritations that so constantly await ill-assorted and ill-regulated unions. The golden rule in married life is Mutual Forbearance. We must never forget that no alliance, however well designed, can ever secure perfect contentment; for it so happens that where people love most, they are apt to be most exacting one to the other. There may be a fanaticism in love as well as in belief, for affection is but the religion of the heart. As with a people the aggregate of individual virtues make up the sum of national greatness, so in domestic life the multifarious duties devolving upon each, faithfully fulfilled, make up the measure of human bliss.

"We urge each not to be the first by whom the harsh word is spoken, nor the last to offer the hand of reconciliation. Beware of jealousies, and vigilantly foster feelings of trust and loving-kindness.

" It is fervently to be hoped that the newly-married pair will prove to each other suitable companions through life, and be knit together, not only with the silken cords of affection, but with a bond that strengthens with years and brightens with age—the bond of congenial tastes and intellectual attachment. Marriage is itself an education, which schools the heart, and directs the affections in the paths of peace. A world of bliss is ever present in that household which is pervaded by the elevating and softening influence of literature and art, which purifies love, and attunes the feelings to harmonious sympathy with all humanity.

"The names husband and wife have a charmed sound, and the married state has a halo around it that dims with its lustre all other relationships of life. Husband and wife are 'all the world to each other,' and they should strive to make their domestic hearth so pure and tranquil, that when they assume the momentous but blissful responsibilities of father and mother, they may feel sure that their children will be born under influences that shall make them dutiful and loving to their parents, and enthusiastic workers for the good of others.

"To the husband we say: Conserve and cherish the sacredness of home; make it the altar at which you worship, and be sure that domestic bliss is within the reach of all who intelligently strive to attain it. It is to be won alone by a manly yet considerate treatment of the one to whom you have dedicated your life, and who will return your affection, however lavish, with boundless interest.

"To the wife we say: Now that you have won a woman's greatest prize, a loving heart, guard it with zealous care, nor ever let the storm of anger rise to wither true affection with its fiery breath. In attaining the consummation of all the gentler feelings which animate a woman's breast, never forget that love, unaccompanied by true companionship, soon droops and perishes under the chilling influence of uncongeniality of mind.

"To husband and wife we say : So live, that when the evening of life arrives, secure in the affection of children and friends, you can exclaim with the poet—
'Not another joy like unto this succeeds in unknown fate.'

"[As Secular Institutions are not licensed as places wherein marriages can be legally performed, the foregoing service can be used in this way: After the couple have been duly 'joined in holy matrimony' at the Registrar's Court, the party can adjourn to the Hall, where the celebration can be held. It will be as well that this should take place on the same day, though that is not absolutely necessary. The reading of the service should be preceded by the singing of poem No. 5 in this Manual, and followed by No. 19, both of which should be set to cheerful and impressive tunes. The reader of the service can introduce a few remarks of a personal nature, if he thinks fit.]

"III. *A Burial Service.*

"BY AUSTIN HOLYOAKE.

"We this day consign to the earth the body of our departed friend; for him life's fitful dream is over, with its toils, and sufferings, and disappointment. He derived his being from the bountiful mother of all ; he returns to her capacious bosom, to again mingle with the elements. He basked in life's sunshine for his allotted time, and has passed into the shadow of death, where sorrow and pain are unknown. Nobly he performed life's duties on the stage of earth; the impenetrable curtain of futurity has fallen, and we see him no more. But he leaves to his sorrowing relatives and friends a legacy in the remembrance of his virtues, his services, his honour, and truth. He fought the good fight of free inquiry, and triumphed over prejudice and the results of misdirected education. His voyage through life was not always on tranquil seas, but his strong judgment steered him clear of the rocks and quicksands of ignorance, and for years he rested placidly in the haven of self-knowledge. He had long been free from the fears and misgivings of superstitious belief. He worked out for himself the problem of life, and no man was the keeper of his conscience. His religion was of this world—the service of humanity his highest aspiration. He recognised no authority but that of Nature; adopted no methods but those of science and philosophy; and respected in practice no rule but that of conscience, illustrated by the common sense of mankind. He valued the lessons of the past, but disowned tradition as a ground of belief, whether miracles and supernaturalism be claimed or not claimed on its side. No sacred Scripture or ancient Church formed the basis of his faith. By his example he vindicated the right to think, and to act upon conscientious conviction. By a career so noble, who shall say that his domestic affections were impaired, or that his love for those near and dear to him was weakened? On the contrary, his independent method of thought tended to develop those sentiments which have their source in human nature—which impel and ennoble all morality—which are grounded upon intelligent personal conviction, and which manifest themselves in worthy and heroic actions, especially in the promotion of truth, justice and love. For worship of the unknown, he substituted duty; for prayer, work; and the record of his life bears testimony to his purity of heart; and the bereaved ones know but too well the treasure that is lost to them for ever. If perfect reliance upon any particular belief in the hour of death were proof of its truth, then in the death of our friend the principles of Secularism would be triumphantly established. His belief sustained him in health; during his illness, with the certainty of death before him at no distant period, it afforded him consolation and encouragement; and in the last solemn moments of his life, when he was gazing as it were into his own grave, it procured him the most perfect tranquillity of mind. There were no misgivings, no doubts, no tremblings lest he should have missed the right path; but he went undaunted into the land of the great departed, into the silent land. It may be truly said of him, that nothing in life became him more than the manner of his leaving it. Death has no terrors for the enlightened; it may bring regrets at the thought of leaving those we hold dearest on earth, but the consciousness of a well-spent life is all-sufficient in the last sad hour of humanity. Death is but the shadow of a shade, and there is nothing in the name that should blanch the cheek or inspire the timid with fear. In its presence, pain and care give place to rest and peace. The sorrow-laden and the forlorn, the unfortunate and the despairing, find repose in the tomb—all the woes and ills of life are swallowed up in death. The atoms of this earth once were living man, and in dying we do but return to our kindred who have existed through myriads of generations.

[*Here introduce any personal matters relating to the deceased.*]

Now our departed brother has been removed, death, like a mirror, shows us his true reflex. We see his character, undistorted by the passions, the prejudices, and the infirmities of life. And how poor seem all the petty ambitions which are wont to sway mankind, and how small the advantages of revenge. Death is so genuine a fact that it excludes falsehood or betrays its emptiness; it is a touchstone that proves the gold and dishonours the baser metal. Our friend has entered upon that eternal rest, that happy ease, which is the heritage of all. The sorrow and grief of those who remain alone mar the thought that the tranquil sleep of death has succeeded that fever of the brain called living. Death comes as the soothing anodyne to all our woes and struggles, and we inherit the earth as a reward for the toils of life. The pain of parting is poignant, and cannot for a time be subdued; but regrets are vain. Every form that lives must die, for the penalty of life is death. No power can break the stern decree that all on earth must part; though the chain be woven by affection or kindred, the beloved ones who weep for us will only for a while remain. There is not a flower that scents the mountain or the plain, there is not a rosebud that opes its perfumed lips to the morning sun, but ere evening comes may perish. Man springs up like the tree: at first the tender plant, he puts forth buds of promise, then blossoms for a time, and gradually decays and passes away. His hopes, like the countless leaves of the forest, may wither and be blown about by the adverse winds of fate; but his efforts, springing from the fruitful soil of wise endeavour, will fructify the earth, from which will rise a blooming harvest of happy results to mankind. In the solemn presence of death—solemn, because a mystery which no living being has penetrated—on the brink of that bourne from whence no traveller returns, our obvious duty is to emulate the good deeds of the departed, and to resolve so to shape our course through life, that when our hour comes we can say, that though our temptations were great—though our education was defective —though our toils and privations were sore—we never wilfully did a bad act, never deliberately injured our fellow-man. The reward of a useful and virtuous life is the conviction that our memory will be cherished by those who come after us, as we revere the memories of the great and good who have gone before. This is the only immortality of which we know—the immortality of the great ones of the world, who have benefited their age and race by their noble deeds, their brilliant thoughts, their burning words. Their example is ever with us, and their influence hovers round the haunts of men, and stimulates to the highest and happiest daring. Man has a heaven too, but not that dreamed of by some—far, far away beyond the clouds; but here on earth, created by the fireside, and built up of the love and respect of kindred and friends, and within the reach of the humblest who work for the good of others and the improvement of humanity. As we drop the tear of sympathy at the grave now about to close over the once loved form, may the earth lie lightly on him, may the flowers bloom over his head, and may the winds sigh softly as they herald the coming night. Peace and respect be with his memory. Farewell, a long farewell!"

"[The foregoing service is suitable to be said over the grave of an adult male; it may, with slight effort, by altering the gender, be made suitable for a female also. It is almost impossible to write that which would be applicable to persons of all ages. It can always be sufficiently individualized by some friend of the deceased introducing a few remarks of a personal nature.]"

Amid all the grotesqueness of these compositions —and they are grotesque, as being a sort of travestie on what we, from our point of view, consider most solemn—still I cannot but regard them as hopeful. I read them as a sign of Secularism against itself. Man may try to limit his ideas to this world, but he cannot; and these very makeshifts attest the fact. I print them in full for that very reason; because I am sure if one only passes from them to the contemplation of the simplest service under revelation, he will see that in the latter case only is life: the soul at last animates the dry bones. Dr. Sexton, who, curiously enough, has pointed my moral in another way by passing from Secularism to the opposite extreme of modern Spiritualism, as it were, anticipates this objection of the *soullessness* attaching to his creed in the following, which I extract from the Secularists' Hymnal:—

THE WORSHIP OF NATURE.
Music by John Lowry.

They tell us that we worship not,
  Nor sing sweet songs of praise;
That love divine is not our lot,
  In these cold modern days;
That piety's calm, peaceful state
  We banish from the earth:
They know not that we venerate
  Whate'er we see of worth:—

The singing of the birds on high,
　The rippling of the stream,
The sparkling stars in yon bright sky,
　The sunlight's merry gleam,
The ocean's wide and watery main,
　The lightning's vivid flash,
The sweet and gentle showers of rain,
　The awful thunder's crash;

The trees and flow'rs that deck the land,
　The soft and grassy mead,
The firm-set earth on which we stand,
　Are worshipful indeed.
We venerate great Nature's plan,
　And worship at her shrine,
While goodness, truth, and love in man,
　We hold to be divine.　　　G. SEXTON.

And so too in the following Benediction, or "Dismission" as it is termed, one is almost tempted to smile as one recognises the old *animus*. I still regard these different compositions as eminently hopeful, because I believe those who used them and felt the need of them would soon find it necessary to put something else in place of "great nature" in the former, and the "social system" in the latter. Even the significant letters which stand for "Common Metre" are witnesses on our side, and bespeak our Secularist friends more ecclesiastical than they have any idea of:—

DISMISSION.

Farewell, dear friends! adieu, adieu;
　In social ways delight;
Then happiness will dwell with you:
　Farewell, dear friends! good-night.

Farewell, dear friends! adieu, adieu;
Remember us this night;
We claim to do the same for you:
Farewell, dear friends! good-night.

Farewell, dear friends! adieu, adieu,
Till we again unite;
The social system keep in view:
Farewell, dear friends! good-night.

MR. BRADLAUGH ON TORYISM.

For one who hungers and thirsts after heterodoxy, whether theological or political, Mr. Bradlaugh is, by his own election and of set purpose, a standing dish where one may " cut and come again." There is this vast advantage about Mr. Bradlaugh that it is impossible to mistake him. None can accuse him of giving an uncertain sound. Theologically he is an atheist, or rather an anti-theist: politically, a republican *pur sang*. In the former capacity I had heard him laboriously and at length deny the existence of God, and defend his position, with the skill of a master in debate, against all comers; and the announcement that he would take, as a Tuesday evening subject at the Hall of Science, " The Queen's Speech and the Premier's Intentions "—that Premier being Mr. Disraeli—assured me that I should hear some equally definite and decisive utterances on political matters. I recognised the invitation as the call of duty, and went. The *National Reformer* fails as a *vade mecum*, from the fact of being, unlike its editor, vague in its statements of forthcoming events. No hour was mentioned for the lecture; so I took it for granted it would come off at the same time as on

Sundays, and consequently got there at seven o'clock, which I found was just an hour and a half too soon. The prospect of ninety minutes on the inhospitable and unattractive flagstones of Old Street, St. Luke's, is sufficient to try one's philosophy; but what is the use of going to the Hall of Science unless one *is* a philosopher? I was philosophic, and waited. What else was I to do? My philosophy resolved itself into necessity.

One thing I could say, at all events, that the rewards of my patience were immediate and appreciable—I got a front seat. The hall was filled completely and early: the twopenny gallery with genuine working men and working women; the fourpenny seats with working men and working women too, but with a large admixture of those whose work, like my own, was of the head and not of the hands. Buyers and sellers throng the aisles of the Temple of Science, and a shrill-voiced lad tempts the waiting audience with such racy pamphlets as "John Brown and the Queen," "Mr. Bradlaugh's letter to the Prince of Wales," "Autobiography of Mr. Bradlaugh." I invested in all three, and may quote from the two last, but certainly not from the first. Immersed in the events of Mr. Bradlaugh's chequered career, I found the time pass quickly enough; and in due course, accompanied as usual by his two daughters, our orator mounted his rostrum amid great applause.

"It was almost a mistake," he said, after a few opening remarks by the chairman, "to have chosen the Queen's Speech for a subject, because there was so little in it. That speech was delivered by commission, and such a proceeding could scarcely fail to suggest the possibility of the Crown itself one day being put into commission altogether. He had lately been in a country where there were thirty-eight parliaments; and he had read some fourteen or fifteen of the Messages addressed to these legislative assemblies. These Messages were real ones. They told you something of what the policy was going to be. The Queen's Speech differed in the fact that it showed what the policy was *not* going to be, or rather it told nothing at all. It began by saying that her Majesty's relations with foreign powers were friendly, and yet we were in the thick of the Ashantee war. The fact was that five of the paragraphs in the speech were copied from former speeches; only two paragraphs had any claim to originality. On the subject of treaty obligations, he warned his hearers that there was danger in the exercise by ministers of what was called the Crown prerogative, by which the country might be first plunged into war, and then the war itself afterwards made the subject of debate. The Abyssinian and Ashantee expeditions had been very expensive; but when we were once embarked in them we were told that 'the honour of the country was involved,' and we must go on. It would be a great thing if it could be made a part of the Constitution that no minister could protect himself in this way, or war entered upon without the consent of Parliament. He saw danger in the fact that both Germany and France were making vast preparations for war. Both countries had larger armies than when the Franco-Prussian war broke out. At one single place on the French frontier provisions for a year and a half had been lately served out to the German troops in the space of four weeks. Italy, France, and Germany each had armies at our doors in numbers utterly disproportionate to their areas. Suppose," he said, " Prussia had seen fit to make a way to the sea for herself by the dismemberment of Belgium, and Mr. Disraeli felt disposed to interfere, what could we do? We could not put fifty thousand men into the field. We had too many troops for peace, but not enough to justify any intervention in European questions.

"Then, as to the marriage of the Duke of Edinburgh, the Queen said :—

"'The marriage of my son, the Duke of Edinburgh, with the Grand Duchess Marie Alexandrowna of Russia, is at once a source of happiness to myself and a pledge of friendship between two great Empires.'

"This was unobjectionable enough. No wonder there had been some rejoicings. It was, no doubt, a source of happiness to the Queen" (this was said with the driest humour). "It might be a pledge of friendship between two great Empires; but between the Russian and English people, no—I can't be expected to rejoice," he proceeded. "I regard the Royal Family as too large already. I don't object to the Royal Family increasing and multiplying, if they would do it at their own expense; but they don't. It was said that this was a love match; and no doubt there were great inducements for the Duke; but, as far as experience had gone, the women had not had much to induce them to marry into our Royal Family. When we saw the people greeting a Russian Princess, could we help thinking of the cries we had once heard on behalf of Poland? And what hope could there be for a people who would lend themselves to such a sham? Is the English nation," he asked, "forgetting its old history? Charles Fox told George III. that he anh his family were but the creatures of a revolution. You seem to have forgotten that. Then with regard to the Ashantee War. If Sir Garnet Wolseley had stopped long enough at the Gold Coast, we should have made a treaty, and if it suited our purpose, perhaps we should have observed its provisions. We were a long-suffering people abroad. We had done all a Christian nation should have done. I hope " he continued, " you understand why the war broke out at all. I don't! Still it did break out—we have been victorious—we have got our trophies—have got (this amid shouts of laughter)—*the umbrella!*

"As to the Bengal famine. India, it must be remembered, had no representative in the House of

Commons. We governed India by a pure despotism. This was not the first famine. We had depopulated Rohilcund (cries of shame). Yes—but he doubted whether that depopulation was a greater shame than the present famine, because we could have prevented it.

"From India we came home again, and met with one of Disraeli's juggling tricks, the Trades' Commission. The Speech said :—

"'Serious differences have arisen and remonstrances been made by large classes of the community as to the working of the recent Act of Parliament affecting the relationship of Master and Servant, of the Act of 1871, which deals with offences connected with trade, and of the law of conspiracy, more especially as connected with these offences. On these subjects I am desirous that, before attempting any fresh legislation, you should be in possession of all material facts and of the precise question in controversy, and for this purpose I have issued a Royal Commission to inquire into the state and working of the present law with a view to its early amendment, if it should be found necessary.'

"So long as the relation of Master and Servant remained, so long there would be a war between Capital and Labour. There had been a time when serfdom prevailed in England; and the law was framed on the supposition that it existed still. Did they know that there was still in force and unrepealed a statute of

George II. which makes misbehaviour—or 'miscarriage,' whatever that might be—on the part of an artizan to his employer punishable with imprisonment and whipping? True that statute was never carried out, and why? Only because Public Opinion was stronger than the law. He defended Mr. Macdonald for taking his seat on this Commission. It was, he knew, one of the wretchedest farces ever enacted; but still, if such a Commission was to be, he thought Mr. Macdonald did quite right in accepting a seat upon it. The Land Question was going to be a big one; and this was how the Speech disposed of it:—

"'The delay and expense attending the transfer of land in England have long been felt to be a reproach to our system of law, and a serious obstacle to dealings in real property. This subject has in former Sessions occupied the attention of Parliament, and I trust that the measures which will now be submitted for your consideration will be found calculated to remove much of the evil of which complaint has been made.'

"There was at that moment a lock-out of the farmers. The farmers told the peasants to go and starve and be damned. Do you know," he asked, in the most measured tones, "what starving men do? Did you ever hear of the Jacquerie? Unless they let the peasants till their own land, some of their titledeeds won't be worth the stamps they've got upon them. Was it not better," he asked, "to create peasant proprietors than paupers? It was not, he held, the fault of the tenant-farmers, but of the superior landlords, that things were in this position. The facility of transfer they wanted was not between the Duke of Westminster and the Duke of Northumberland, but from the Duke to Harry, Dick, or Hodge, with a large family and a starving wife all drifting fast to a pauper's grave!

"It would indeed be a shame for us if we were going back, as some had said, to old Toryism. I deny it," he thundered out. "They dared not make one backward step. What had been the history of the Tory party? It had lent itself to some liberal measures, but when? When it was out of office, and wanted to come in. What had it ever conserved for us? Since 1760, labour had been continually getting cheaper and bread dearer. They had conserved debt. Twenty-seven millions of tax was conserved by a Tory Government. Those who talked about Conservative working men simply did not understand English. Not, however, that there was much to choose between Whig and Tory. It was like the two slaves, Pompey and Sambo. When they were lost and their master advertised them, he said that they were very much alike, only Pompey was a little more like Sambo than Sambo was like Pompey. The only difference was, the Tories were a little more open and honest in their rascality than the Whigs. How was it that such a cheap paper as that he held in his hand was possible? Why, because working men went to jail to make it so. Catholic Emancipation and Reform had only been conceded through fear. I ask you, Tories, can you stop one republican club or lecture in London? You sent men to prison in '39 for speaking as I am speaking now. Dare you send me to jail? (Immense applause.) And if you can't stop the mouth of one man, how will you stop the men in the Northumberland mines, the Durham pits, and the workshops of Lancashire?"

He concluded by picturing the great parks of the nobility, given up to hares and pheasants and keepers, and surrounded by starving peasants, and sat down, saying abruptly, by way of summary, "I deny your Conservative Reaction."

Such are the very plain words of this plain speaker as they may be heard almost any week at the Hall of Science. It may be interesting to know from his own words how he first attained to his present state of opinion. The following are extracts from his Autobiography:—

"I was born on the 26th September, 1833, in a small house in Bacchus Walk, Hoxton. My father was a solicitor's clerk with a very poor salary, which he supplemented by law writing. He was an extremely industrious man, and a splendid penman. I never had the opportunity of judging his tastes or thoughts outside his daily labours, except in one respect, in which I have followed in his footsteps. He was passionately fond of angling. Until 1848 my life needs little relation. My schooling, like that of most poor men's children, was small in quantity, and, except as to the three R's, indifferent in quality. I remember at seven years of age being at a National school in Abbey Street, Bethnal Green; between seven and nine I was at another small private school in the same neighbourhood; and my 'education' was completed before I was eleven years of age at a boys' school in Coalharbour Street, Hackney Road. When about twelve years of age I was first employed as errand lad in the solicitor's office where my father remained his whole life through. After a little more than two years in this occupation, I became wharf clerk and cashier to a firm of coal merchants in Britannia Fields, City Road. While in their employment the excitement of the Chartist movement was at its height in England, and the authorities, frightened by the then huge continental revolution wave, were preparing for the prosecution of some of the leaders amongst the Chartists. Meetings used to be held almost continuously all day on Sunday, and every week-night in the open air on Bonner's Fields, near where the Consumption Hospital now stands. These meetings were in knots of from fifty to five hundred, sometimes many more, and were occupied chiefly in discussions on theological, social, and political questions, any bystander taking part. The curiosity of a lad took me occasionally in the week evenings to the Bonner's Fields gatherings. On the Sunday I, as a member of the Church of England, was fully occupied as a Sunday-school teacher. This last named fashion of passing Sunday was broken suddenly. The Bishop of London was announced to hold a confirmation in Bethnal Green. The incumbent of St. Peter's, Hackney Road, the district in which I resided, was one John Graham Packer, and he, desiring to make a good figure when the Bishop came, pressed me to prepare for confirmation, so as to answer any questions the Bishop might put. I studied a little the Thirty-nine Articles of the Church of England, and the four Gospels, and came to the conclusion that they differed. I ventured to write the Rev. Mr. Packer a respectful letter, asking him for aid and explanation. All he did was to denounce my letter to my parents as Atheistical, although at that time I should have shuddered at the very notion of becoming an Atheist, and he suspended me for three months from my office of Sunday-school teacher. This left me my Sundays free, for I did not like to go to church while suspended from my teacher's duty, and I, instead, went to Bonner's Fields, at first to listen, but soon to take part in some of the discussions which were then always pending there.

"At the commencement I spoke on the orthodox Christian side, but after a debate with Mr. J. Savage, in the Warner Place Hall, in 1849, on the 'Inspiration of the Bible,' I found that my views were getting very much tinged with Free-thought, and in the winter of that year, at the instigation of Mr. Packer, to whom I had submitted the 'Diegesis' of Robert Taylor, I—having become a teetotaller, which in his view brought out my infidel tendencies still more vigorously—had three days given me by my employers, after consultation with my father, to 'change my opinions or lose my situation.' I am inclined to think now that the threat was never intended to have been enforced, but was used to terrify me into submission. At that time I hardly knew what, if any, opinions I had, but the result was that sooner than make a show of recanting, I left home and situation on the third day, and never returned to either.

"I was always a very fluent speaker, and now lectured frequently at the Temperance Hall, Warner Place, Hackney Road, at the small Hall in Philpot Street, and in the open air in Bonner's Fields, where at last on Sunday afternoons scores of hundreds congregated to hear me. My views were then Deistical, but rapidly tending to the more extreme phase into which they ultimately settled. . . . .

"I studied hard everything which came in my way, picking up a little Hebrew and an imperfect smattering of other tongues. I tried to earn my living as a coal merchant, but at sixteen, and without one farthing in my pocket, the business was not extensive enough to be profitable. I got very poor, and at that time was also very proud. A subscription offered me by a few Freethinkers shocked me, and awakened me to a sense of my poverty; so, telling no one where I was going, I went away, and on the 17th December, 1850, was, after some difficulty, enlisted in the Seventh Dragoon Guards. With this corps I remained until October, 1853, being ultimately appointed orderly-room clerk; the regiment, during the whole of the time I remained in it, being quartered in Ireland. While I was in the regiment I was a teetotaller, and used often to lecture to the men in the barrack-room at night; and I have more than once broken out of Portobello barracks to deliver teetotal speeches in the small French Street Hall, Dublin. Many times have I spoken there in my scarlet jacket, between James Haughton and the good old father, the Rev. Dr. Spratt, a Roman Catholic priest, then very active in the cause of temperance. While I was in the regiment my father died, and in the summer of 1853 an aunt's death left me a small sum, out of which I purchased my discharge, and returned to England, to aid in the maintenance of my mother and family."

In reference to more recent times, he says:—

"During the Franco-Prussian struggle I remained neutral until the 4th of September. I was against Bismarck and his blood-and-iron theory, but I was also utterly against the Empire and the Emperor; so I took no part with either. I was lecturing at Plymouth the day the *déchéance* was proclaimed, and immediately after wrote my first article in favour of

Republican France. I now set to work, and organized a series of meetings in London and the provinces, some of which were co-operated in by Dr. Congreve, Professor Beesly, and other prominent members of the Positivist party. . . . .

"When the great cry of thanksgiving was raised for the recovery of the Prince of Wales, I could not let it pass without protest. While he lay dangerously ill I had ceased to make any attack on himself or family, but I made no pretence of a grief I did not feel. When the thanksgiving day was fixed, and tickets for St. Paul's were sent by the Lord Chamberlain to working men representatives, I felt it right to hold a meeting of protest, which was attended by a crowded audience in the New Hall of Science. . . . .

"It is at present too early to speak of the Republican movement in England, which I have sought, and not entirely without success, to organize on a thoroughly legal basis. It is a fair matter for observation that my lectures on 'The Impeachment of the House of Brunswick,' have been delivered to crowded audiences assembled in some of the finest halls in England and Scotland, notably the Free Trade Hall, Manchester, the Town Hall, Birmingham, the Town Hall, Northampton, and the City Hall, Glasgow. It is, as far as I am aware, the first time any English citizen has, without tumult or disorder, and in buildings belonging to various Municipalities, directly challenged the hereditary right of the reigning family.

"In penning the foregoing sketch I had purposely to omit many facts connected with branches of Italian, Irish, and French politics. I have also entirely omitted my own struggles for existence. The political parts are left out, because there are secrets which are not my own alone, and which may not bear full telling for many years to come. The second, because I hope that another year or two of hard work may enable me to free myself from the debt load which for some time has hung heavily round me."

As a specimen of Mr. Bradlaugh's power of irony, I quote the other pamphlet I spoke of as being sold at the Hall of Science, omitting, for obvious reasons, some few passages. It is entitled—

"*A Letter from a Freemason*

TO

"General H.R.H. ALBERT EDWARD, PRINCE OF WALES, Duke of Saxony, Cornwall, and Rothesay; Earl of Dublin, Colonel 10th Hussars, Colonel-in-Chief of the Rifle Brigade, Captain-General and Colonel of the Hon. Artillery Company, K.G., G.C.S.I., K.T., G.C.B., K.P., etc. etc. etc.

"Dear Br.—I do not ask you to pardon this, to the profane, perhaps, an apparently too familiar style of address, although I do pray pardon if I have unintentionally omitted any of your numerous titles in the formal superscription to this letter. I have never written before to a Prince, and may lack good manners in thus inditing; but to my brother Masons I have often written, and know they love best a plain, fraternal greeting, if the purpose of the epistle be honest.

"You have voluntarily on your part, and unsought on my side, commenced by accepting me as a brother, and you have cemented this fraternity by specially swearing to protect me on appeal in my hour of danger; and though history teaches me that sworn promises are less well kept than steadfast, manly pledges, and that Princes' oaths are specially rotten reeds to lean upon; yet in the warmth of newly-created brotherhood, I am inclined to believe you, brother —for we are brethren, you and I—not brothers perhaps as we should be of the same common humanity—for in this land I know that Princes are no fair mates for those who are pauper born; but we are brothers by your own choice, members of the same fraternity by your own joining; men self-associated in the same grand Masonic brotherhood, and it is for that reason I write you this letter. You, though now a Past Grand Master, are but recently a free and accepted Master Mason, and probably yet know but little of the grand traditions of the mighty organization whose temple doors have opened to your appeal. My knowledge of the mystic branch gained amongst the Republicans of all nations is of some years' older date. You are now, as a Freemason, excommunicate by the Pope—so am I. It is fair to hope that the curse of the Church of Rome may have a purifying and chastening effect on your future life, at least as efficacious as the blessing of the Church of England has had on your past career. You have entered into that illustrious fraternity which has numbered in its ranks Swedenborg, Voltaire, and Garibaldi. These are the three who personify grand Idealism and Poetic Madness; Wit and Genius, and true Humanity; manly Energy, sterling Honesty, and hearty Republicanism. My sponsor was Simon Bernard—yours, I hear, was the King of Sweden.

"In writing, dear brother, I do not address you as a Prince of Wales, for some of our Princes of Wales have been drunken, riotous spendthrifts, covered in debt, and deep in dishonour; but you, dear brother, instead of being such an one, figure more reputably as the erudite member of a Royal Geographical Society, or as a steady fellow of the Worshipful Company of Fishmongers. Happily there is no fear that in your case a second Doctor Doran may have to pen the narrative of a delicate investigation. If Junius were alive to-day, his pen would not dare to repeat its fierce attack on another Prince of Wales. Junius charged George, Prince of Wales, with quitting the arms of his wife for the endearments of a wanton, with toying away the night in debauchery, and with mocking the sorrows of the people with an ostentatious prodigality. But your pure career, your sober and virtuous life, would win laudations even from Junius's ghost. You are an English gentleman, as well as Prince of Wales; a good and kind husband in spite of being Prince of Wales; with you woman's honour is safe from attack, and sure of protection. The draggled and vice-stained plumes on your predecessors' escutcheons have been well-cleaned and straightened by modern journalism, and the Prince of Wales' feathers are no longer (like the Bourbon fleur-de-lis) the heraldic ornament of a race of princes *sans foi, sans mœurs*. Fit were you as profane to make the journeys to the Altar, for fame writes you as sober and chaste, as high-minded and generous, as kind-hearted and truthful. These are the qualities, oh Albert Edward, which hid your disability as Prince, when you knelt bare-kneed in our audience chamber. The brethren who opened your eyes to the light, overlooked your title as Prince of Wales in favour of your already famous manhood. Your career is a pleasant contrast to that of George Prince of Wales. Yet because you are as different from the princes whose bodies are dust, while their memories still remain to the historian as visible monuments of shame, I write to you, not as English Prince, but as brother Master Mason. Nor do I address you in your right as one of Saxony's princes, for amongst my memories of other men's readings, I have thoughts of some in Saxony's electoral roll, who were lustful, lecherous, and vile; who were vicious sots and extravagant wasters of their people's earnings, who had lured for their seraglios each fresh face that came within their reach : while you, though Duke of Saxony, have joined a brotherhood whose main intent is the promotion of the highest morality. I do not indeed regard your title of Duke at all in writing you, for when we find a Duke of Newcastle's property in the hands of Sheriffs' Officers, his title a jest for bankruptcy messengers, and the Duke of Hamilton's name an European byeword, it is pleasant to be able to think that the Duke of Cornwall and Rothesay is not as these Dukes are; that this Duke is not a runner after painted donzels, that he has not written cuckold on the forehead of a dozen husbands, that he is not deep in debt, has not, like these Dukes, scattered gold in filthy gutters, while deaf to the honest claims of justice. We know, brother, that you would never have voluntarily enrolled yourself in the world's grandest organization, if you had been as these. It would have been perjury if you had done so—perjury which, though imperially honoured at the Tuileries, would be scouted with contempt by a Lancashire workman. . . . .

"You are a prince, but dare you be a man; for the sake of the Danish flower, whose bloom should gladden your life; for the sake of the toiling millions who are loyal from habit, and who will revolt reluctantly, but for peace will pay taxes readily; for the sake of the halo that history will show round your head in its pages? If you dare, let us see it. Go to Ireland—not to Punchestown races, at a cost to the people of more than two thousand pounds—but secretly amongst its poor, and learn their deep griefs. Walk in London, not in parade at its horse shows, where snobs bow and stumble, but in plain dress and unattended; in its Spitalfields, Bethnal Green, Isle of Dogs, and Seven Dials; go where the unemployed commence to cry in vain for bread, where hunger begins to leave its dead in the open streets, and try to find out why so many starve. Don corduroy and fustian, and ramble through the ploughed fields of Norfolk, Suffolk, Northamptonshire, Wiltshire, and other counties, where thirteen shillings per week are high wages, out of which the earner has to feed and clothe man, wife, and family, and pay rent.

"Brother, before you die you will hear cries for a Republic in England, cries that will require the brains of a grand man to answer, cries which are gathering now, cries from the overtaxed, who pay, without thought and without inquiry, many more pounds in unearned pensions, for yourself and brother princes, than they will by-and-by pay shillings, unless indeed you all work miracles, and make yourselves worth your money to the nation. Yet even this you might do; you might—you and your fellow princes in Europe—if you would disband your standing armies, get rid of the tinselled drones and gaudy court caterpillars, the State Church leeches, and hereditary cormorant tax-eaters, and then there would be a renewed lease of power for you, and higher happiness for the people. But whatever you determine to do, do quickly, or it will be too late. The *Vive la République* now heard from some lips in Paris, Lyons, Marseilles, Bordeaux, will soon be the voice of France, and there is an electric force in the echo of that cry—a force which evokes the lightning-like flash of popular indignation with such directness against princes who mock peoples, against kings who rule for themselves, and against peers who govern for their own class, that as in a moment the oak which has stood for centuries, is stripped of its brown bark, and left bleached and blasted to wither, so is royalty stripped of its tinselled gilding and left naked and defenceless to the cold scorn of a justly indignant nation. As a Freemason you are bound to promote peace, but peace makes the strength of peoples, and discovers the weakness of princes. As a Freemason you are bound to succour the oppressed of the world, but then it will be against your fellow princes. As a Freemason you are bound to aid in educating the ignorant, but if you do this you teach them that the sole authority kings can wield they derive from the people; that a nation may elect a chief magistrate to administer its laws, but cannot give away their liberties to a master who shall have the right to bequeath his authority over their children to his child. As a Freemason you are bound to encourage the development of Free-thought, but Free-thought is at war with the Church, and between Church and

Crown there has ever been most unholy alliance against peoples. You were a prince by birth, it was your misfortune. You have enrolled yourself a Freemason by choice, it shall either be your virtue or your crime—your virtue if you are true to its manly dutifulness; your crime if you dream that your blood royalty is of richer quality than the poorest drop in the veins of

"A FREE AND ACCEPTED MASON."

THE LAND AND LABOUR LEAGUE.

It is not always possible to follow rigorously my method of treating first of all descriptively, each body, religious or political, which I make my subject of study. It has happened, especially in the case of political associations, that no public meeting has occurred during the period of my examination, and I am therefore reduced to the necessity of throwing myself on the courtesy of the secretary or some other official for the information I require. In that case, I state openly my object, enclosing a stamped envelope for reply, and in most cases, or at all events in many cases, have received a prompt response. What the motive may be for refusing information I cannot of course do more than surmise, and must leave my readers to draw their own conclusions. It may be remembered by the readers of "Unorthodox London" that two only out of all the multitudinous sects I dealt with thus refused information. The Irvingites did not wish for publicity, though they have been advertising and holding public meetings furiously ever since; and the Particular Baptists refused to answer my letters. The Positivists only declined courteously to adopt anything which might appear to savour of propagandism through the press, but have since supplied me with everything I required. I regret to find that some "heterodox" societies appear to be following the evil example of the Particular Baptists.

Such, let me hasten to say, was far from being the case with the "Land and Labour League," the secretary whereof, in reply to my inquiries, obligingly wrote me the following letter, and added the documents which I herewith append, on the principle of allowing every religious or political body to speak for itself.

"80, WHITECROSS STREET, E.C.

"DEAR SIR,—Please accept as apology for the delay in answering your letter my illness, which having confined me to the house, has prevented me from attending to correspondence. I enclose you two publications which will give you some idea of the principles advocated by the League.

"We are out of other publications we have issued. It is also our intention shortly to invite combined action of other Radical and Liberal Associations, in support of the principles of our League.

"About a twelvemonth ago we published five reasons for opposing Mr. Mill's proposition for Free Trade in Land, which probably you have seen either in the *Examiner*, or the *National Reformer*, or the *Eastern Post*. The *Standard* also took a favourable view of our opposition at Mr. Mill's meeting at Exeter Hall, where we moved a counter resolution. I also enclose you a copy of songs in elucidation of our principles.

"We have sent copies of the circular headed 'Deus Rex' to several of the Lent Preachers at the Chapel Royal. And now for a few remarks which you will please receive as coming from me. It seems to me that the Heterodoxy of London owes its life to the Infidel way in which professors and teachers of religion have pretended to teach God's truth. They have all along ignored what I may rightly call Material Christianity, that is, a Christianity suitable for man in his material existence; and then the arguments, or rather assertions without argument or reason, by which they support their Spiritual Christianity are so contrary to reason, Divine justice and truth, that they must have driven many from accepting even Spiritual Christianity; while millions cannot at all reconcile the present state of society and suffering, as in accordance with the love of Him who is represented as a God of love. The fact is the religious world, are endeavouring to engraft religion upon a state of society the fundamental principles of which are the very opposite of those social principles laid before us in the Bible; hence there is no unity between the practical and theoretical, or I may say Theocratical. Take for instance one simple land-law of the Bible, 'The land shall not be sold for ever, for the land is Mine.' Therefore it appears that as long as 'The earth is the Lord's' it is not rightly, and never should become a marketable commodity.—Our rulers 'frame mischief by a law,' and 'are not valiant for the truth upon the earth.' They will not accept the doctrine that the land is made for the people, and that God never appointed a rent collector.

"Should anything unforeseen occur, or any movement of the League within a short period, I will advise you. I shall look out for 'Heterodox London,' as doubtless it will contain much that is in harmony with my own sentiments.

"Yours faithfully,
(Signed) "F. RIDDLE,
"*Secy. L.L.L.*"

I have a shrewd suspicion that Mr. Riddle, aware of my clerical status, was poking a sly homily at me in this letter; but the courtesy of his remarks made me a willing listener, and I shall always be glad to "sit under" him or any other lay-preacher who will give me a novel light upon my duties and responsibilities. Indeed, the clerical profession seems, not unnaturally, to be a great object of the League's attentions. The following is the text of the circular distributed among them; and I venture to hope some of my reverend brethren have taken the hint, and "improved" the very suggestive text named therein :—

"DEUS REX.

"LAND AND LABOUR LEAGUE,
"80, WHITECROSS STREET, LONDON, E.C.

"REV. SIR,—By a resolution of the Council of this League, under date October 27th, 1873, I am directed to suggest to you—'The propriety and utility—under the present circumstances of society—of directing or requesting the various Clergy, Ministers, and others, to give Sermons or Addresses on Nehemiah, chapter v. verses 1 to 13 inclusive.'

"It will be obvious to you that the misery, destitution, deaths from starvation and disease, now existing amongst a large number of the honest, toiling industrial classes of Great Britain, are mainly, if not entirely due to a neglect of duty on the part of those who have constituted themselves the governing classes, and who, under a pretence of legislation, have fraudulently and dishonestly appropriated to themselves for their own use, a monopoly of the Land and material resources of Great Britain—the which they could alone rightly *hold in trust* for the benefit of the people —and who have also made such laws in reference to Currency, National, Local, Harbour and Public Works, Bonds and Debts, and the permission of unlimited usury and extortion, as altogether have practically subjected and enslaved the Workers to the Capitalists.

"The Land and Labour League respectfully urges that the Clergy and Ministers have hitherto preached to the poor alone the words of the tent-maker Paul,

'That if any would not work, neither should he eat.'

Working men contend that this doctrine should be preached with equal impartiality to their antagonists and enemies, the non-producing classes; and if neither the consideration of duty to God nor the motive of love to man, has been sufficiently powerful to induce those who have voluntarily taken charge of the moral, mental and material welfare of the people, to abolish the infamous monopolies — the Land and Labour League would urge upon all interested, the consideration of the question of how far, or whether it would be wise under present circumstances to delay a just and equitable reparation of these wrongs—until the working classes shall have determined to vindicate for themselves their just, natural and lawful rights as human beings.

"Signed on behalf of the Land
"and Labour League,
"FREDERIC RIDDLE,
"*Secretary.*"

The specific objects of the League, however, will be best gathered from the two pamphlets enclosed by Mr. Riddle, which I abridge without, I hope, omitting any material point:—

I.

Address of the Land and Labour League to the Working Men and Women of Great Britain and Ireland.

" FELLOW WORKERS,—The fond hopes held out to the toiling and suffering millions of this country thirty years ago have not been realized. They were told that the removal of fiscal restrictions would make the lot of the labouring poor easy; if it could not render them happy and contented it would at least banish starvation for ever from their midst. They raised a terrible commotion for the big loaf, the landlords became rampant, the money lords were confounded, the factory lords rejoiced—their will was done—Protection received the *coup de grace*. A period of the most marvellous prosperity followed. At first the Tories threatened to reverse the policy, but on mounting the ministerial benches, in 1852, instead of carrying out their threat, they joined the chorus in praise of unlimited competition. Prepared for a pecuniary loss, they discovered to their utter astonishment that the rent-roll was swelling at the rate of more than 2,000,000*l.* a year. Never in the history of the human race was there so much wealth—means to satisfy the wants of man—produced by so few hands, and in so short a time, as since the abolition of the Corn Laws. During the lapse of twenty years the declared value of the annual exports of British and Irish produce and manufactures—the fruits of your own labour—rose from 60,000,000*l.* to 188,900,000*l.* In twenty years the taxable income of the lords and ladies of the British soil increased, upon their own confession, from 98,000,000*l.* to 140,000,000*l.* a year; that of the chiefs of trades and professions from 60,000,000*l.* to 110,000,000*l.* a year. Could human efforts accomplish more?

"Alas! there are stepchildren in Britannia's family. No Chancellor of the Exchequer has yet divulged the secret how the 140,000,000*l.* are distributed amongst the territorial magnates, but we know all about the trades-folk. The special favourites increased from sixteen, in 1846, to one hundred and thirty-three, in 1866. Their average annual income rose from 74,300*l.* to 100,600*l.* each. They appropriated one fourth of the twenty years' increase. The next of kin increased from three hundred and nineteen to nine hundred and fifty-nine individuals: their average annual income rose from 17,700*l.* to 19,300*l.* each: they appropriated another fourth. The remaining half was distributed amongst three hundred and forty-six thousand and forty-eight respectables, whose annual income ranged between 100*l.* and 10,000*l.* sterling. The toiling millions, the producers of that wealth—Britannia's Cinderellas—got cuffs and kicks instead of halfpence.

"In the year 1864 the taxable income under Schedule D increased by 9,200,000*l.* Of that increase the metropolis, with less than an eighth of the population, absorbed 4,266,000*l*., or nearly a half. 3,123,000*l*. of that, more than a third of the increase of Great Britain, was absorbed by the City of London, by the favourites of the one hundred and seventy-ninth part of the British population: Mile End and the Tower, with a working population four times as numerous, got 175,000*l*. The citizens of London are smothered with gold; the householders of the Tower Hamlets are overwhelmed by poor-rates. The citizens, of course, object to centralization of poor-rates purely on the principle of local self-government.

"During the ten years ending 1861 the operatives employed in the cotton trade increased 12 per cent.; their produce 103 per cent. The iron miners increased 6 per cent.; the produce of the mines 87 per cent. Twenty thousand iron miners worked for ten mine owners. During the same ten years the agricultural labourers of England and Wales diminished by eighty-eight thousand one hundred and forty-seven, and yet, during that period, several hundred thousand acres of common land were enclosed and transformed into private property to enlarge the estates of the nobility, and the same process is still going on.

"In twelve years the rental liable to be rated to the poor in England and Wales rose from 86,700,000*l*. to 118,300,000*l*.: the number of adult able-bodied paupers increased from one hundred and forty-four thousand five hundred to one hundred and eighty-five thousand six hundred.

"These are no fancy pictures, originating in the wild speculations of hot-brained incorrigibles; they are the confessions of landlords and money lords, recorded in their own blue books. One of their experts told the House of Lords the other day that the propertied classes, after faring sumptuously, laid by 150,000,000*l.* a-year out of the produce of your labour. A few weeks later the President of the Royal College of Surgeons related to a jury, assembled to inquire into the causes of eight untimely deaths, what he saw in the foul ward of St. Pancras.

"Hibernia's favourites too have multiplied, and their income has risen, while a sixth of her toiling sons and daughters perished by famine, and its consequent diseases, and a third of the remainder were evicted, ejected and expatriated by tormenting felonious usurpers.

"This period of unparalleled industrial prosperity has landed thousands of our fellow toilers—honest, unsophisticated, hard-working men and women—in the stone yard and the oakum room; the roast beef of their dreams has turned into skilly. Hundreds of thousands, men, women and children, are wandering about—homeless, degraded outcasts—in the land that gave them birth, crowding the cities and towns, and swarming the highroads in the country, in search of work to obtain food and shelter, without being able to find any. Other thousands, more spirited than honest, are walking the treadmill to expiate little thefts, preferring prison discipline to workhouse fare, while the wholesale swindlers are at large, and felonious landlords preside at quarter sessions to administer the laws. Thousands of the young and strong cross the seas, flying from their native firesides, as from an exterminating plague; the old and feeble perish on the roadside of hunger and cold. The hospitals and infirmaries are overcrowded with fever and famine-stricken: death from starvation has become an ordinary everyday occurrence.

"All parties are agreed that the sufferings of the labouring poor were never more intense, and misery so widespread, nor the means of satisfying the wants of man ever so abundant as at present. This proves above all that the moral foundation of all civil government, 'THAT THE WELFARE OF THE ENTIRE COMMUNITY IS THE HIGHEST LAW, AND OUGHT TO BE THE AIM AND END OF ALL CIVIL LEGISLATION' has been utterly disregarded. Those who preside over the destinies of the nation have either wantonly neglected their primary duty while attending to special interests of the rich to make them richer; or their social position, their education, their class prejudices have incapacitated them from doing their duty to the community at large or applying the proper remedies: in either case they have betrayed their trust.

"Class government is only possible on the condition that those who are held in subjection are secured against positive want. The ruling classes have failed to secure the industrious labourer in the prime of his life against hunger and death from starvation. Their remedies have signally failed; their promises have not been fulfilled. They promised retrenchment; they have enormously increased the public expenditure instead. They promised to lift the burden of taxation from your shoulders; the rich pay but a fractional part of the increased expenses; the rest is levied upon your necessaries—even your pawn tickets are taxed—to keep up a standing army, drawn from your own ranks, to shoot you down if you show signs of disaffection. They promised to minimise pauperism: they have made indigence and destitution your average condition—the big loaf has dwindled into no loaf. Every remedy they have applied has but aggravated the evil, and they have no other to suggest—their rule is doomed. To continue is to involve all in a common ruin. There is one, and only one, remedy. Help yourselves. Determine that you will not endure this abominable state of things any longer; act up to your determination, and it will vanish.

"A few weeks ago a score of London working men talked the matter over. They came to the conclusion that the present economical basis of society was the foundation of all the existing evils—that nothing short of a transformation of the existing social and political arrangements could avail, and that such a transformation could only be effected by the toiling millions themselves. They embodied their conclusions in a series of resolutions, and called a conference of representative working-men, to whom they were submitted for consideration. In three consecutive meetings those resolutions were discussed and unanimously adopted. To carry them out a new working-men's organization, under the title of the 'Land and Labour League,' was established. An executive council of upwards of forty well-known representative workingmen was appointed to draw up a platform of principles arising out of the preliminary resolutions adopted by the conference, to serve as the programme of agitation by means of which a radical change can be effected.

"After mature consideration the Council agreed to the following :—

" 1. Nationalization of the Land.
" 2. Home Colonization.
" 3. National, Secular, Gratuitous and Compulsory Education.
" 4. Suppression of Private Banks of Issue. The State only to issue Paper Money.
" 5. A direct and progressive Property Tax, in lieu of all other Taxes.
" 6. Liquidation of the National Debt.

" 7. Abolition of the Standing Army.

" 8. Reduction of the Number of the Hours of Labour.

" 9. Equal Electoral Rights, with Payment of Members.

" The success of our efforts will depend upon the pressure that can be brought to bear upon the powers that be, and this requires numbers, union, organization, and combination. We therefore call upon you to unite, organize, and combine, and raise the cry throughout Ireland, Scotland, Wales, and England ' The LAND FOR THE PEOPLE,'—the rightful inheritors of nature's gifts. No rational state of society can leave the land, which is the source of life, under the control of, and subject to the whims and caprices of, a few private individuals. A government elected by, and as trustee for, the whole people is the only power that can manage it for the benefit of the entire community.

" Insist upon the State reclaiming the unoccupied lands as a beginning of its nationalization, and placing the unemployed upon it. Let not another acre of common land be enclosed for the private purposes of non-producers. Compel the Government to employ the army, until its final dissolution, as a pioneer force to weed, drain, and level the wastes for cultivation, instead of forming encampments to prepare for the destruction of life. If green fields and kitchen gardens are incompatible with the noble sport of hunting, let the hunters emigrate.

"Make the Nine points of the League the Labour programme, the touchstone by which you test the quality of candidates for parliamentary honours, and if you find them spurious reject them like a counterfeit coin, for he who is not for them is against you.

"You are swindled out of the fruits of your toil by land laws, money laws, and all sorts of laws. Out of the paltry pittance that is left you, you have to pay the interest of a debt that was incurred to keep your predecessors in subjection; you have to maintain a standing army that serves no other purpose in your generation, and you are systematically overworked when employed, and underfed at all times. Nothing but a series of such radical reforms as indicated on our programme will ever lift you out of the slough of despond in which you are at present sunk. The difficulty can be overcome by unity of purpose and action. We are many; our opponents are few. Then working men and women of all creeds and occupations claim your rights as with one voice, and rally round, and unite your forces under the banner of the 'LAND AND LABOUR LEAGUE' to conquer your own emancipation!

"JOHN WESTON, *Treasurer.*

"MARTIN J. BOON,
"J. GEORGE ECCARIUS, } *Secretaries.*"

II.

"*The Land Question.*

"Resolutions submitted to the Conference held at the 'Bell Inn,' Old Bailey, on Wednesday evening, October 13th, 1869, and adjourned to Wednesday, the 20th, and succeeding Wednesday evenings, at the same place.

"PREAMBLE.

"Whereas the existence and rapid increase of poverty and pauperism amongst the industrial classes, side by side with the equally rapid increase and development of the scientific appliances of production, is an anomaly that demonstrates the existence of radical and fundamental defects in the arrangements of society, which it is the incumbent and imperative duty of all classes of Reformers to use their utmost endeavours to discover and remove, this Conference recommends that a vigorous, outspoken, and manly exposition of the causes of this anomalous state of things, with a view to its eradication, be forthwith set on foot by an Association to be now formed under the title of the 'Political and Social Reform League,' on the basis of the following Resolutions, and pledges itself individually and collectively to support such a movement :—

"RESOLUTIONS.

"FIRST.—That the good of the community, individually and collectively, requires that the Government of the country should be conducted in strict accordance with the principles of justice and impartiality, and with a paternal regard for the moral, social, intellectual, and material welfare of all the inhabitants: That justice to all is the interest of each, and injustice to any an injury to all: That the present monopoly in land and practice of usury are diametrically opposed to these philosophic and unassailable truths, and lie at the bottom of all the evils, social and moral, that afflict society.

"SECOND.—That the natural elements—earth, air, and water—with their natural products, are the rightful inheritance and birthright equally of all the inhabitants of a country, of which no human power or authority can justly deprive them: That the creation of private property in land, and its alienation from the great mass of the people, was a blunder and a crime that laid the foundation for the system of falsehood, fraud, and deception that now obtains—a system in which vice becomes virtue and virtue vice—that has resulted in incalculable mischief and confusion; in universally 'muzzling the ox that treadeth out the corn'; in poverty, pauperism, starvation, and premature death to the 'hewers of wood and drawers of water,' and in piling up mountains of wealth for the enjoyment of the idle and worthless, thereby engendering vice, crime, and immorality blacker than 'Egyptian darkness,' obliterating the Creator's image in man, sinking him immeasurably below the brute creation, banishing from his being all that is noble and godlike in humanity, and converting him into a very fiend and a demon, delighting in the cruelty and injustice he perpetrates, and in the damnation and death he inflicts: That the mitigation and removal of these evils can only be effected by the rectification of the errors that have occasioned them;—viz. the restoration of the land to its rightful inheritors—the People—and abolishing the accursed system of usury.

"THIRD.—That the present system of land-holding and letting having caused such manifold evils, a new arrangement, whereby the land shall be held by the State as trustee for the people, to be used for their sole benefit, HAS BECOME AN IMPERATIVE NECESSITY, in order to avert the otherwise inevitable calamity of violent convulsions, and the terrible alternative—a sanguinary and bloody revolution—as no power could control the exasperation and rage for vengeance that would necessarily ensue should the mass of the people become fully aware of the heinousness of the system by means of which they have for ages been robbed and murdered, ere steps had been taken to peaceably effect its removal.

"FOURTH.—That while it would be entirely in accordance with the principles of justice and equity to call upon the landlords unconditionally to surrender the land, and not only the land, but likewise a little of the hundreds of millions of money they have levied on the people for its use, yet, as such a course might in some few instances, where the ownership had recently changed hands, be attended with some degree of hardship, to avoid which, and in order to make the transition from the old to the new order of things as rapid and as smooth as possible, the present holders should be entitled to receive such compensation, in the form of terminable annuities, payable out of the national revenue, as a parliament elected by universal or manhood suffrage should determine.

"FIFTH.—That having recovered possession of the land, the Government should lay down such terms and conditions for its occupancy and cultivation as might be deemed necessary and expedient to protect and advance the interests of the community, and, at the same time, create such a feeling of confidence and security amongst the cultivators of the soil, and such inducements to industry as would leave no excuse for idleness in men capable of wielding the implements of husbandry while there remains an acre of land waiting to be cultivated, or of reclaimable waste or bog to be reclaimed: That to this end the land should be let in such quantities as to suit, as far as practicable, the circumstances and aspirations of all persons or associations desirous of placing themselves upon the land, and, where necessary, loans or grants of money should be made, either in compensation for improvements effected or in progress, or on the security of the crops, and the holdings, on the fulfilment of the required conditions, should be of a fixed and permanent character.

"SIXTH.—That along with the abolition of the landlords, it is also imperatively necessary to cancel and abolish their eight hundred million power patent for plunder, misnamed the National Debt, with its twin iniquity and monument of folly and wickedness, the standing army, consuming between them wealth to the enormous amount of a million a week, every pennyworth of which is ground out of the bone and muscle of down-trodden and famishing industry; that the maintenance of a large standing army in time of peace, at an enormous cost—while millions of Her Majesty's subjects are perishing of cold and hunger—is incapable of any other interpretation the working classes can accept, than that it is kept up for the sole purpose of maintaining the ascendancy of aristocratic imbecility, folly, and blindness—of perpetuating their well-worn 'privilege' of wholesale 'picking and stealing,' and stemming the approaching recognition of the dignity of labour: That the so-called National Debt (money borrowed of themselves for themselves), having been contracted by the aristocracy and moneyocracy to further their own selfish and wicked designs, they, and they alone, are responsible for its liquidation and settlement, and ought to be specially taxed for that purpose, and not another farthing should be levied on industry for the payment of either the principal or interest, nor for the maintenance and education of a mighty host of useless consumers and professional cut-throats.

"SEVENTH.—That the object and duty of the POLITICAL AND SOCIAL REFORM LEAGUE shall be to disseminate and enforce the views and declarations set forth in the preceding resolutions, and to show that no administration or party in the State who are not prepared gradually to carry out the reforms they propose, with many others not stated, but equally necessary to bring the Government into unison and harmony with the principles laid down in the first resolution, are worthy of the confidence and support of the industrial classes; and that all their professions of sympathy for the poor or of a desire to inaugurate a career of 'Justice to Ireland,' or anywhere else, are mere shams and pretences, which it is their bounden duty to treat with unmitigated derision and contempt."

From the poetry of the League, which I am unromantic enough not to like so well as the prose, I cull two extracts, selecting one as a specimen of the sublime, and the other of—well, of the reverse :—

Songs of Freedom and Right for the People.

GOD SAVE THE PEOPLE.

Great God the people save,
Bless them with length of days,
    God save us all.
 Make us victorious,
 Triumphantly glorious
 O'er those who misrule us,
    God save us all.

O Lord our God arise,
Teach aristocracies
    To heed thy law.

Confound their politics,
Frustrate their knavish tricks,
On Thee our hopes we fix,
    God save us all.

Thy plenteous gifts in store,
On us be pleased to pour,
    Long may we live.

May we defend Thy Laws,
And ever have true cause,
With heart and voice to sing,
    God is our King.

NOT FOR RAD.

Tune—"Not for Joe."

I don't care what you call my name,
 My friends all call me Rad,
I'm up to many a Tory trick,
 And sure they're very bad.
So long you've bled you scarce can tell
 Why your suff'rings are so sad,
But if they try my sense to gull
 I tell them not for Rad.

Chorus—Not for Rad, not for Rad,
  He's too wide awake you know,
  No, no, no, not for Rad,
  Not for Raddy, oh dear no.

I used to wonder what it was
 That made the world so bad,
At last, my friends, I found the cause
 Why 'tis things are so sad.
Now the other day I asked for a crib,
 Was told that trade's so bad,

Then Bobby poked me in the rib,
　Says he, I'll have you, Rad.
SPOKEN—Well now, said I, no, no, by Gad.
　　　Chorus—Not for Rad, not for Rad,
　　　　He's too wide awake you know,
　　　　No, no, no, not for Rad,
　　　　I told Bobby not for Rad.

There's fellers called most noble Lords,
　They does no work at all,
They're always giving us hard words,
　And pays us very small.
Ten shill'ns a week they'll give to us,
　" Take that and be content,
And sure you needn't make a fuss,
　You scarce pay any rent."

SPOKEN—Well says I, I really think you ought to gi'e me more; myself, my wife, and kids, we make up half a score, we really cannot live on that.
　　　Chorus—Not for Rad, not for Rad,
　　　　He's too wide awake you know,
　　　　No, no, no, not for Rad,
　　　　Not for Raddy, oh dear no.

I read a book the other day
　When I'd no work to plan,
It told me what they would not say,
　" God gives the land to man."
And the secret then I found at last,
　This land they've ta'en away,
That's how 'tis they're rich so fast
　And we so little pay.

SPOKEN—Fancy hundreds of thousands of acres of land—the people's lands too—for one man, and they *makes* us pay rent to work it, and when we've made such lots of wealth, they doles us our starvation's mite and says " Rest and be contented."
　　　Chorus—What! Content!! Not for Rad,
　　　　He's too wide awake you know,
　　　　No, no, no, not for Rad,
　　　　Not for Raddy, oh dear no.

I think you've heard enough from Rad
　　To set you all in thought,
And though things now go bad and bad,
　　Don't be so cheaply bought.
Make up your minds at once, my lads,
　　Proclaim your rights aloud,
And be no longer lordlings' cads,
　　Although so long you've bowed.

SPOKEN—I say, mind you teach your fellows that the Land of Britain belongs by God's own gift to Britain's men, and that

　　　　Chorus—'Tis for Rads, 'tis for Rads,
　　　　　　They're so wide awake I guess,
　　　　　　Yes, yes, yes, 'tis for Rads,
　　　　　　'Tis for Raddies, oh dear yes.

　　　　　　Hurrah, hurrah, hurrah,
　　　　　　The land, the land, the land.

THE KANSAS CO-OPERATIVE COLONY.

It must not be supposed from the easy-going *couleur de rose* descriptions which my readers meet with in these different chapters, that the hunter after Heterodoxy always has a successful run. Covers are often drawn blank for a long time, sometimes altogether, and such, at the time of sitting down to write the present account, appears to be the case with the Working Men's Co-operative Colony, Kansas, U.S.A., the Association for promoting which advertise Sunday Evening Lectures in the *National Reformer*, and name two gentlemen as corresponding secretaries; but they steadily refuse to correspond with me. I have written on two occasions, enclosing stamped envelope for reply, but as yet, can only say, in the language of Bradshaw, "no information received."

However, I was not going to be done by the coyness of the Kansas secretary, so on a certain Sunday evening I arrayed myself in my garb of *ouvrier*, and set out to beard that retiring gentleman in his den. A public meeting was advertised as usual in the *National Reformer* thus :—

"WORKING MEN'S CO-OPERATIVE COLONY, KANSAS, U.S.A.—Public meetings in the Large Room on the first floor at the Eclectic Hall, 18, Denmark Street, Soho, every Sunday evening, at 8.30, at which lectures are delivered and progress at the Colony reported. J. F. Murray, Cor. Sec., A. Days, Assist. Cor. Sec."

This looked all fair and above-board enough, and in due season I reached Denmark Street, which is close by St. Giles's Church, and found the Eclectic Hall without difficulty. I passed at once into the meeting-room, and saw a goodly assemblage gathered. I had got it; the reason of the secretary's reticence was they had so many volunteers for Kansas that they had no time to answer letters. I sidled up to a working-man next me, who was making notes in what looked like a washing-book, and asked him when the lecture was to commence. To my great joy he informed me there were to be three speakers, so I flattered myself I should soon know all about the Kansas co-operatives; when he followed up his information by asking me—somewhat inconsequentially, I thought—whether I was an abstainer. Coyly as the Kansas secretary himself I answered I was not, and asked him whether abstinence was a part of the Kansas scheme. The man glared at me for a moment, and then the truth flashed upon him and me simultaneously. I had strayed into the wrong room. A teetotal lecture was impending here, and my Kansas co-operatives gathered on the first floor.

To the first floor I mounted, and entered what could only be by a stretch of courtesy called a "large" room, where I found about eight or ten men and two or three women seated on forms, with two individuals, rather more jauntily dressed than the others, at a table. One, a red-headed, bright-eyed young man, with a nosegay in his button-hole, scrutinized me severely when I came in, as indeed did all the assembled except the second secretary, who was an austere-looking gentleman, in reverend black, writing hard, after the manner of actors on the stage. I have a supreme conviction that he was writing nothing; but he kept on perseveringly at it all the time I was there. I could not get to feel at my ease; for all the other folks in the room seemed to know one another, and kept up a constant conversation about people and things utterly unknown to all except the initiated. The chief topic of talk was a Mr. Radford, who it appeared had just set sail with his wife and family for the Colony, and who, the dapper secretary remarked in a semi-official tone, would at that time be feeling very sick—the secretary used an inelegant but perhaps more expressive synonym for that disagreeable process.

I waited about an hour listening to this not very edifying conversation, and watching men and boys paying their pence to the officials—I presume subscriptions to this mystic Association. Mystic it was in the strictest sense of the term, for nothing in the shape of a public lecture took place, and no one whit of information could I extract beyond what cropped up in conversation; which was to the effect that Mr. Radford having got out to the Colony would want some funds to go on with, and a committee was formed to discuss the problem of ways and means.

One fine bearded working-man, whose brother had gone out with Mr. Radford, was disposed to be communicative; but he could not command the publications of the Association, which the jaunty secretary kept all to himself; so I passed downstairs into the teetotal lecture room, where my friend of an hour since was inveighing against alcohol to his heart's content. As for me, I had the disagreeable sensation of having lost an evening by being decoyed to the Eclectic Hall under promise of a public lecture, when none such was forthcoming. I was prepared to sympathize greatly with the objects of the Association as far as I could infer them from its title; but I confess I cannot understand why, if the scheme is *bonâ fide* intended for the public good, the Association should be converted by its officials into a secret society.

Certainly the Kansas Colony Association has the most remarkable way of doing things. While the above remarks were being printed, and the Association still steadily refusing to answer my letters, I received a copy of the *Leamington, Warwickshire, and Centre of England Chronicle,* the London letter of which contained the following paragraphs relative to the Kansas Colony carefully marked for my inspection. If the mission of Mr. Radford be "the most interesting event that has happened since the creation of the world," and the Kansas "chick" really anxious to " peck up applicants for membership," one would fancy the secretary might, at all events, receive instructions to be ordinarily civil to inquirers, instead of treating them in this circumlocutory backstairs kind of manner. However, the Association has full right to conduct its affairs in its own way. My commission simply is to chronicle facts, and leave others to draw their own inferences. Subjoined are the remarkable paragraphs in question :—

"If we speculate on the prospective future from the completion of present actions, a meeting that was held in the Large Hall in Denmark-street, to present a testimonial to Mr. Radford on his departure to America, to take the stewardship of the Kansas Co-operative Colony, was the most interesting event that has happened since the creation of the world. I am bound to explain why I use such an apparently exaggerated estimate of the night's proceedings. The Kansas Colony has been wallowing in all but insurmountable difficulties, with a strain on the pockets of the promoters that literally deprived them of butter for their daily bread. What with the instalments for the land payments, the land tax of the State of Kansas, the raising money to send out Mr. Radford, his wife, and seven children, one would have thought philanthropy would have found out these fighters for a noble purpose, and poured in aid to enable them to do without the strain of attempting the next to impossible. Would it be credited that they have subscribed, in five years, something over two thousand pounds, and all—with perhaps the exception of say £50—by men earning weekly wages? They had been attempting a mortgage; but an American mortgage is not looked at by English capitalists. Luckily, on the occasion of the meeting, the chairman of the Company was enabled to announce that a mortgage had at last been obtained, and that now they, on release from the anxiety for immediate subscriptions, could take their time, as the repayments for the mortgage were in small sums that the Colony could easily meet when once the land was under cultivation; and as repayment did not begin for three years from the date of signing, they could now breathe freely, and exert all their powers for the development of the Colony. This is very satisfactory, but it does not justify the statement that it was the most important meeting that has been held since the world began. You may think I have forgotten the labourers' meeting under the tree at Wellesbourne, but that was to raise wages, not actual emancipation. True; but why it is so is because the system they intend to follow out is the redemption of society—in mutual co-operation—labour exchange—the nationalization of the land, which means that no individual can ever own the land, as it will always belong to the Company; and even the present mortgage is not out of the Company, for it is the chairman himself who has made the promise of a personal repayment of the mortgage by spreading its re-payment over a certain time, so that the members have nothing to do with its liquidation. But as the chairman had only lately joined the Company, the real battle had been fought by the Society, just as the English won the battle of Waterloo before the Prussians came up to the front. The land is never to be sold, but each colonist, at home or abroad, can occupy ten acres as an everlasting occupancy, so that the idea of home shall be a fact—of generation following generation to the crack of doom; I presume, with the right of the Colony, on an improvement or alteration being required, of giving him not less than double compensation, if required, to surrender his occupancy. But as such a requisition is all but impossible, save in the village for a town-hall or new street, so on his ten acres he can build his house as a castle that is impregnable. You may say a man and his family cannot live on ten acres; true, but they have some 250 acres for a co-operative farm, at which he can employ his time; and the probabilities are, that as soon as the estate secures the prospect of the re-payment, the Company will buy land, not only in America but in England, and so make their principles a practical example for the public, which hitherto has had to be contented with paper proposals. You may say, Why is the Company not more known? The answer is, that people do not like joining a Society in difficulties; but now that the difficulties are removed, and the egg satisfactorily hatched, the chick will peck up applicants for admission to membership, which means immediate emancipation from the troubles that now encompass the man who is born into the world with the right to work—if those who want work think it right to give it to him, if not, he is left to starve. I say, therefore, that a Society on its legs, with such intentions, is the first institution that has recognised the authority of the community, in combination with the sovereignty of the individual; and being the first, its principles, as noble, just, equitable, and promoting the welfare of all, will now spread like wildfire among the oppressed, either to join it or to go and do likewise. I wish Mr. Radford's speech, in conclusion, could have been reported, for I never listened to a speech of such heartfelt eloquence, tempered with the moderation of common sense. If the labourers have an Arch over them, the mechanics have a doorway."

AT SUNDAY SCHOOL.

It is a very significant evidence of heterodoxy when a religious body, foregoing the ordinary appellation of church or chapel, bestows on its place of Sunday meeting the philosophic title of "school." Such is the case with the Positivists, or followers of Auguste Comte, who gather week by week on Sunday morning and evening in a small lecture room in Chapel Street, Bedford Row, on which they bestow the old appellation of the Positivist School. I have visited this school on two recent occasions, and heard lectures by the chief apostles of Positivism in London, Dr. Congreve and Dr. Bridges, each of which seems sufficiently distinctive to merit a report.

There would seem to be a tendency on the part of most religious bodies, in these days of keen competition, to push to the front, and no longer elect to "blush unseen;" and even that coy and demure damsel, Philosophy, is catching the contagion from her more impulsive and gushing sister. A year or two ago, when I was collecting materials for my "Unorthodox London," two religious bodies stood rigidly aloof and refused me all information. They did not want to be "done." These were the Irving-

At Sunday School. 243

ites (or Catholic Apostolic Church) and the Particular Baptists. The former seemed to think ventilation in the columns of a penny paper *infra dig.* and un-Apostolic; the latter never answered my letter at all. Since then the Irvingites have come out strongly in the advertising way. It seems to have struck them that, though penny papers were not, of course, an institution in Apostolic times, yet still their existence is a necessary and legitimate development of civilization. Be that as it may, the Catholic Apostolic Church rivals Professor Holloway in the extent of its advertisements, and seeks a platform in every hall in London, while it must have pretty well made the fortune of its bill-poster. The Catholic Apostolic Church is wise in its generation; not so the Particular Baptists. They blush unseen as ever, and still vend their "Earthen Vessels" down the little chapel in Johnson Street, as though there was no world at all outside Notting Hill.

So when I entered the Positivist School a few Sundays since, I did so much in the same way as a gentleman likely to be "wanted" presents himself at one of Ned Wright's exclusive suppers. I secreted my note-book as furtively as I had my cigar on the Metropolitan Rail. But it was no use. Some men, as Malvolio says, have greatness thrust upon them; and since the publication of "Unorthodox London," I cannot enter a conventicle without being "spotted" forthwith. A cheery gentleman who had given me most of the information I had gathered on a previous visit, some years before, was warming his hands at a stove, and no doubt his heart simultaneously by talking to a young lady—I presume a Positivist, but I know pretty. I saw from his manner he remembered me. I believe if I were to go in the garb of an Ashantee chief they would still find me out. However, we said nothing, except about the weather, and such other safe topics; and in course of time the lecturer and his small audience arrived. This lecturer was Dr. Congreve, who had on my previous visit firmly but courteously declined to give me information, simply on the quite intelligible ground that the Positivists did not seek publicity. They were glad to see all who came, and were, of course, open to be reported; but they wished criticism to come purely from without—a canon which none will deem other than sound.

There were very few Sunday scholars at school that morning. The weather outside was miserable; and inside Dr. Congreve was on a heavyish subject, namely, the Positivist Doctrine of Submission. The special phase, however, to be treated that particular morning was a very fascinating one indeed, being an inquiry as to whether the great leaders of thought in past ages believed in the bases they laid down for their teachings. Dr. Congreve, at some length, divided the past and present experience of humanity into three epochs, which he named respectively the

Initial, the Transitional, and the Final. In the organic periods of the Great Theocracies and of the Highest Catholicism, he thought there was no doubt that the leaders of thought *did* believe the doctrines they proclaimed. The success and prevalence of the doctrines were an evidence that they did so. Even in times of dissolution, like those of Aristotle, there was in this philosopher, for instance, a respectful toleration of the old Polytheism, though quite different from that of Plato. So in the cases of Bacon and Descartes, there was no attack on the ancient faith, but a reverent acquiescence which, nevertheless, was only provisional. When the dissolution was very advanced the attitude became more daring. The higher speculative minds demanded change; the lower would still hold on provisionally to old faiths and forms. "We have," said Dr. Congreve, "for the time being eliminated the name of God; but there is no reason why in process of time it should not be replaced, though standing, of course, as the representative of a new idea, namely, Humanity."

Well, this was a bit profound; and as I dared not use my note-book, lest the lecturer should see and denounce me, I fear I carried away but a few fragments of a masterly discourse. Professor Beesly was among the scholars, or audience, or congregation—I never know which to call it—and, as soon as the lecture was over, I prepared to go: but not a bit of it. My cheery friend fished me out, and presented me incontinently to the lecturer as the author of "Unorthodox London." I hope I blushed; I honestly tried to. At all events, I smilingly reminded the Doctor of our previous correspondence, and he repeated to me once more what were his sole and certainly reasonable objections to giving me information. The Positivists are very far above puffing themselves; that was all. He told me that on Sunday evenings Dr. Bridges was delivering a course of lectures on the Great Names in the Positivist Calendar —those to which the months are dedicated. The subject for that evening was Dante; for the next, Gutenberg; for the following, Shakspeare. I selected what the French call the "noble Williams," and went accordingly.

I found the school quite full now, as they told me I should. Many members of trades' unions attend in the evening, the teaching of this Sunday school being quite as much political as moral or religious; and we were then in the thick of politics, for it was the first day of the great election week.

Dr. Bridges had commenced, with something more than punctuality, before I got there, and I could only struggle into a bad seat at the back. They seemed to be all *bonâ fide* working men around me; and there were a good many who looked like working women too: many who might have been decent domestic servants spending their "Sunday out" in that most unlikely of all places. The *savans* and strong-minded ladies (if there were any of the latter) were more in front. Mr. Odger came some time after me, with a little knot evidently of his Southwark supporters round him, and passed up to the chief seat in the synagogue, as if he had been on the floor of St. Stephen's already.

"The original purpose of Art," said Dr. Bridges, "was to enable man to live outside the present, in the past or the future. Art was not of necessity beautiful or imitative; but this was of its essence, that it should supply the necessity which all felt of escaping from the present. Narrow-minded moralists preached the advisability of becoming absorbed in duty; politicians bade us be absorbed in the State; but this Life of Memory was essential to all. It should only co-exist with and not supplant the life of Common Duties; for," said he, "the most degraded of all is the ultra art-life of self-indulgent Epicureanism. For healthy existence the two lives were necessary. But the question might be asked, How could this extend to the degraded classes? It was true of them, as of us, that they needed this double life. If not, they would satisfy their craving by drunkenness. What was not done by art would be done by gin. The function of art, both good and bad, was to give a pleasurable excitement outside of self. Bad art, for instance, was that of Holywell Street, or of modern novels. It was a *Di-version* in the literal sense of the word—a turning away from self, that was sought.

"This function of Art in old times was always associated with religion, as in the Hindoo and Hebrew poetry; but the era to be considered was that of the Renaissance, or, in other words, the fifteenth century, when there took place the revival of beauty, of free thought, and of the old classical spirit. But there was more than this; it was not merely a revival that then occurred. It was a continuance. An onward step was made. There was a blossoming out of the Middle Ages. As in Dante the Catholic side, so in Shakspeare the chivalrous side of Mediævalism was represented. Ariosto was emphatically the Poet of Chivalry; and chivalry meant loyalty, courage, firmness, tenderness, and truth — especially towards woman. The Greek and Roman women had been wholly or partially degraded. Hence it was a new type of poetry which was embodied in Ariosto and Calderon."

The working men in front of me began to fidget and speculate as to when he was "a-coming to Shakspeare." They were, in fact, but overgrown boys, and Ariosto and Calderon were a little beyond them.

"Shakspeare," said Dr. Bridges—as if he had heard the honest artisans—"was the representative of this renaissance spirit in England. Chaucer had been the contemporary of Petrarch; but after his time came the French Wars, the Wars of the Roses, and the Reformation. Life had been too unsettled for the revival. Shakspeare especially, like Corneille, opened up the pages of Roman History. It had been said he was aristocratic. The fact was that Art idealizes the actual, and that the virtues with which it could deal lived in mediæval times only among the upper classes. The Positivist is, *quâ* Positivist, neither Aristocrat nor Democrat, but Sociocrat. He wants to level up, not down: to raise the general level of society. The type of Bayard was a perfect combination of courage, truth, and tenderness, seldom seen before his time or since. The nearest approach perhaps, was Garibaldi. Others might be discerned in the best of Cromwell's Puritans, or the best of the Paris workmen. The self-sacrifice of these latter was worthy the knights of the Middle Ages.

"Art at present," concluded Dr. Bridges, after giving a lengthened analysis of "King Lear" (which sent me to sleep), "was now confined to drawing-rooms, where Browning and Tennyson were simpered out to coteries. It was not national, because society was disturbed. English society was, for the present, given over to money-making; and therefore there was no national Art. In Parliament Street, only the day before, he had seen the most shameless electioneering placard—he knew not of which party—which exemplified that aspect of modern society. It exhorted people to 'vote for those who defend trade against co-operative societies, and are ready to amend the law against adulteration!' That meant really, 'vote for the right to charge more for goods than they are worth, and to adulterate *ad libitum.*' He was," he said, "careless as to which party got in as things are at present; but this selfishness was fatal to Art. All we could do was to use the Art of the past as best we might; and the comfort for Positivists lay in the fact that the noblest sphere of the Art of the future lay in the Religion of Humanity. One word as to electioneering. He had said he viewed the question of parties with indifference. There were reasons which might incline him to either side. He hoped to see disestablishment compassed. He hoped workmen would be elected who would push forward social problems. All these matters deserved serious attention; but there was no chance of success in the present elections; at least the success could only be partial. Even the prevention of further establishment —which was involved in the Education Act—was scarcely to be hoped for. He hoped that such men as should be elected would join for an uncompromising use of their powers; but he doubted whether they might not do more good outside than inside Parliament, in forming a healthy state of public opinion. At all events, it was to be hoped that the few thoroughgoing men in Parliament would continue so, and not consent to feeble compromises."

Such were some of the teachings of this strange Sunday School; and, as I passed out into sanctimonious Bedford Row, I saw the good people coming out of St. John's, and Mr. Odger girding up his loins to address his followers on the flagstones; but I had imbibed instruction enough for one while, so passed on and left him orating.

There is no part of my present task which I have approached with so much diffidence as the description of the outward and visible signs of Positivism, or in the execution of which I am so conscious of deficiency. The outward and visible sign conveys so little of the inward meaning; and the process by which the Positive Philosophy passes into the Religion of Humanity is so complicated and delicate, that I feel my best plan will be simply to transcribe a few extracts from Mr. G. H. Lewes's "History of Philosophy," and refer my readers to that work, together with the prolific literature of Positivism, or, better still, counsel them to adopt the same course of personal observation which I myself put in practice.

The first two essays of Comte were: I. "Plan des Travaux Nécessaires pour Reorganizer la Société;" II. "Considérations Philosophiques sur les Sciences et les Savants." "These form," says Mr. Lewes, "an excellent introduction to the study of Positivism; and in them it is shown (1) that all phenomena, even those of politics, are subject to invariable laws; (2) that the human mind passes from initial theological conceptions to final positive conceptions, through the transition of metaphysical conceptions; (3) that human activity, in like manner, passes through three phrases, from the conquering military régime to the pacific industrial régime, through the transitional state of a defensive military régime; (4) that everywhere, and at all times, the state of opinions and manners determines the institutions, and that the nature of the general beliefs determines a corresponding political régime; (5) that philosophy (or general beliefs) in passing from the theological to the positive stage, must bring about the substitution of the industrial for the military régime; and, finally, that the spiritual reorganization, which is the necessary condition of all social reorganization, must repose upon the authority of demonstration; it must be based on science, with a priesthood properly constituted out of the regenerated scientific classes. In other words, the spiritual authority must issue from a philosophy which can be demonstrated, not from a philosophy which is imagined."

Some years ago, when the subject was quite new to me, I alluded to it in one of my Sunday evening sermons, and found the congregation greatly interested in the subject. I hope it is not egotistical to quote one's self again. The passage I subjoin, referring to Comte's separation from his wife and subsequent connexion with Clotilde, explains in some degree the evolution of the Religion out of the Philosophy. It must be remembered under what circumstances the words were spoken; I prefer to insert them as they were then delivered, instead of modifying them as I might perhaps be inclined to do now:—

"Mary of Bethany I would make the type of that trite and rudimentary truth—man's deep need of religion. Yes; the truth is trite and rudimentary enough. It is a truism as well as a truth; but it came to me supplemented with an illustration which may prove as interesting to you as to me.

"Some of you may be aware—others are not—that there is a system in our midst, represented, slenderly perhaps, but still represented, by individuals whose names are well known, which system professes to have outgrown all belief in, or need of, God and supernatural agencies; nay, to have also outstripped metaphysics, the science of mind, and to have reduced everything to positive knowledge.

"This you may say is simply the position of Atheism; but this is not quite the case; and *why* and how it is not so is the most curious part of the system. The man who elaborated that system for many years found it answer his purpose. At length, in face of an experience precisely the same as befel the sisters of Bethany, he found himself obliged to supplement his philosophy with a religion. One whom he loved died, and then his system failed him. Then there came home to the mind of this philosopher for the first time, as it would appear, a conviction of that poor truism which seemed just now so rudimentary—man's deep need of religion. But what was he to do? He had cut the ground from beneath his feet. He had ceased to believe, and made his many followers cease to believe in God. They did not even believe in the noblest part of self. What then was left him? A 'Religion of Humanity' as it is termed. So grew up, out of its founder's sorrow, this strange system. The year is divided into thirteen lunar months, each named after some great man. Every day is dedicated to some minor celebrity—one day to the dead in general, one other to the memory of holy women. The calendar is studded with *fête* days just like a calendar of the saints. This is not the place to discuss the merits or demerits of the system; but this *is* the the place, and now, when that system is growing up in our midst, is surely the time for the preacher to put the fact in its true significance as a curious, a marvellous piece of evidence of that other fact (not so rudimentary as it might seem) of man's *deep need of religion*.

"Starting in absolute Atheism about the beginning of this century, it has resulted in this strange form of religion. The founder, only some fifteen years dead, actually preached and performed the marriage and burial services. Surely the deduction from this strange history is, not only man's deep need of religion, but the further truth that 'the old is better.' The God of Revelation is surely more worthy our worship than the God of Humanity—the God of Self, that is. The Church, with all her defects, all the fluctuations in her history, has surely served her purpose better, and presents to us in the roll of her noble army something more worthy of our acceptance than a calendar which enshrines the names of Orpheus and Solon, and even condescends to chronicle S. Paul, but has no place for the name of Jesus of Nazareth.*

"There is nothing perhaps more useful than new and striking enforcements of old and familiar truths. You were, very likely, half inclined to resent the statement of such an elementary fact as man's need of religion. But I ask you, has not God's Finger written down a curious sanction of it in this growing system? The men who profess it are intellectual giants; they are active and energetic in all works of practical and social well-doing. But this is not enough; and they have unconsciously written down the fact for us that it is not enough. Man that is, has not only a body to be tended, and a mind to be educated, but a spirit to be trained for a life beyond the present.

"We are told that Society thus growing out of its need of God and belief in God, growing up to the merest materialism is typed by the life of the individual. Often too truly it is the case. The man,

---

* On a subsequent occasion I inserted the following :—"I have this afternoon listened to an able exposition of this doctrine; and being anxious to ascertain how *any* religious system could grow up in Comte's brain, was informed that Comte was insane when he was religious—though how to distinguish between Comte sane and Comte insane, we were not told. Comte certainly was insane, but at an early period of his life, when he formed his philosophy and *not* his religion!"

grown up from childhood *seems* to have outgrown God—*seems* to forget the nobler part of self—*seems* to be immersed in things of this world. *Seems*, but is not. You know—such of you as have at all experienced this in self—that, however far you seemed to get from God—however much you were led to sacrifice the higher to the lower impulses of your nature, there were times when this could not be the case. The spirit *would not* be ignored any more than the mind or the body. You could no more starve the spirit of communion with God than you could starve the body with impunity, or prevent the mind appropriating something to itself from surrounding influences.

"And oftenest—as in this Bethany household, and as in this strange system—it is sorrow that calls out the true self, and teaches the man or the woman what one would at first fancy the familiar lesson of their own inner needs."

On the subject of Comte's separation from his wife and subsequent connexion with Clotilde, Mr. Lewes writes thus:—"Into the domestic question I cannot enter. Be the blame of the failure chiefly hers or chiefly his, the failure sprang from conditions we cannot accurately appreciate. That the separation was her deed and not his, seems indisputable. . . . . It is clear, from many indications, that they quarrelled frequently and violently; their views of life were different, and probably the worldly views of the one were a continual exasperation to the other; but it is also clear that he did not regard her as having done anything to forfeit his respect and admiration. He continued for some years to correspond with her on affectionate terms.

"It was," continues Mr. Lewes, "in the year 1845 that he first met Madame Clotilde de Vaux. There was a strange similarity in their widowed conditions. She was irrevocably separated from her husband by a crime which had condemned him to the galleys for life; yet, although morally free, she was legally bound to the man whose disgrace overshadowed her. Comte was also irrevocably separated from his wife by her voluntary departure; and, although morally free, was legally bound. Marriage being thus unhappily impossible, they had only the imperfect, yet inestimable, consolation of a pure and passionate friendship. He was fond of applying to her the lines of his favourite Dante—

> Quella che imparadisa mia mente
> Ogni basso pensier dal cor m'avulse.

Every one who knew him during this brief period of happiness will recall the mystic enthusiasm with which he spoke of her, and the irrepressible overflowing of his emotion which led him to speak of her at all times and to all listeners. It was in the early days of this attachment that I first saw him; and in the course of our very first interview he spoke of her with an expansiveness which was very interesting. When I next saw him he was as expansive in his grief at her irreparable loss; and the tears rolled down his cheeks as he detailed her many perfections. His happiness had lasted but one year."

The context reminds one forcibly of a passage in the "Autobiography of John Stuart Mill." "Her death," continues Mr. Lewes, "made no change in his devotion. She underwent a transfiguration. Her subjective immortality became a real presence to his mystical affection. The remainder of his life was a perpetual hymn to her memory. Every week he visited her tomb : every day he prayed to her, and invoked her continual assistance. His published invocations and eulogies may call forth mockery from frivolous contemporaries—intense convictions and disinterested passions easily lending themselves to ridicule—but posterity will read in them a grave lesson, and will see that this modern Beatrice played a considerable part in the evolution of the Religion of Humanity.

"The increasing notoriety of the name of Auguste Comte is significant of a spreading sympathy and a spreading dread. In grave treatises, and in periodical works, his opinions are silently adopted, openly alluded to, and discussed with respect; but much oftener they furnish a flippant sentence to some jaunty journalist, or pander to the austere dishonesty of some polemical theologian. Indignation, scorn, and ridicule are poured forth with all the greater freedom, because usually unhampered by any first-hand knowledge.

"Meanwhile," it is so Mr. Lewes concludes his subject, " anarchy continues, and the Faith is slow in spreading."

I very much hope that, although I wrote these words first of all for a Manchester newspaper, I do not come under Mr. Lewes's category of a "jaunty journalist," as I am sure I do not under that of a polemical theologian. To me there is no problem half so interesting as that proposed for solution by the Positivist body; and I rejoice, whenever I have the opportunity, to transform myself into a disciple in the Chapel Street School. Plaster busts of the great of all ages stand on brackets round the walls, and pictures of sacred and secular subjects are hung between and beneath them. Of worship there is nothing, as far as I have seen; the object of the meeting being simply to listen to a lecture. I must confess I should vastly like to see the full ritual as organized by Comte himself carried out; but, as far as I can ascertain, this Chapel Street School is the only focus of the faith in London. I only wish that the other visits which I have had to pay in the execution of my now almost completed task were half so agreeable and instructive as those at the "Sunday School."

The following are the Positivist Calendar, and the course of Lectures thereupon, one of which I have reported above:—

POSITIVIST CALENDAR, ADAPTED TO ALL YEARS EQUALLY.
By AUGUSTE COMTE, *Founder of the Religion of Humanity.*

Days of the Week.	Days of the Civil Calendar.	FIRST MONTH. **MOSES.** THE INITIAL THEOCRACY.		Days of the Civil Calendar.	SECOND MONTH. **HOMER.** ANCIENT POETRY.	
Mon.	Jan. 1	1 Prometheus	*Cadmus.*	Jan. 29	1 Hesiod	
Tues.	" 2	2 Hercules	*Theseus.*	" 30	2 Tyrtæus	*Sappho.*
Wed.	" 3	3 Orpheus	*Tiresias.*	" 31	3 Anacreon	
Thur.	" 4	4 Ulysses		Feb. 1	4 Pindar	
Fri.	" 5	5 Lycurgus		" 2	5 Sophocles	*Euripides.*
Sat.	" 6	6 Romulus		" 3	6 Theocritus	*Longus.*
Sun.	" 7	7 **NUMA**		" 4	7 **ÆSCHYLUS**	
Mon.	" 8	8 Belus	*Semiramis.*	" 5	8 Scopas	
Tues.	" 9	9 Sesostris		" 6	9 Zeuxis	
Wed.	" 10	10 Menu		" 7	10 Ictinus	
Thur.	" 11	11 Cyrus		" 8	11 Praxiteles	
Fri.	" 12	12 Zoroaster		" 9	12 Lysippus	
Sat.	" 13	13 The Druids	*Ossian.*	" 10	13 Apelles	
Sun.	" 14	14 **BUDDHA**		" 11	14 **PHIDIAS**	
Mon.	" 15	15 Fo-Hi		" 12	15 Æsop	*Pilpay.*
Tues.	" 16	16 Lao-Tseu		" 13	16 Plautus	
Wed.	" 17	17 Meng-Tseu		" 14	17 Terence	*Menander.*
Thur.	" 18	18 The Theocrats of Thibet		" 15	18 Phædrus	
Fri.	" 19	19 The Theocrats of Japan		" 16	19 Juvenal	
Sat.	" 20	20 Manco Capac	*Tamehameha.*	" 17	20 Lucian	
Sun.	" 21	21 **CONFUCIUS**		" 18	21 **ARISTOPHANES**	
Mon.	" 22	22 Abraham	*Joseph.*	" 19	22 Ennius	
Tues.	" 23	23 Samuel		" 20	23 Lucretius	
Wed.	" 24	24 Solomon	*David.*	" 21	24 Horace	
Thur.	" 25	25 Isaiah		" 22	25 Tibullus	
Fri.	" 26	26 St. John the Baptist	*[III.*	" 23	26 Ovid	
Sat.	" 27	27 Haroun-al-Raschid	*Abderrahman*	" 24	27 Lucan	
Sun.	" 28	28 **MAHOMET**		" 25	28 **VIRGIL**	

Days of the Week.	Days of the Civil Calendar.	THIRD MONTH. **ARISTOTLE.** ANCIENT PHILOSOPHY.		Days of the Civil Calendar.	FOURTH MONTH. **ARCHIMEDES.** ANCIENT SCIENCE.	
Mon.	Feb. 26	1 Anaximander		Mar. 26	1 Theophrastus	
Tues.	" 27	2 Anaximenes		" 27	2 Herophilus	
Wed.	" 28	3 Heraclitus		" 28	3 Erasistratus	
Thur.	Mar. 1	4 Anaxagoras		" 29	4 Celsus	
Fri.	" 2	5 Democritus	*Leucippus.*	" 30	5 Galen	
Sat.	" 3	6 Herodotus		" 31	6 Avicenna	*Averhoes.*
Sun.	" 4	7 **THALES**		April 1	7 **HIPPOCRATES**	
Mon.	" 5	8 Solon		" 2	8 Euclid	
Tues.	" 6	9 Xenophanes		" 3	9 Aristæus	
Wed.	" 7	10 Empedocles		" 4	10 Theodosius of Bithynia	
Thur.	" 8	11 Thucydides		" 5	11 Hero	*Ctesibius.*
Fri.	" 9	12 Archytas	*Philolaus.*	" 6	12 Pappus	
Sat.	" 10	13 Apollonius of Tyana		" 7	13 Diophantus	
Sun.	" 11	14 **PYTHAGORAS**		" 8	14 **APOLLONIUS**	
Mon.	" 12	15 Aristippus		" 9	15 Eudoxus	*Aratus.*
Tues.	" 13	16 Antisthenes		" 10	16 Pytheas	*Nearchus.*
Wed.	" 14	17 Zeno		" 11	17 Aristarchus	*Berosus.*
Thur.	" 15	18 Cicero	*Pliny the Younger.*	" 12	18 Eratosthenes	*Sosigenes.*
Fri.	" 16	19 Epictetus	*Arrian.*	" 13	19 Ptolemy	
Sat.	" 17	20 Tacitus		" 14	20 Albategnius	*Nasir-Eddin.*
Sun.	" 18	21 **SOCRATES**		" 15	21 **HIPPARCHUS**	
Mon.	" 19	22 Xenocrates		" 16	22 Varro	
Tues.	" 20	23 Philo of Alexandria		" 17	23 Columella	
Wed.	" 21	24 St. John the Evangelist		" 18	24 Vitruvius	
Thur.	" 22	25 St. Justin	*St. Irenæus.*	" 19	25 Strabo	
Fri.	" 23	26 St. Clement of Alexandria		" 20	26 Frontinus	
Sat.	" 24	27 Origen	*Tertullian.*	" 21	27 Plutarch	
Sun.	" 25	28 **PLATO**		" 22	28 **PLINY THE ELDER**	

Days of the Week	Days of the Civil Calendar	FIFTH MONTH. CÆSAR. MILITARY CIVILIZATION.	Days of the Civil Calendar		SIXTH MONTH. SAINT PAUL. CATHOLICISM.
Mon.	Apr. 23	1 Miltiades	May	21	1 St. Luke .... St. James.
Tues.	" 24	2 Leonidas	"	22	2 St. Cyprian
Wed.	" 25	3 Aristides	"	23	3 St. Athanasius
Thur.	" 26	4 Cimon	"	24	4 St. Jerome
Fri.	" 27	5 Xenophon	"	25	5 St. Ambrose
Sat.	" 28	6 Phocion .... Epaminondas.	"	26	6 St. Monica
Sun.	" 29	7 **THEMISTOCLES**	"	27	7 **ST. AUGUSTIN**
Mon.	" 30	8 Pericles	"	28	8 Constantine
Tues.	May 1	9 Philip	"	29	9 Theodosius
Wed.	" 2	10 Demosthenes	"	30	10 St. Chrysostom .... St. Basil.
Thur.	" 3	11 Ptolemy Lagus	"	31	11 St. Pulcheria .... Marcian.
Fri.	" 4	12 Philopœmen	June	1	12 St. Genevieve of Paris
Sat.	" 5	13 Polybius	"	2	13 St. Gregory the Great
Sun.	" 6	14 **ALEXANDER**	"	3	14 **HILDEBRAND**
Mon.	" 7	15 Junius Brutus	"	4	15 St. Benedict .... St. Antony.
Tues.	" 8	16 Camillus .... Cincinnatus.	"	5	16 St. Boniface .... St. Austin.
Wed.	" 9	17 Fabricius .... Regulus.	"	6	17 St. Isidore of Seville ..... St. Bruno.
Thur.	" 10	18 Hannibal	"	7	18 Lanfranc .... St. Anselm.
Fri.	" 11	19 Paulus Æmilius	"	8	19 Heloise .... Beatrice.
Sat.	" 12	20 Marius .... The Gracchi.	"	9	20 The Architects of the Middle Ages
Sun.	" 13	21 **SCIPIO**	"	10	21 **St. BERNARD** Bennet the Less
Mon.	" 14	22 Augustus .... Mæcenas.	"	11	22 St. Francis Xavier Ignatius Loyola.
Tues.	" 15	23 Vespasian .... Titus.	"	12	23 St. Ch. Borromeo Fredk. Borromeo.
Wed.	" 16	24 Hadrian .... Nerva.	"	13	24 St. Theresa ...St. Catherine of Siena.
Thur.	" 17	25 Antoninus .... Marcus Aurelius.	"	14	25 St. Vincent de Paul Abbé de l'Epée.
Fri.	" 18	26 Papinian .... Ulpian.	"	15	26 Bourdaloue .... Claude Fleury.
Sat.	" 19	27 Alexander Severus .... Ætius	"	16	27 William Penn .... George Fox.
Sun.	" 20	28 **TRAJAN**	"	17	28 **BOSSUET**

Days of the Week	Days of the Civil Calendar	SEVENTH MONTH. CHARLEMAGNE. FEDERAL CIVILIZATION.	Days of the Civil Calendar		EIGHTH MONTH. DANTE. MODERN EPIC POETRY.
Mon.	June 18	1 Theodoric the Great	July	16	1 The Troubadours
Tues.	" 19	2 Pelayo	"	17	2 Boccaccio .... Chaucer.
Wed.	" 20	3 Otho the Great ...Henry the Fowler.	"	18	3 Rabelais .... Swift.
Thur.	" 21	4 St. Henry	"	19	4 Cervantes
Fri.	" 22	5 Villiers .... La Valette.	"	20	5 La Fontaine .... Burns.
Sat.	" 23	6 Don John of Austria John Sobieski.	"	21	6 De Foe .... Goldsmith.
Sun.	" 24	7 **ALFRED**	"	22	7 **ARIOSTO**
Mon.	" 25	8 Charles Martel	"	23	8 Leonardo da Vinci .... Titian.
Tues.	" 26	9 The Cid .... Tancred.	"	24	9 Michael Angelo ...... Paul Veronese.
Wed.	" 27	10 Richard I. .... Saladin.	"	25	10 Holbein .... Rembrandt.
Thur.	" 28	11 Joan of Arc .... Marina.	"	26	11 Poussin .... Lesueur.
Fri.	" 29	12 Albuquerque ...... Sir W. Raleigh.	"	27	12 Velasquez .... Murillo.
Sat.	" 30	13 Bayard	"	28	13 Teniers .... Rubens.
Sun.	July 1	14 **GODFREY**	"	29	14 **RAPHAEL**
Mon.	" 2	15 St. Leo the Great .... Leo IV.	"	30	15 Froissart .... Joinville.
Tues.	" 3	16 Gerbert .... Peter Damian.	"	31	16 Camoens .... Spenser.
Wed.	" 4	17 Peter the Hermit	Aug.	1	17 The Spanish Romancers
Thur.	" 5	18 Suger .... St. Eligius.	"	2	18 Chateaubriand
Fri.	" 6	19 Alexander III. .... Becket.	"	3	19 Walter Scott .... Cooper.
Sat.	" 7	20 St. Francis of Assisi ...... St. Dominic.	"	4	20 Manzoni
Sun.	" 8	21 **INNOCENT III.**	"	5	21 **TASSO**
Mon.	" 9	22 St. Clotilde	"	6	22 Petrarca [and Bunyan.
Tues.	" 10	23 St. Bathilda St. Mathilda of Tuscany.	"	7	23 Thos. à Kempis ...Louis of Grunada
Wed.	" 11	24 St. Stephen of Hungary ...Mat. Cor-	"	8	24 Mme. de Lafayette ...Mme. de Staël.
Thur.	" 12	25 St. Elizabeth of Hungary [vinus.	"	9	25 Fénelon .... St. Francis of Sales.
Fri.	" 13	26 Blanche of Castile	"	10	26 Klopstock .... Gessner.
Sat.	" 14	27 St. Ferdinand III. .... Alfonso X.	"	11	27 Byron Eliza Mercœur, Shelley.
Sun.	" 15	28 **SAINT LOUIS**	"	12	28 **MILTON**

At Sunday School.

Days of the Week.	Days of the Civil Calendar.	NINTH MONTH. GUTENBERG. MODERN INDUSTRY.	Days of the Civil Calendar.	TENTH MONTH. SHAKSPEARE. THE MODERN DRAMA.
Mon.	Aug. 13	1 Marco Polo .... *Chardin.*	Sept. 10	1 Lopez de Vega .... *Montalven.*
Tues.	„ 14	2 Jaques Cœur .... *Gresham.*	„ 11	2 Moreto .... *Guillem de Castro.*
Wed.	„ 15	3 Vasco de Gama .... *Magellan.*	„ 12	3 Rojas .... *Guevara.*
Thur.	„ 16	4 Napier .... *Briggs.*	„ 13	4 Otway
Fri.	„ 17	5 Lacaille .... *Delambre.*	„ 14	5 Lessing
Sat.	„ 18	6 Cook	„ 15	6 Goethe
Sun.	„ 19	**7 COLUMBUS** .... *Tasman.*	„ 16	**7 CALDERON**
Mon.	„ 20	8 Benvenuto Cellini	„ 17	8 Tirso
Tues.	„ 21	9 Amontons .... *Wheatstone.*	„ 18	9 Vondel
Wed.	„ 22	10 Harrison .... *Pierre Leroy.*	„ 19	10 Racine
Thur.	„ 23	11 Dollond .... *Graham.*	„ 20	11 Voltaire
Fri.	„ 24	12 Arkwright .... *Jacquard.*	„ 21	12 Metastasio .... *Alfieri.*
Sat.	„ 25	13 Conté	„ 22	13 Schiller
Sun.	„ 26	**14 VAUCANSON**	„ 23	**14 CORNEILLE**
Mon.	„ 27	15 Stevin .... *Torricelli.*	„ 24	15 Alarcon
Tues.	„ 28	16 Mariotte .... *Boyle.*	„ 25	16 Mme. de Moteville ... *Mme. Roland.*
Wed.	„ 29	17 Papin .... *Worcester.*	„ 26	17 Mme. de Sévigné ... *Lady Montagu.*
Thur.	„ 30	18 Black	„ 27	18 Lesage .... *Sterne.*
Fri.	„ 31	19 Jouffroy .... *Fulton.*	„ 28	19 Madame de Staël ... *Miss Edgeworth.*
Sat.	Sept. 1	20 Dalton .... *Thilorier.*	„ 29	20 Fielding .... *Richardson.*
Sun.	„ 2	**21 WATT**	„ 30	**21 MOLIERE**
Mon.	„ 3	22 Bernard de Palissy	Oct. 1	22 Pergolesi .... *Palestrina.*
Tues.	„ 4	23 Guglielmini .... *Riquet.*	„ 2	23 Sacchini .... *Grétry.*
Wed.	„ 5	24 Duhamel (du Monceau) ... *Bourgelat.*	„ 3	24 Gluck .... *Lully.*
Thur.	„ 6	25 Saussure .... *Bouguer.*	„ 4	25 Beethoven .... *Handel.*
Fri.	„ 7	26 Coulomb .... *Borda.*	„ 5	26 Rossini .... *Weber.*
Sat.	„ 8	27 Carnot .... *Vauban.*	„ 6	27 Bellini .... *Donizetti.*
Sun.	„ 9	**28 MONTGOLFIER**	„ 7	**28 MOZART**

Days of the Week.	Days of the Civil Calendar.	ELEVENTH MONTH. DESCARTES. MODERN PHILOSOPHY.	Days of the Civil Calendar.	TWELFTH MONTH. FREDERICK II. MODERN POLICY.
Mon.	Oct. 8	1 Albertus Magnus *John of Salisbury.*	Nov. 5	1 Marie de Molina
Tues.	„ 9	2 Roger Bacon .... *Raymond Lully.*	„ 6	2 Cosmo di Medici the Elder
Wed.	„ 10	3 St. Bonaventura .... *Joachim.*	„ 7	3 Philip de Comines ...... *Guicciardini.*
Thur.	„ 11	4 Ramus .... *The Cardinal of Cusa.*	„ 8	4 Isabella of Castile
Fri.	„ 12	5 Montaigne .... *Erasmus.*	„ 9	5 Charles V. .... *Sixtus V.*
Sat.	„ 13	6 Campanella .... *Sir Thomas More.*	„ 10	6 Henri IV.
Sun.	„ 14	**7 ST. THOMAS AQUINAS**	„ 11	**7 LOUIS XI.**
Mon.	„ 15	8 Hobbes .... *Spinoza.*	„ 12	8 L'Hôpital
Tues.	„ 16	9 Pascal .... *Giordano Bruno.*	„ 13	9 Barneveldt
Wed.	„ 17	10 Locke .... *Malebranche.*	„ 14	10 Gustavus Adolphus
Thur.	„ 18	11 Vauvenargues ...... *Mme. de Lambert.*	„ 15	11 De Witt
Fri.	„ 19	12 Diderot .... *Duclos.*	„ 16	12 Ruyter
Sat.	„ 20	13 Cabanis .... *George Leroy.*	„ 17	13 William III.
Sun.	„ 21	**14 LORD BACON**	„ 18	**14 WILLIAM THE SILENT**
Mon.	„ 22	15 Grotius .... *Cujas.*	„ 19	15 Ximenes
Tues.	„ 23	16 Fontenelle .... *Maupertuis.*	„ 20	16 Sully .... *Oxenstiern.*
Wed.	„ 24	17 Vico .... *Herder.*	„ 21	17 Mazarin .... *Walpole.*
Thur.	„ 25	18 Fréret .... *Winckelmann.*	„ 22	18 Colbert .... *Louis XII.*
Fri.	„ 26	19 Montesquieu .... *d'Aguesseau.*	„ 23	19 D'Aranda .... *Pombal.*
Sat.	„ 27	20 Buffon .... *Oken.*	„ 24	20 Turgot .... *Campomanes.*
Sun.	„ 28	**21 LEIBNITZ**	„ 25	**21 RICHELIEU**
Mon.	„ 29	22 Robertson .... *Gibbon.*	„ 26	22 Sidney .... *Lambert.*
Tues.	„ 30	23 Adam Smith .... *Dunoyer.*	„ 27	23 Franklin .... *Hampden.*
Wed.	„ 31	24 Kant .... *Fichte.*	„ 28	24 Washington .... *Kosiusko.*
Thur.	Nov. 1	25 Condorcet .... *Ferguson.*	„ 29	25 Jefferson .... *Madison.*
Fri.	„ 2	26 Joseph de Maistre .... *Donald.*	„ 30	26 Bolivar ...... *Toussaint L'Ouverture.*
Sat.	„ 3	27 Hegel .... *Sophie Germain.*	Dec. 1	27 Francia
Sun.	„ 4	**28 HUME**	„ 2	**28 CROMWELL**

At Sunday School. 263

Days of the Week	Days of the Civil Calendar	THIRTEENTH MONTH. BICHAT. MODERN SCIENCE.		Festival of all THE DEAD	Festival of HOLY WOMEN	Complementary Day (Dec. 31)	Additional Day in Leap-year	Note.—In Leap-years the first of March and all subsequent days will coincide with the day following that to which they are placed opposite in this Calendar. The names in Italics are those of the persons who, in Leap-years, take the places of their Principals.
Mon.	Dec. 3	1 Copernicus	*Tycho Brahé.*					
Tues.	,, 4	2 Kepler	*Halley.*					
Wed.	,, 5	3 Huyghens	*Varignon.*					
Thur.	,, 6	4 James Bernouilli	*John Bernouilli.*					
Fri.	,, 7	5 Bradley	*Roemer.*					
Sat.	,, 8	6 Volta	*Sauveur.*					
Sun.	,, 9	7 **GALILEO**						
Mon.	,, 10	8 Vieta	*Harriott.*					
Tues.	,, 11	9 Wallis	*Fermat.*					
Wed.	,, 12	10 Clairaut	*Poinsot.*					
Thur.	,, 13	11 Euler	*Monge.*					
Fri.	,, 14	12 D'Alembert	*Daniel Bernouilli.*					
Sat.	,, 15	13 Lagrange	*Joseph Fourier.*					
Sun.	,, 16	14 **NEWTON**						
Mon.	,, 17	15 Bergmann	*Scheele.*					
Tues.	,, 18	16 Priestley	*Davy.*					
Wed.	,, 19	17 Cavendish						
Thur.	,, 20	18 Guyton Morveau	*Geoffroy.*					
Fri.	,, 21	19 Berthollet						
Sat.	,, 22	20 Berzelius	*Ritter.*					
Sun.	,, 23	21 **LAVOISIER**						
Mon.	,, 24	22 Harvey	*Ch. Bell.*					
Tues.	,, 25	23 Boërhaave	*Stahl.*					
Wed.	,, 26	24 Linnæus	*Bernard de Jussieu.*					
Thur.	,, 27	25 Haller	*Vicq d'Azyr.*					
Fri.	,, 28	26 Lamarck	*Blainville.*					
Sat.	,, 29	27 Broussais	*Morgagni.*					
Sun.	,, 30	28 **GALL**						

A Course of Lectures, by DR. BRIDGES, *upon the Principal Names of the* POSITIVIST CALENDAR. *These names are as follows:—*

I.	MOSES, with whom are associated	{ Numa, Buddha,	Confucius, Mahomet.
II.	HOMER, with whom are associated	{ Æschylus, Phidias,	Aristophanes, Virgil.
III.	ARISTOTLE, with whom are associated	{ Thales, Pythagoras,	Socrates, Plato.
IV.	ARCHIMEDES, with whom are associated	{ Hippocrates, Apollonius,	Hipparchus, Pliny.
V.	CÆSAR, with whom are associated	{ Themistocles, Alexander,	Scipio, Trajan.
VI.	ST. PAUL, with whom are associated	{ St. Augustin, Hildebrand,	St. Bernard, Bossuet.
VII.	CHARLEMAGNE, with whom are associated	{ Alfred, Godfrey of Bouillon,	Innocent III. St. Louis.
VIII.	DANTE, with whom are associated	{ Ariosto, Raphael,	Tasso, Milton.
IX.	GUTENBERG, with whom are associated	{ Columbus, Vaucauson,	Watt, Montgolfier.
X.	SHAKSPEARE, with whom are associated	{ Calderon, Corneille,	Molière, Mozart.
XI.	DESCARTES, with whom are associated	{ St. Thomas Aquinas, Bacon,	Leibnitz, Hume.
XII.	FREDERIC OF PRUSSIA, with whom are associated	{ Louis XI. William the Silent,	Richelieu, Cromwell.
XIII.	BICHAT, with whom are associated	{ Galileo, Newton,	Lavoisier, Gall.

These Lectures, like all others given at the Positivist School, are Free to all.

SPOUTING AT COGERS' HALL.

Down one of the slummy byeways which diverge from Fleet Street—that wondrous centre of the newsmongers, where they spend their time in learning or telling some new thing, like the Athenians of old—there stands a public-house bearing the title, at once pretentious and convivial, of Cogers' Hall. I am no antiquary, and never busied myself to inquire into the origin of the appellation; nor have I any notion where the apostrophe ought to stand in the word, or even whether there should be an apostrophe at all. Cogers' Hall was known to me when I was a Slave of the Lamp on the London Press, as a supper house where I was wont to beguile an hour in the course of the evening by eating a capital Welsh rarebit, smoking a long clay, and moistening my own clay with a glass of whisky and water, whilst I listened simultaneously to discussions *de omnibus rebus et quibusdum aliis*. A knot of clever tap-room orators—I hope the term is not an offensive one—gather nightly at Cogers' Hall and discourse learnedly on all things in heaven, on earth, and under the earth, but chiefly on British politics. It was a nice free and easy way of combining instruction, not exactly with amusement, but with nutrition; and although I am no more sorry to have left my nightwork behind me than I am to have discarded my boyish tunic and corduroys, still I like to look in at Cogers' occasionally, just as we all like to go back to the old schoolhouse and look at the name we carved on the desk at the time when we inhabited the tunic and trousers aforesaid. Perhaps the pleasure I feel is due to contrasting my present state of freedom with that past condition of bondage. I often wonder whether ordinary, unromantic prisoners in Newgate, or the places whither small debtors gravitate, feel the same sort of attachment to their dungeons as Silvio Pellico did, and whether that accounts for the large number of second convictions we read and hear of. It was rather like a privileged Peri voluntarily quitting Paradise and taking a look at Purgatory; but I determined to kick off my slippers and shake myself clear of my dressing-gown the other night, and start for Fleet Street. It was a thoroughly characteristic evening I selected. In fact, I would not give a straw to visit these haunts except under conditions of proper local colour. Fleet Street on a bright moonlight night is a mistake. I used to run so as not to see the summer dawn when I left the newspaper office in the small hours. About midsummer I could not escape it, of course. It would steal incongruously over the chimney-pots, making the cats and policemen who monopolized the streets look real ridiculous—as Sam Slick says. But the evening I chose for my visit to Cogers' was a thoroughly appropriate one. The whole scene was suggestive of pea-soup. It lay in native fluidity on the roads and pavements. It was vapourized into fog and Scotch mist above. The sky was palpable *purée aux croutons*. The whole scene resembled a very turbid Turner's picture, utterly uncomfortable, but highly picturesque and quite *sui generis*.

Let no one whose object is simply to hear the oratory of the Ancient Society of Cogers—"established 1755," as the lamp over the doorway informs him—present himself at the portal before half-past nine o'clock, for he will have to wait until that somewhat untimely hour before the fun begins. As I was a "chiel takin' notes," it did not matter in my case. I wanted to look about me; and I had ample time, for I got there at eight o'clock. By a placard outside the door, I learnt that the subject of discussion for the evening was, "The Newcastle Election," which was to be treated by a "Dispassionate Eclectic." The gentleman who had assumed this mystic alias, however, had no wish to conceal his identity, for he was also described by his ordinary title of Mr. M'Gilchrist. I do not know that the subject was particularly attractive, but I remember the opener of the debate as a racy speaker, and thought I might as well go in at once as stop outside in the pea-soup, the more liquid portion of which was beginning to come down in the shape of something more than a drizzle. Some half-dozen *habitués* were scattered over the long room as I entered, earlier even than myself, and among them, in seediest of attire, the well-remembered form of Mr. M'Gilchrist himself. He was in close confab with another man, and looked as little likely to "orate" as any one I ever saw. Two respectable tradesmen were discussing the comparative merits of red and yellow pine planks at a centre table, and a feeble old man, destined as "Vice" to occupy a chair at the nether end of the room, uncomfortable as a monkish Miserere, was dothering about the place, and finally settled down to coffee. I supped and read the "Siliad," which I had bought *en route* in Booksellers-row; but was astonished to find that scarcely thirty people had gathered when it was time to begin. Having smoked a cigar and eaten several lumps of loaf sugar, the Dispassionate Eclectic took his seat on the right of the chair, which was itself filled by a sharp bead-eyed little man, who smoked a long clay pipe, and had a steaming glass of something comfortable before him. Somebody proposed that the opener of the debate should refresh prior to commencing his harangue; and the Dispassionate Eclectic, expressing audibly his opinion that such a process would do him no harm, ordered, "Hot rum." He divided his modicum into two portions, so as to take it hot and hot during his speech. I could not help noticing that he spoke almost deferentially to the waiter when he asked for a second tumbler, and I felt an old sensation coming over me that Mr. M'Gilchrist's talents deserved a better sphere.

At length, in deference to a decisive "go on," he went on. He began by explaining and defending his title of a Dispassionate Eclectic. He simply meant, he said, that he was not prone to perform an act of servile homage (of which I cannot even hint the nature) to Mr. Gladstone, as the *Daily Telegraph* did, nor, on the other hand, did he long to apply his foot offensively to that gentleman's person after the manner of the *Standard*. If I succeed, in this veiled way, to convey to my readers the forcible but inelegant manner in which this Dispassionate Eclectic opened, I shall have justified forthwith his being included in the somewhat heterodox list of names I have to do with. He contrasted the scantiness of the present Liberal majority in Newcastle with the larger numbers of previous years, and confessed that the discrepancy was significant. In terse and telling sentences he sketched the position of Newcastle as comparatively isolated, unlike the other large towns of the north which lay "in a pack," and so virtually still the metropolis of Northumbria. Joe Cowen—it was thus familiarly he spoke of the nascent M.P.—was the son of a father who took his daughters to church on Sundays; but Joe had got mixed up with the Holyoake lot, and was moreover a teetotaller in a city where there were 1200 publicans. He had against him, then, Toryism *en masse*, alcohol *en masse*, and also the frightened Whigs. The working men who sought to vote for Joe, were prevented by the crowded state of the booths during dinner hour, so that they lost their only chance, and Joe's majority was thereby narrowed.

But, in the first place, said our Dispassionate Eclectic, this event reminded us that we wanted to get rid of the "infernal nuisance" of elections turning so entirely on the Permissive Bill and alcohol questions—the Beer and Pump interests, as he would term them. People merged all political differences in hatred of grog, and elevated water into a cardinal virtue. What use was it to grumble if a cure could not be found for drinking? Here the Dispassionate Eclectic raised his tumbler of "hot rum" to his eloquent lips, and the coincidence caused a laugh among his audience. You may laugh, he said, but can you find the cure? In the opinion of the Eclectic the Government ought once and for all to declare its policy on this liquor question.

A second "infernal nuisance" was the Home Rule question; but on this point "Joe," he held, had given in his adhesion when he spoke generally in favour of local self-government. But the third, and most important point was that, though "Joe" had not actually risen from the ranks, he was strong on all Radical measures. Whiggism—and this was really the question raised by our Dispassionate Eclectic—had been practically effete since 1868. Sir George Grey had made a virtue of retiring from Morpeth, but it was really because five-sixths—if not seven-eighths—of the constituency had solicited a working man's candidate to stand. When asked to explain the attitude of Mr. Gladstone, the *Daily Telegraph* said he was " resting on his oars," the *Times* that " people were tired of sweeping changes." So he took this Newcastle election as a type of what the general election would be. We were apathetic now, but should be excited then; and, although he seldom indulged in vaticination, he prophesied that there would be few candidates on the old Whig programme, but lots like " Joe." That was the bone of contention he threw down for the Cogers to discuss.

A bearded man named French replied, and confessed himself disappointed with the Dispassionate Eclectic. When a man gave himself that name, he generally found him turn out a rabid Radical; and he was sorry to find that Mr. M'Gilchrist had done so on this occasion. He held that the so-called effete Whigs were the men of the future. People were tired of the " blazing" policy of Gladstone and the no-policy of Disraeli. On the liquor subject the question was grog or no grog. It was a question between despotism and freedom. We ought to be able to drink when we wanted. He, as a press man, wanted to drink just at the time when the publics were closed. Somebody suggested that the Ben Jonson had an exceptional licence in favour of press men, and was open all night, to which Mr. French replied that the Ben Jonson made its monopoly an excuse for vending inferior liquids. No, Whiggism was not effete—witness the Lancashire elections. As comes the voice of Lancashire, so—said Mr. Gladstone himself—comes the voice of England. The narrow majority of "Joe" was practically a defeat.

The little dark man in the chair laid aside his churchwarden and spoke discursively, but nobody listened. Some Newcastle men, who had eaten Welsh rarebits and drunk stout on the side benches, rose up and went. The "Vice" had more coffee, and the Dispassionate Eclectic was supplied condescendingly by the waiter with a huge lump of cheese and bread and a foaming glass of beer. As I rose to go I saw—and saw with pain—a kindly old gentleman, who was sitting next the Dispassionate Eclectic, and eating a plate of cold meat, surreptitiously transfer half of his portion on to the plate of the Dispassionate Eclectic, who clearly thought this would do him no harm, and proceeded to eat it accordingly; but the waiter, who was ubiquitous and all-seeing, as his craft mostly are, espied the transfer, and looked indignantly at the Dispassionate Eclectic, as though he had lent himself to an irregular and heterodox proceeding. There was a good deal of very plain speaking at Cogers' Hall, besides the inelegant exordium I have been unable to report; but I could not help thinking that places like these act very much as safety valves, enabling these rabid Radicals and Dispassionate Eclectics to let off the steam. Perhaps if other countries had some kindred institutions we should hear of fewer *coups d'état* and political complications in general.

So meditating, I passed out into the pea-soup, as did most of the rest, and the harmless little bead-eyed chairman was "left speaking."

SOMERS TOWN ON BIBLE SLAVERY.

OF all the unholy haunts into which my pursuit of heterodoxy has led me, decidedly the unholiest is Somers Town. There is a suburban sound in the title which ill prepares one for the reality; and although I cannot say I expected anything very romantic, I was not prepared for the actual slumminess which supervened upon me when, in consequence of information I had received from the columns of the *National Reformer*, I went one Tuesday evening to hear the latter of two discussions at Middlesex Hall on the interesting question, "Does the Bible teach Slavery?" I had only the vague idea that Somers Town was somewhere near King's Cross Station; and when I reached that point I was really adrift: but, passing behind the cathedral-like structure of the Midland Railway Station, soon found myself, as usual too early, in the precincts of Middlesex Hall. Turning to my right from the Euston Road, I had to turn to my left to get into Chapel Street, and to my right again to reach Middlesex Street. Such were the directions I received from an aborigine outside a flaunting public-house. Chapel Street I found to be one of the most characteristic localities I ever visited.

There was a sort of permanent market going on there; a double row of costermongers' trucks lining the street, while the shops were driving a busy trade too, so that there were four rows of emporiums all in full action at once in busy Chapel Street. The shops were chiefly devoted to boots and shoes of fabulous cheapness, or composed of butchers' stalls where garrulous salesmen exhorted non-existent "ladies" to "buy, buy." The roadway was very much absorbed in the dissemination of vegetables, salads, &c., all of which looked temptingly fresh, and were arranged in thumping penny "lots;" though here too there were trucks for the sale of liver, tripe, &c., which did not look by any means so attractive. I have reason to believe that anything from a boot-lace to a round of beef could be purchased in the great bazaar of Chapel Street, Somers Town.

My mission in these heretical expeditions of mine seems, I regret to state, very often to resolve itself into scandalizing some good orthodox people. I paced Middlesex Street from end to end, and there was only one building I could see in the most distant degree resembling a "Hall," and that turned out to be a Sunday school. I went in, emboldened by success in many a previous expedition, and anxious only on the score of being a quarter of an hour before time; when, on inquiring whether that were the arena for discussion on Biblical Slavery, I was answered in a pert negative by a pug-nosed little pupil teacher, and referred to the other end of the street, on the opposite side of the way. While I went out the occupants of the Sunday school commenced a sort of defiant psalm-singing, levelled, I have no doubt, at myself; for I ought to mention that in those evening escapades I array myself in the seediest of overcoats, with a brigand hat, which I purchased specially for Grafton Hall on St. Patrick's Day, unclerical trousers, with a fierce stripe down the sides, and boots which have seen very much better days. In fact, I try to impersonate the not-very-well-to-do working-man of advanced opinions, and sometimes wish I wore a beard and could induce the signs of labour on my hands; for I find where the people do not know me they glance very suspiciously at me—I fancy, on the score of my Jacob-like chin and my in-artistic hands. Gloves, of course, would betray me on the spot.

From beneath a low-arched passage higher up the street, and on the other side of the way, as Miss Pug-nose had said, I heard the sounds of an awful brass band proceeding, and thought possibly that might be a preliminary flourish of trumpets before the impending Bible study. It was Middlesex Hall, sure enough, and a placard outside announced the discussion which had attracted me; but I thought I would let them get the overture—if such it should prove to be—done before I went in. I therefore paced Middlesex Street, and took another turn through the

Chapel Street Bazaar. When I came back the minstrelsy had ceased. In I went, therefore, and was directed to pass to the reserved seats; somebody would come by-and-by and take my twopence.

It was the usual type of "Hall," and a gentleman, who afterwards turned out to be the chairman, was engaged in propping up the rickety balustrade of the platform with pieces of firewood, and then tying the desk which it supported with a piece of string; for the whole affair swayed about on the slightest provocation, and might really prove dangerous if speakers waxed warm in debate. This done, the audience having assembled, and somebody volunteered to collect the pence, the chairman assumed his place, and the two disputants, each bearing a newspaper parcel of books for quotation, took chairs on his right and left; an attendant at the same time putting a jug of water, almost as big as an ewer, and a glass on a box within easy reach of the speakers.

As this was the second lecture or discussion, it may be as well briefly to post up my readers in the first by quoting the report of the *National Reformer*:—

"MIDDLESEX HALL, MIDDLESEX STREET, SOMERS TOWN.—The first of two evenings' debate on the question, 'Does the Bible Teach Slavery?' took place here on Tuesday evening last, between Messrs. W. Hale and T. Harrington. The former opened in the affirmative, by quoting Noah's curse of Canaan, and the several laws relating to the subject to be found in the Pentateuch, such as that the Jews were to purchase bondmen and bondmaids of the heathen round about, as a possession for ever; supplementing his quotations by the authority of men eminent in the Christian Church, to the effect that these texts justified slave-dealing and slave-holding. Mr. Harrington denied that the texts quoted proved his opponent's case, because, according to Kalisch, the Hebrew word used did not mean slave, and proceeded to deal with the several passages on this understanding, and stated that where a man was said to be sold, he had simply sold himself for a given number of years. He also quoted texts against cruelty and injustice, and contended that these were incompatible with slavery as known in modern times. A vote of thanks to the chairman (Mr. Turpin) closed the proceedings. The debate will be concluded next Tuesday evening, April 7th, at 8.15. Admission 1d.—A. E. JACKSON."

On this occasion, Mr. Harrington, a respectable and somewhat youthful working man, opened the debate and drew attention to the disadvantage he laboured under in having to do so on the negative side. He alluded ironically to his opponent's previous practice in debate, whereas he himself was only a plain man, fitter to sit at the feet of such a Gameeliel (*sic*) than to argue with him. He read a long definition of slavery as it existed in Greece and Rome, from

Professor Bekker, and then launched forth into a really eloquent picture of a gathering of slaves at some great pagan centre, such as Corinth or Ephesus—slaves who were reduced to the condition of human chattels from no fault or crime of their own, but simply because their skin was black instead of white. A reader came among them and read Christ's Golden Rule and other texts, which the speaker quoted in great abundance, and made them exclaim, "Listen to what that man is *a-saying of*. He says we are all one family, and that no man has a right to own us." He quoted from Barnes an apposite story, of a man who had bought a "bright-haired girl" in a slave-market, and afterwards found she was his own sister. Such was the discovery which the slaveholder made under Christianity; and the speaker urged with much warmth, and not without a certain rough eloquence, that there was in the New Testament no explicit statement in favour of slavery. Even in Paul's Epistle to Philēmon (I was afraid he would call him so, and he did), he urged, after reading nearly the whole letter, (1) that there was no positive evidence that Onesimus was a slave in our sense of the term. The Greek word δοῦλος, he said, meant a servant in any capacity; (2) there was no evidence that Paul forced or even advised Onesimus to return; (3) even if he were a slave, it was questionable whether he returned to that condition; and (4) it was distinctly said, in v. 16, that after his return he was to be no more considered a servant. When Ignatius wrote his Epistle to the Ephesians, the bishop of that Church was named Onesimus, and was supposed by commentators to be this identical person. Cheever, whom his opponent had allowed on a previous occasion to be a just and good man, and whose words he argued must therefore be true, had said that it was quite impossible to carry out Christ's Golden Rule in the case of a slave, and that the whole Bible from Genesis to Revelation was one continual line of fire against this iniquity. The duties of husbands towards their wives, and children towards their parents, became impossible in a state of slavery. Thomas Paine himself said that Jesus Christ preached excellent morality, and taught the equality of man; and Robert Owen, that He required all men to love one another; and how could this be if He sanctioned the idea that man was a chattel?

Mr. Harrington's half-hour was now up, and Mr. Hale advanced to the gingerbread balustrade, quaffing a long draught from the washing jug as he did so. In fact, both the disputants were profuse in their potations of cold water.

He complained, in broad provincial dialect, of Mr. Harrington's quotation of irrelevant texts, and assured him he had no intention of resting his case only on Philemon—the quantity of whose penultimate he relieved me by correcting. After making severe onslaughts on Mr. Harrington's numerous quotations from sacred and secular writers, Mr. Hale thus clinched the case. His opponent had—so he said—conceded the fact that slavery did exist in the Old Testament, though slaves were to be manumitted at the Year of Jubilee. Christ, in Matt. v. 17—" I will give you chapter and verse if you want it," he said, triumphantly—had stated it to be His mission " not to destroy but to fulfil the Law," *ergo* He did not destroy the legal institution of slavery. The passages which bade men not resist evil, and turn to the smiter the smitten cheek, were, he said, calculated to sanction any iniquity, moral or physical; and St. Paul, in his Epistle to the Romans, said "the powers that be are ordained of God," and were not to be resisted. Were slaveholders not a power? He read a long passage from Theodore Parker, defending the conduct of Judas Iscariot on these grounds. He was bound to betray Christ—in fact, both Christ and the Apostles upheld the system then in vogue, and advised obedience to masters, not only to the good and gentle, but likewise to the froward.

Each of the disputants had now had half an hour for main speech; and then followed a quarter of an hour's reply on both sides. In their second speeches, however, they left the case very much where it was before; and I was less interested in the debate itself than in the keen, eager faces of the listeners, who followed it attentively, and applauded equally when a point was made on either side. They were mostly genuine working-men, in their working clothes, and with signs of the day's toil upon them; and it was really a curious problem as to how they could be brought to feel interest in an archaic question like that proposed. There was only one woman present at the debate, and she looked like a decent matronly person returning from a day's charing or washing—very much the same sort of congregation one gathers at a school or cottage lecture, only—and this it was that struck me—with the preponderance of numbers on the men's side. Why should we not organize orthodox discussions, where everybody should have the chance of ventilating his opinions, and all command a "clear stage and no favour?"

Good might be done, I could not help thinking, as I passed once more through busy Chapel Street, by thus coming down from Coward's Castle and inducing a healthy collision of thought. Why should we leave this Socratic method entirely to the heterodox and the heretical?

A further idea struck me too in reference to this discussion. If it did nothing else, it made both sides read their Bibles. If one tripped at a text the other was down upon him in a moment. It may be a little Jesuitical, perhaps, but an energetic curate who believed in Bible-reading would do well to invite any Freethinker in his parish to a discussion in the schoolroom, if only with the ulterior object of forcing him to post himself up in the *litera scripta* of the Sacred Writings.

VEGETARIANISM.

If Heterodoxy be understood according to its etymology as thinking differently from other people, there can be no question as to the title of this particular "ism" to stand on my voluminous list of religious and social heresies.

A "good cut at a sirloin" has always been considered the standard of dietetic excellence for the full-blooded Englishman; and to exchange that standard for a leguminous or farinaceous one has certainly never been dreamed of in our philosophy until the present crisis in the kitchen. But there is a noticeable tendency at the present moment to go to the basis of things, and accept nothing as final until proved by argument or experience. The age that has opened the question whether alcohol is wholesome may be expected—after some inevitable delay perhaps—to enter on the more revolutionary question still, whether flesh be a necessity of diet, at all events in anything like the proportions it has hitherto borne. Having the question forced upon me, then, not only as the social topic of the hour, but as an item of housekeeping assuming every day more formidable proportions, I resolved to open up in the most practical way possible the whole question of dietary. I sought, and soon found, a gentleman who had been a vegetarian for a quarter of a century, and who, I heard, had brought up a stalwart family of nine on a system of housekeeping from which flesh meat was rigidly excluded. This was the very man I wanted. Of course, like everybody with a hobby, he was glad of an opportunity to ventilate his. The following is the result of my colloquy :—

I must not, of course, violate confidence by giving even the slightest hint as to my informant's name and local habitation, though, as I was a perfect stranger to him, I have every reason to believe he would as readily impart to any member of the community the results of his experience as he did to me. As I sat in his office there entered to me—as the stage phrase goes—a well-built man of middle height, lacking equally the emaciation or the adiposity which one is accustomed to associate with the adoption of a vegetable diet. He looked neither thin, like our conventional Yankee, nor fat, like a priest towards Eastertide, but was a lithe, active-looking, healthy paterfamilias, decidedly juvenile for a progenitor of nine. He will, I am sure, excuse this pen-and-ink photograph. The portrait, though faithful, will be flattering; and it is most pertinent to my present purpose. Had my typical vegetarian been too thin or too stout, too sallow or too rubicund, I might have been discouraged at the outset. This healthy-looking gentleman, with the crisp curly hair and beard one always attributes to a Hercules, startled me with a favourable impression as to the flesh-making and health-sustaining properties of whatever pabulum he might have adopted. Another point that told immensely in his favour with me was that he was the reverse of pig-headed, which is not always the case with men who have ideas or hobbies. He began by assuring me that, though he was a vegetarian and a water-drinker, he had made no savage vows in either capacity. He would sometimes, upon compulsion, not from choice, pick a bit of fish, fowl, or even flesh; he was not guiltless of an occasional glass of brandy and water, though, from long disuse, he always felt more or less uncomfortable after either. The solid was not easily assimilated, and the alcohol left an unpleasant tingling in his system for four-and-twenty hours, as though to give him a gentle reminder that he had been trespassing.

I checked—politely I trust—a tendency on the part of my friend to wander back to the Garden of Eden. I quite conceded the point that a vegetable diet was all that could be gathered from Genesis, and even that the use of flesh meat might be a part of the Fall; but, to come to the question at issue in my mind—

"What, Sir," I said, "did you have for breakfast this morning? What will you have for dinner, tea, and supper?"

Smiling at the practical form my questions took, he

told me he had just partaken of two slices of Neville's bread, with some figs and a glass of water. "This," he added, handing me a paper bag containing two or three slices of plum-cake, "with a draught of water from yonder decanter will be my dinner. For tea I shall have a bowl of milk and some bread and butter, and for supper bread and cheese, with a salad."

In answer to my suggestion that one might probably tire of plum-cake and water for dinner, he reminded me that the *carte* of most men, tied like himself to the City during the day, was almost as monotonously limited to the routine of "chop or steak." "Besides," he added, "there are endless varieties of vegetarian cookery for those who seek a relish. I am detailing, as you asked me, the regimen I myself have adopted. Vegetables, fruits, and farina afford quite as large a field as fish, flesh, and fowl."

He was loud in praise of oatmeal and beans. He pointed to the fact that whilst in England the men were ill-fed, and the horses in fine condition, the reverse was the case in Scotland, where the men were muscular and the cattle comparatively ill-conditioned; from which he inferred that we gave to our cattle that nutrition which the canny Scot wisely reserved for himself.

But still I was not satisfied. What, if I might make bold to ask, was the nature of my interlocutor's life; and did he never feel that vacuum which—British like—I had got to think could only be filled with beefsteak and stout, or their equivalents?

His calling, he told me, besides chaining him for many hours each day to the office, took him into the most squalid parts of the East-end of London; and so it was he had found the cruel nature of the fallacy, that meat and beer were the staples of existence, forced in still more strongly on his conviction. "To secure such," he said, "these poor people sacrifice all the decencies of life. They cannot buy best joints. They feed on liver, tripe, and such offal, where, if at all, disease is sure to lurk.

"I really began to see what a powerful agent of civilization a sensible diet-table might be made." Saying thus, he pointed out triumphantly to a tabular form hanging in his office, and especially drew my attention to the name of the non-vegetarian chemist who subscribed it:—

"*Composition of Food.*

Weight.	THE FOLLOWING ARTICLES OF DIET:	CONTAIN:		SUPPLY TO BODY:		
		Solid Matter.	Water.	Flesh forming Principle.	Heat forming Principle.	Ashes.
lb.		lb.	lb.	lb.	lb.	lb.
100	Turnips	11·0	89·0	1·0	9·0	1·0
,,	Red Beet Root ...	11·0	89·0	1·5	8·5	1·0
,,	Carrots	13·0	87·0	2·0	10·0	1·0
,,	Potatoes	28·0	72·0	2·0	25·0	1·0
,,	Butcher's Meat ...	36·6	63·0	21·5	14·3	·8
,,	Bread (stale)	76·0	24·0	10·7	64·3	1·0
,,	Peas..................	84·0	16·0	29·0	51·5	3·5
,,	Lentils...............	84·0	16·0	33·0	48·0	3·0
,,	Barley-meal	84·5	15·5	14·0	68·5	2·0
,,	Wheat-meal	85·5	14·5	21·0	62·0	2·5
,,	Beans	86·0	14·0	31·0	51·5	3·5
,,	Sago	88·0	12·0	3·4	84·0	·6
,,	Maize-meal.........	90·0	10·0	11·0	77·0	2·0
,,	Oat-meal............	91·0	9·0	12·0	77·0	2·0
,,	Rice..................	92·4	7·6	8·4	82·0	2·0

"Grain and other nutritious vegetables yield us, not only in starch, sugar, and gum, the carbon which protects our organs from the action of oxygen, and produces in the organism the heat which is essential to life, but also in the form of vegetable fibrine, albumen, and caseine, our blood, from which the other parts of our body are developed. These important products of vegetation are especially abundant in the seeds of the different kinds of grain, and of peas, beans, and lentils, and in the roots and juices of what are commonly called vegetables. They exist, however, in all plants, without exception, and in every part of plants, in larger or smaller quantity." Again :—" Vegetable fibrine and animal fibrine, vegetable albumen and animal albumen, hardly differ, even in form; if these principles be wanting in the food, the nutrition of the animal is arrested; and when they are present, the graminivorous animal obtains in its food the very same principles on the presence of which the nutrition of the carnivora entirely depends." The next statement is very important to be remembered. " Vegetables produce in their organism the blood of all animals, for the carnivora, in consuming the blood and flesh of the graminivora, consume, strictly speaking, only the vegetable principles which have served for the nutrition of the latter."—*Liebig.*

Another strong point which my voluble friend put forward was his comparative immunity from adulteration. He needed no analyst to examine his fruit, his vegetables, his occasional egg, and filtered water. He even argued warmly against cooking fruit—though here I know the homœopathists, whom I had always considered the most consummate masters of diet, would join issue with him. "Nature gave them to us as they are, ready to eat; and what do we find? Edible in their original state, these fruits—such as the apple, cherry, or plum—are not palatable, when cooked, without sugar;" and sugar he seemed to regard as the very concentration of all adulterations. Tea and coffee he also patronized but slenderly, preferring the Paradisiacal spring water.

And how do we think this active gentleman amused himself when work was over, and he retired to the suburban residence of his nine vegetarian olive-branches? As an amateur carpenter and joiner. Vegetarianism, in one word, according to his representation, had kept him sound in wind and limb, as well as clear in head, for a quarter of a century. Barring the arrivals of the nine, and an accident or two, his doctor's bill had not been 10*l*. during all that period. Remembering what my butcher, brewer, wine merchant, and doctor had derived from me during a far shorter period, it was all I could do to prevent myself from rushing into a greengrocer's, purchasing an enormous salad, and, bearing it triumphantly home, resolving my little household into graminivora on the spot. But, like Wordsworth's pertinacious querist in the pretty poem "We are Seven,"

I ventured on one more question, as I stood hat in hand to depart. Did he not find it inconvenient in social life, and especially when travelling? There was no vegetarian restaurant even in London, I believed, or I should have immediately adjourned to it. There was none, he said; but there was no difficulty, he submitted, in culling from the *carte*, especially of foreign restaurants in town, such dishes as suited him. In travelling, the landlords of rural hostelries generally looked on him as a "foreigner," and were tolerant of his little weaknesses. So, in social life, he was saluted by his intimate friends with the remark, "In the name of the Prophet, figs!" from that fruit forming so large a portion of his diet. At public dinners he could pick his way among the various dishes, affecting chiefly the leguminous ones; and, if necessary, he could, being free from all vows, partake of a slice of meat or a glass of wine, though certain —perchance like some of his fellow-guests—to feel the retributive "morning after."

Such was my interview with a vegetarian. He forwarded me afterwards a number of pamphlets on the subject, which I proceed to analyse. The long-defunct "Vegetarian Messenger," one of those volumes, represents a period in the history of the system when it appeared likely to take firmer hold of popular esteem than afterwards proved to be the case. It is full of recipes for savoury vegetarian dishes, the mere reading of which makes one's mouth water; and

British housewives would do well to consult its pages, if only to provide a stopgap for meat whilst famine prices rule.

Take for instance the following recipes, which certainly, in these days of deep culinary study, may well alternate with, if they do not supplant, the ordinary courses of fish, flesh, and fowl:—

"TWELVE VEGETARIAN RECIPES.

"1. *Breadcrumb Omelet.*—One pint of breadcrumbs, a large handful of chopped parsley, with a large slice of onion minced fine, and a teaspoonful of dried marjoram. Beat up two eggs, add a teaspoonful of milk, some nutmeg, pepper, and salt, and a piece of butter the size of an egg. Mix altogether, and bake in a slow oven till of a light brown colour. Turn out of dish and send to table immediately.

"2. *Yorkshire Pudding.*—Flavour your batter with pot marjoram, lemon thyme, and sweet balm powdered, a little chopped parsley, and an onion minced fine. Bake in moderate oven; serve hot with gravy.

"3. *Macaroni Pudding.*—Two ounces of macaroni; boil till tender, drain the water from it, and add half a pint of new milk, and half an ounce of parsley, chopped fine. A teaspoonful of lemon thyme powdered, some lemon peel, pepper, and salt, and dash of nutmeg. Put it in a well buttered dish, and bake twenty minutes. If wanted richer, beat up an egg in the milk.

"4. *Buttered Onions.*—Take enough (rather small) onions to make a dish; let them all be of like size; peel them, and throw them into a stew-pan of boiling water with some salt. Boil for five minutes, drain them, put them into a saucepan with a good thick piece of butter, a sprinkling of nutmeg, pepper, and salt; toss them about over a clear fire until they begin to brown; add a tablespoonful of mushroom ketchup, and a dessert-spoonful of sage and marjoram and parsley. Do them gently for a quarter of an hour, and serve upon toast moistened in lemon juice.

"5. *Mushroom Pudding.*—One pint of mushrooms, half a pound of breadcrumbs, and two ounces of butter. Put the butter in the breadcrumbs, adding pepper and salt, and as much water as will moisten the bread; add the mushrooms, cut in pieces; line a basin with paste, put in the mixture, cover with paste, tie a cloth over, and boil an hour and a half. It is equally good baked.

"6. *Buttered Eggs or Rumbled Eggs.*—Break three eggs into a small stew-pan, put a tablespoonful of milk and an ounce of fresh butter, add a saltspoonful of salt and a little pepper. Set the stew-pan over a moderate fire, and stir the eggs with a spoon, being careful to keep every particle in motion until it is set. Have ready a crisp piece of toast, pour the eggs upon it, and serve immediately. [This mode of dressing eggs secures that the white and the yolk shall be perfectly mixed. The white, which is so very nutritious, is insipid and unpalatable when the egg is simply boiled, fried, or poached.]

"7. *Potted Lentils or Haricots.*—Stew a teacupful of lentils in water, with a morsel of butter and some mushroom powder. Beat up to a smooth paste. When cold, add an equal quantity of fine brown breadcrumbs, with seasoning of salt, mace and cayenne, and the size of a walnut of old cheese. Beat all together with two ounces of butter. Press firmly into pots. (Haricot beans may be used instead of lentils.) If it is to be kept long, hot butter must be poured on the top.

"8. *Baked Potatoes with Sage and Onion.*—Peel as many potatoes as you require; put them in a pie-dish, and a good-sized onion, with half a teaspoonful of dried sage, two ounces of butter, and enough water to cover the bottom of the dish. Season with salt and pepper.

"9. *Barley Soup.*—Soak four tablespoonfuls of Scotch barley in cold water for an hour. Put it in stew-pan with about a pint of cold water. Set it on a moderate fire; let it stew gently, and add three good-sized onions, two small turnips, a carrot, and a head of celery. Season to taste with salt and pepper. When quite soft, add a tablespoonful of mushroom ketchup.

"10. *Groat Pudding.*—Pick and wash a half pint of groats, and put them in a dish with a pint of water, a large onion chopped small, a little sage or marjoram, a good lump of butter, pepper and salt. The groats may be steeped thus for some hours before baking. Apples may be added, or substituted, for the onions and herbs. If substituted, use sugar instead of the seasoning. Bake in a moderate oven till the groats are tender.

"11. *Savoury Pie.*—Pare several potatoes and two or three onions. Slice them, if large. Place these in a buttered pie-dish, in layers, with a little well steeped tapioca, pepper, salt, and powdered sage upon each, also mushroom powder, or fresh mushrooms if liked. Slices of cold bread omelet, or a few Brussels sprouts, may be inserted. Cover with a plain crust; one made of ordinary bread dough, with a very little butter, is preferable to anything heavy. Keep the bottom of the pie supplied with hot water while baking, or it will be without gravy.

"12. *Vegetarian Gravy.*—This may be flavoured either with mushroom powder or browned onion, and coloured with a little chicory, the basis being made as plain melted butter, with less flour or thickening, and seasoned with pepper, salt, and mace, if approved.'"

Professor Francis William Newman, whose theological proclivities have already claimed our notice, is a tower of strength to the Vegetarians, and in dealing with the current literature of the subject I give the preference to his lectures. I only regret that I cannot find space to print in full the Address of 1872; but I select those passages which have a present interest, on account of their economical bearing, and also those which bring the subject into connexion with the known theological opinions of our author:—

"When the name and practice of Vegetarianism is brought casually before an English man or woman, it is very generally regarded as fanciful and ridiculous. I will not deny that while I knew it myself only from a distance, I thought it a strange, perhaps even a silly fancy; hence I cannot be surprised that others, equally uninformed as I then was, so regard it. I have often heard the rather scornful question, made in a peculiarly decisive tone : 'What *is* the use of it?' Of course the questioner implies the true and obvious answer to be, 'Absolutely none whatever.' Now, by way of reply, I will take the liberty of asking some questions in return. Did you ever hear of such a thing as Cattle Murrain? Did you ever hear of Diseased Meat in the Market? or of Contagious Disease spreading among foul eaters? or are you at all aware of butchers' meat becoming very dear? inconveniently dear for most, ruinously dear to hand-workers? Well, if these matters are familiarly known to you, I have one more question—Did you ever reflect on the *causes* of these things? for you can hardly believe that they come without a cause. It is possible that many present have never inquired into the causes, and my first attempt will be to aid in the research, by recalling many obvious and notorious facts.

"The easiest question to answer is—What is the cause of the high price of butchers' meat? The reply is—An enormous increase of demand. The whole series of events is in the easy memory of those who are no longer young, yet may need to be shortly recapitulated to the new generation. I will first remark, that any great murrain in cattle (however caused), would naturally be followed by an increased price of meat. I do not overlook this, when I refer to the increase of demand as the main and steady cause of the rise in price. In fact, it was distinctly predicted by far-seeing economists in 1846 and the previous years, during the contest for the abolition of the old Corn Laws. The late General Perronet Thompson illustrated popularly his economic prediction, by saying: 'When, through the cheapening of bread, a man finds he has an unexpected sixpence in his pocket, he is very apt to want a mutton-chop.' On this ground he foretold that the abolition of the Corn Laws would make the artisans eat, not more bread, but more butchers' meat, and that the price of such meat would rise. Accordingly, he and Colonel Torrens prophesied that the farmers would become enriched by the sale of agricultural *luxuries*, in proportion as the one agricultural *necessary* (bread) became cheaper: for most persons expected that bread would permanently be reduced in price. In fact, it has only been saved from great fluctuations, and its indefinite rise hindered. Higher wages and steadier work, rather than cheaper bread, have made our artisans able to demand flesh meat; and this increased demand was a marked fact already in 1848. Importation of foreign cattle for immediate consumption has been on the increase thenceforward. With the development of the railway system the prices have become more equalized, not by a fall in the towns, but by a rise in the more secluded rural districts. At length it became worth while to turn Irish arable land into grazing, for the production of more cattle. This must be the tendency everywhere, at a certain point of price, if butchers' meat go up, or bread go down; for land is husbanded, not for the cultivator's mouth, but for his purse (or what here amounts to the same, for the landlord's purse); hence, unless our present career be checked, we have a very dreary prospect before us. . . . .

"It may be replied, that the working classes are wilful and besotted, and will of course grasp at every luxury in their power. See, it will be said, how recklessly they spend their money on beer or gin, or if not on drink, then on tobacco-smoking, or perhaps on both. There are many exceptions. Nevertheless, I concede, they are a minority. I admit and press, that so long as all who are rich enough to get an article, insist on getting it, the poorer will covet it, will count it a luxury, and will often ruin their finance by eagerness for it. But what then? Why, then, this is precisely the reason why the richer should set them a different example. 'I will eat no meat while the world standeth,' said the great Paul, 'if it make my brother to offend.' If there is not enough sound flesh meat for all, and it be not necessary for our welfare, why should we, who are richer, rush in to clutch at it?

"But I turn to another side of the subject, hardly less important. Just alarm is widely spread concerning a fact too broad to be denied—the growth of our towns, and the disproportionate emptiness of our country. This is everywhere the symptom of progressive national decay. The Roman poet Horace saw it already before his eyes in Italy. Small freeholds had become rare. On the great estates were beautiful villas, splendid parks cultivated for elegance, not for service. The fruit-tree was 'evicted' (to use his phrase) by the barren tree. The towns were full, and the country empty. Grazing superseded agriculture; cattle took the place of robust freemen, and were tended by a sparse population of slaves. A Gaulish chieftain, soon after, in urging his countrymen to revolt against Rome, used the argument, 'Italy is poor in men;' and Pliny echoed it in the utterance, 'Broad estates have ruined Italy.' In modern Turkey we have the same deplorable phenomenon, from widely different causes—well filled towns and empty country. The historian Sismondi attests that it characterized every land, which was in its turn ruined by the Roman empire. No impartial and well-informed person can look on Great Britain without discerning the same alarming phenomenon in contrasting our rural districts to our towns. The country places do not support their own births; the rustic population flock to the towns. Now, I am not about to say that this is directly caused by flesh eating; it undoubtedly depends on circumstances of landed tenure, which cannot here be treated. Nevertheless, the evils are aggravated by the demands of the wealthy towns for cattle and their products; this fact alone makes it worth a landlord's while to keep arable in pasture. If the towns renounced flesh eating, we should see in a single generation, even without improved land tenure, a tide of migration set the other way, from towns into the country. Rustic industry would be immensely developed. All motive for expatriation of our robustest youth would for a long time yet be removed, and the country might be enormously enriched, not in an upper stratum of great fortunes, but (if national morality kept pace with wealth) down to the bottom of the community. Our strength is proportioned to the number of our industrious and loyal citizens. The country would then bear a great increase of population without effort; for it is certain that ordinary arable land will produce easily four times as much human food as the same land devoted to grazing. Of course there is land where the soil barely covers the rock—where a plough cannot be driven, or where mere steepness forbids—on which nevertheless grass can grow. No one wishes to get rid of all grazing land. But where the soil has moderate depth cultivation improves it; if there be but enough labourers. The area for which twenty men suffice to tend oxen grazing on it, might need the labour of a thousand (including rustic artisans) if it were duly laid out for crops. I do not forget or dissemble that a large part of cattle food, especially the winter supply, is provided by cultivation, as beans and oats for horses, turnips and other roots for sheep and oxen. Still, the movement towards Vegetarianism would be a movement for native cultivation and rustic industry. . . . .

"But it may occur to you that I have said nothing of fish. It is true that the economic objections to butchers' meat do not apply against fish from the sea; nor is the moral objection to killing them equal to that against killing birds. Fish do not displace crops on the soil, and are a real addition to the food of a nation. But except on the sea-coast, fish on the average is dearer than mutton; I believe I may say, by far dearer; and has less nourishment, pound for pound. Flabby fish, which is very unnutritious, and will not bear transport, is not coveted, and may remain cheap. But the really solid kinds are not cheap anywhere, I believe:* and are in general enormously dear, as turbot and salmon. Salmon, I know, recently in Clifton, where I live, was selling at 3s. 6d. a pound, and 2s. 6d. is a common price. I do not know that a pound of salmon gives more nourishment than a pound of mutton, even to those who are able to digest it; hence until the price of fish is enormously reduced, it is difficult to say much in their favour from the economic side, except so far as they are used as condiment, like anchovy, herring, sardines, or even sprats. Vegetarians being desirous of attesting that their strength is not supported on fish, any more than on beasts and fowls, think it right to abstain even from these condiments; but it is not likely that they will devote any large portion of their zeal to dissuade people from them. Rather they will take for granted that those who on the whole see reasons for abstinence from flesh, will think it wiser, in the present state of opinion, when the example of every abstainer tells for something, to aim at that completeness in a broad principle which all alike are sure to understand.

"Perhaps some of you are disappointed, that I have not entered into any proofs that farinaceous food suffices for strength and health. Indeed doctrine so opposite is sedulously preached by men who ought

---

* Perhaps I ought to except *Skate*. I have always wondered that so solid and nourishing a fish, so palatable when thoroughly dressed, is so cheap in the London market. The rich seem to despise it for its cheapness.

to know, that I think it rather better to refer you to those who can speak with authority on this question; else I must perhaps have devoted the entire lecture to it. But as our Society has printed a four page tract of testimonies from celebrated physiologists— few of them Vegetarians—who assert that farinaceous food and pulse, suffice abundantly for strength, and tend eminently to health and long life—I have requested a supply of these to be provided at hand, so that all of you may be able to read the testimonies at leisure.

"I therefore content myself with saying, that the inhabitants of county Kerry and county Cork are by impartial testimony singularly beautiful and strong, though nourished on potatoes with, at most, buttermilk; that the Scotch, living on oatmeal, are on the whole stronger and healthier than the English; that the porters and boatmen of Turkey equal the strongest navvies of the English railways; and that I am persuaded, a general survey of the broad facts of the human race show it to be a delusion, that flesh meat ever gives to men who labour with body or mind any advantage whatever.

"In conclusion, I beg to state the pleasure with which I have delivered this lecture within a Friends' Institute. The Friends from their origin have emphatically taken as their motto—Be not conformed to this world. Accordingly they have espoused the most unpopular causes for the sake of truth and justice, defying dominant opinion, prevalent practices, fashions, and power. They have been foremost against that greatest of iniquities which is now dying out, Chattel Slavery. They have championed the rights of Woman, and nearly every form of mercy. I will not call them our forlorn hope, but in apparently the most hopeless assaults on evil they have been leaders. No foreign victims of evil so call on them now as the most wretched of our own population, who cannot indeed be raised by any one form of action, but only by many combined. Yet I boldly assert, that it is simply impossible to lift them out of their misery and rottenness, unless they are trained to avoid ensnaring drink and expensive eating. Though I cannot claim a first rank for Vegetarianism in elevating the people, yet it is only secondary to abstinence from alcoholic liquors. It directly promotes that gentleness of heart which abhors bloodshed, and indirectly that hatred of war for which the Friends have always been eminent."

But, advanced as Professor Newman may be, it is naturally to America that we turn for the most progressive ideas on this or any other subject; and I cannot refrain from quoting a few passages from Dr. Traill's address, delivered at the eleventh annual meeting of the Vegetarian Society, noting especially those which refer to the moral aspect of the matter:—

"As a reform, Vegetarianism may be said to underlie many other reforms which have made vastly more noise in the world, the temperance cause particularly. Without the co-operation of this, they can never achieve but partial and temporary success. Talk about politics, commerce, navies, armies, annexations, and secessions, unions, and constitutions! What are all these compared with the institution of victuals and drink? . . . .

"Philanthropists, statesmen, politicians, are always busy discussing multitudinous, and in some respects very conflicting schemes of reform, improvement, and progress; and they keep the nation perpetually agitated about banks and tariffs, parties, platforms, squatter sovereignties, extensions, non-interventions, fusions, and confusions, each of which may, perhaps, be of some importance to somebody, but altogether sink into insignificance, as affecting the permanent prosperity of our country, or the weal and woe of the human race, when compared with this matter of eating and drinking. Douglas, Breckenridge, Bell, Lincoln, are all important personages no doubt, and each very useful in his way; but none of these orators have thus far, during the pendency of the presidential campaign, broached any subject so vitally important to the voters as that of beef *versus* bread, hog *v.* hominy, mutton *v.* squash, oysters *v.* peaches, chickens *v.* whortle-berries. 'A sound mind in a sound body' is the best possible platform, not only for all political, but for all human purposes.

"Food supplies the elements of our tissues. We are literally made of what we eat. Our mental manifestations are dependent on the quality of our bodily structures. According to our dietary will be the condition of the 'house we live in'—this bodily tenement of the immortal spirit, which we are commanded by its Author to keep pure, holy, and undefiled.

"I know it is customary with some clergymen, while magnifying the spiritual laws of the Supreme Being, wholly to ignore his physical laws. But I cannot see why one law of the Deity should not be as dear to Him as another. All laws in the universe are laws of nature; and nature's laws are God's laws; and I cannot understand why He should look with any less complacency on the transgression of a law which we call *physical*, because it relates to the body, than He does on the violation of a law which we term *moral*, because it relates to the soul. Certain it is that penalty and punishment equally follow the infraction of any law of the universe.

"And history, which is said to be 'philosophy teaching by example,' informs us that all nations of the earth have gone up or down, have risen or fallen, as they ate and drank.

"Turkey, not long since a powerful nation, is now dying of narcotic poisons. The swarming millions of China are becoming rapidly demoralized and deteriorated with opium. And who so blind that he cannot see that the four yet great and powerful nations of the earth — England, France, Russia, and the United States—are taking a serpent to their bosoms, yea, many serpents, which are bound ere long to have their best heart's blood, unless they in some way, and that speedily, rid themselves of them? It is enough to name that triune demon — alcohol, opium, and tobacco. These physiological fiends are just as sure to sink all these mighty empires to barbarism, sooner or later, provided the people generally persist in their use, as effect is sure to follow cause; so surely as there is law in the universe; so surely as God reigns. . . . .

"Well, what has all this to do with Vegetarianism? Much, very much! I look upon dietetic reform as one of the essential pre-requisites of any general and successful temperance or anti-tobacco reform. The demand for liquor and tobacco is founded in perverted appetences, and so long as these morbid appetites are kept up by gross food, so long will these pernicious habits do their work of destruction. . . . .

"And now, what is the basis of our Vegetarian creed? The arguments *pro* and *con* may be viewed from various stand-points.

"Some persons are Bible Vegetarians. They think that this book inculcates this doctrine.

"Some are scientific Vegetarians. They believe that nature teaches it.

"Some are Vegetarians from benevolence. They regard it as cruel to kill animals for food. They can see no 'peace on earth and good-will to man' while cruelty, even to animals, prevails.

"Some are æsthetic Vegetarians. They see the sublime and the beautiful in human nature, only in circumstances which dispense with slaughter-houses, fowl-pens, and piggeries.

"Others are economical Vegetarians. They perceive a vast saving in soil and territory, and in the wear and tear of human machinery, and an immense diminution of the most degrading toil and drudgery, in abstinence from animal food.

"Others, still, are Vegetarians from experience. They have in some way learned that others have subsisted very well, and perhaps improved, on the adoption of a vegetable diet, and so they try it as an experiment, sometimes just to see if it will agree with their constitutions. Unfortunately, too many of these, not being well-grounded in the theory, are very apt, in some moment of uncomfortable experience, to murmur, as did the children of Israel for the flesh-pots of Egypt, and like the children of Israel, they are often *cursed* with the permission to eat again what their souls lust after.

"And yet others are Vegetarians from necessity. This is altogether the most numerous class. They are mostly invalids, and are quite numerous at some of the Water-cures, which, by the way, are quite as much

Diet-Cures as Water-Cures. They cannot recover health, and many of them cannot even live much longer, without adopting a rigidly simple and strictly Vegetarian diet. Although these persons always get more or less benefit to themselves, they do not very well commend our system to the public. Being generally the worst class of invalids—many of them possessing but the mere relics of ruined constitutions—they do not serve our system very well as advertisements. If they speak ever so well of it, and declare that it has prolonged their lives, and even rescued them from death, those who see and hear them are very apt to regard them as partially demented, and look upon them as frightful examples of the dangerous effects of Vegetarianism.

"But there is one argument yet to be named. We all have our 'isms,' our hobbies. Mine is the *truth* argument. *Vegetarianism is true.* This is why I adopt it; and this I consider reason enough. . . . .

"No animal organization can create or form food of any kind. All that the animal can do is to use or appropriate what nutrient material the vegetable kingdom has provided. The vegetable kingdom is intermediate between the mineral and the animal kingdoms. The vegetable kingdom, of the elements of the inorganic world, compounds or creates alimentary principles, as albumen, casein, fibrin, gum, sugar, starch, &c. These alimentary principles are not properly food in their separate states: they are merely the proximate elements of food. Food, or aliment proper, is the compound of these alimentary principles, as in the potato, the apple, the grain, &c. And all of these proximate aliments of food (alimentary principles) are produced in the vegetable kingdom, and in the processes of formation, growth, development; in the *green* or growing state.

"Hence the error of those who would medicate diseases by plying the system with *inorganic* or *chemical elements*, or animal excretions, to nourish the tissues, as the preparations of iron, phosphates, or hypophosphites of lime, magnesia and soda, cod-liver oil, and other specimens of 'blood-food,' as they are called. The thing cannot be done. Nature abhors the plan. The animal organism will not receive and cannot assimilate inorganic elements or compounds, nor effete matters of any kind. They must first be reduced to their primary elements, and then compounded by the vegetable kingdom. Medicating the human system by means of fertilizers, as we *may* manure the earth for vegetables, is a sad mistake on the part of medical men—a mistake which is sending the human family, old, young, and middle-aged, in great and constant droves, to premature graves, and sadly damaging those constitutions which are not wholly destroyed by this practice.

"Animals may, indeed, feed on other animals; and human beings may feed on other human beings, or on animals. But food, once used, is more or less changed, vitiated. And all of the flesh, and blood, and fat of animals contains more or less of the effete or waste matters, together with any morbid secretions, diseased products, or accidental poisons or impurities which may happen to be present. Hence, as the animal furnishes nothing that it does not derive from the vegetable, the logical deduction is irresistible, that if we would have the best and the purest food, we must take it *directly* from the vegetable kingdom, and not *indirectly* through an animal organism. . . . .

" People raise the anatomical objection, and this is pretty much all resolved into the teeth argument. And what about the teeth?

" Why, we are solemnly assured that man has *carnivorous teeth*, and, therefore, consequently, he is bound in some sort to 'play the dog.' It is not pretended that there is anything inhuman in or about his face otherwise. There is nothing bestial in his form or features. His hands seem better fitted to pluck the luscious fruit and gather the waving grain, than to rend and tear the quivering flesh. ' He walks erect, with face upturned to heaven,' instead of prowling on all fours, like a predaceous brute in search of his feast of blood. He does not crawl along the ground like a reptile hunting a frog for his dinner, nor does he skulk in sly corners and dark places, like the hideous hyena, to pounce on some weaker creature, and drink his fill of gore. And were it not for those *carnivorous teeth* we read so much about in medical books, we should, perhaps, never suspect him of any murderous disposition at meal-times.

"But there they are—the carnivorous teeth—in the books, I mean. If we undertake to argue with a medical man, we are summarily snubbed off with the statement that man has teeth like a hog or a dog—and, *ergo*, he should eat like a pig or a puppy. I can never mention Vegetarianism to a flesh-eating medical gentleman, who does not introduce the teeth argument as the conclusion of the whole matter, as he asks triumphantly, ' What were carnivorous teeth put into our jaws for if not to eat flesh ?'

"I have a short answer. *They were never put there at all.* If they really exist in particular cases, it must be by some accident. They were no part of the original constitution of humanity. And in truth they have no existence at all, except in the imagination of medical men, in medical books and journals, in the public newspapers, and in the jaws of carnivorous animals.

"I take the ground that man should not have animal teeth, because he is not an animal. He is endowed with mental powers which relate him to a future state, and to an immortality of existence, and which impel him to improve his condition from generation to generation—viz., hope, ideality, conscientiousness, spirituality, &c. No animal possesses the least trace of any of these phrenological organs. Hence man is not 'a higher animal,' but a *human being*.

"And now I propose to put this matter of the teeth to the proof. Hearing may be believing, but seeing is the naked truth. I ask medical men to *show their teeth;* to extend their jaws and let their teeth be seen. Let us have the light to shine in upon this dark and perplexing question. I appeal from their statements to their faces; from their books and schools to their own anatomy.

"Is there a person here who believes that, in the anatomy of his teeth, he is only *part human?*—that he is a compromise of human and brute? Let him come forward and open his mouth, not to asseverate his carnivorousness, but to let us see, with our own eyes, what manner of creature he really is. Let us see if he is not created *wholly* in the image of God, who lives eternally, and not in any respect in the image of the beast that perishes.

"I think, if we make a careful examination, we shall readily discover that he is, *toothatically* considered, neither predaceous nor bestial; that he is dietetically, neither swinish nor *tigerocious;* neither *dogmatical* nor *categorial;* nor is he exactly graminivorous, like the cattle; he is not even *sheepish;* but simply, wholly, and exclusively *human.*

"True, there are some resemblances between the teeth of men, women, and children, and the teeth of cats, dogs, lions, tigers, hogs, horses, sheep, cattle, crocodiles, and megalosauruses, (*sic.*) But there are differences, too. And the differences are just as significant as are the resemblances. There is a resemblance between a man's face and the countenance of a cod-fish. There is also a striking difference. There is some resemblance between a man's features—especially if he does not shave—and the features of a bear. There is some resemblance between a woman's hair and a peacock's feathers; between a man's finger-nails and a vulture's talons; between his eye-teeth and a serpent's fangs. But, luckily for us, they are not the same, not precisely alike. Man resembles, more or less, every animal in existence. He differs, too, more or less, from all animals.

"There is one class of scholars who are competent, and qualified by their studies, to give an opinion on the question of the natural dietetic character of man. I mean naturalists who have studied comparative anatomy with especial reference to this question. And it gives me pleasure to inform medical gentlemen that all of them, without a single exception, with the great Cuvier at their head, have testified that the anatomical conformation of the human being, teeth included, is strictly *frugivorous*. . . . .

"And now, in conclusion, I object to animal food because everything about it — the breeding, the butchering, the cooking, and the eating—is sensualizing and depraving. It gives a morbid, unbalanced, and, in some respects, a precocious development. It gives preponderance to the lower propensities at the expense of the moral and intellectual nature. It cultivates, in a thousand ways, the spirit of cruelty and selfishness. It engenders strife in society, and wars among the nations.

Just as the twig is bent, the tree's inclined.

"It distorts the development of childhood and perverts the instincts of youth. It leads directly to liquor-drinking and tobacco-using. It interferes with the law of harmonious development. Every structure, every organ, every faculty, and every power should have its equal, its normal, its proportionate development. All are good in themselves. Rightly educated and properly directed, all conduce to the perfect being. But when we so train and develop the organism as to place the spiritual nature under the dominion of morbid propensities and perverted instincts, the whole being becomes a *lusus naturæ* and a moral monstrosity, and we may well build prisons and penitentiaries, for they will be needed; and we may well organize temperance, and peace, and moral reform, and female guardian societies, for all will have enough to do."

After these tremendous sentences it is difficult to imagine any of us sitting down coolly and complacently to our accustomed chop, or calmly taking a slice from the family joint. The only wonder, indeed, is not that we are so bad as we are nowadays, but that we are not a great deal worse. My Vegetarian friend was, as I have conceded, a very fair average specimen of humanity; and I am, I believe, rather celebrated among my friends and acquaintances for my modest demeanour and imperfect appreciation of my own merits; but I am not sure that I felt so immeasurably that gentleman's inferior as I perhaps ought to have done. I suppose the truth is that, just as some of us are better than our creeds, so some are worse; or else really these vegetarian people being so purged and purified of all the ills, physical, intellectual, and moral which flesh is heir to, would be uncongenial people to live with, until they shall have levelled the rest of us up to their own lofty ideal.

WEST-END SECULARISM.

By what appears to me a manifest defect of arrangement, nearly all the secular "events" in London seem to "come off" at the same time—namely, on Sunday evening. Not only does this fritter away the strength of the persuasion by extending the force along the whole line instead of massing it on a single point, but—what is of more immediate consequence to me—it renders the examination of the different Secularist bodies a work of time, or would do so, had I not, from lengthened experience as a newspaper "Special," learned the art of being in several places at the same time. "How it's done" is my secret, which I may perhaps unbosom some day, like Dr. Lynn the conjuror.

To this rule there are, of course, exceptions, but scarcely more than enough to prove it. Among these are the meetings in Tarlington Hall, Church Street, Paddington, which take place on a Thursday evening, and which I remembered to have seen claiming in the *National Reformer* to represent the secularism of the West-end of London. It has long been a source of surprise to me that Free-thought should seem to eschew the higher strata of society, and work at the

East-end of London, and down by-streets. I fail to see the necessary antagonism between Free-thought and "respectability" which some of the professors of the former, it appears to me, make a mistake (from their point of view) in conceding. There are surely examples, which it would be invidious to specify, of very advanced thought in high places which need not make a West-end crusade quite a forlorn hope. I fancied I had discovered the basis of operations for such crusade in Tarlington Hall, and to Tarlington Hall I went.

I was not so far misled by the palatial name of the place as to be very much staggered when I found that Tarlington Hall stood in the rear of a boot shop near the well-known public-house called the Wheatsheaf, where the Paddington omnibuses change horses, or that you had to go almost through the bootmaker's emporium to get to it; but I *was* shocked when, on turning the handle of the only door I could see, I found myself in that respectable tradesman's back parlour. He soon reassured me, however, by emerging as I closed the door, and informing me that in consequence of the weather (it was raining hard) there would be no lecture that evening, but the same subject, that namely of "Jonah," would be taken on the following Thursday. I was disappointed, I own, for I had come a long way through soaking rain to hear about Jonah; yet I masked my disappointment with a mild joke, saying that I fancied a little rain more or less would not have mattered much to that particular prophet; but the man did not appear to appreciate the mild innocent pleasantry, and retreated to the back parlour whose privacy I had invaded. I could not help realizing the conviction, however, that the number of West-end Secularists must be very small, when a lecture could be thus summarily put off in consequence of a drop of rain; and I must confess I saw no other disappointed individual leaving the boot shop except myself.

I had a second experience of an equally infructuous character at the only other West-end focus of Secularism I could find out. This, I may mention, was situated in the very parish where I formerly held my curacy—St. George's, Campden Hill, Kensington—and Uxbridge Street, where the "Progressive Club" stands, was in my own district; but, of course, I never dared go near Progressive Clubs in those days. It was bad enough to write about Unorthodox London—most of the old ladies thought *that* wrong; I should have been a blacker sheep than ever had I entered anything so heterodox as a Progressive Club then.

I need not have endangered my character on this particular evening either; for the meeting, although advertised in my *vade mecum*, the *National Reformer*, was strictly a business one, consisting of contributions for the sufferers from the Farmers' Lock-out, and the passing a vote of thanks to the Bishop of Manchester for the part he had taken in the agriculcultural question. Reference was also made to the forthcoming Hospital Saturday; but all was too ephemeral to find a place in these pages, or be elevated into a type of West-end Secularism. Uxbridge Street, however, is decidedly nattier and much more convivial than the other places I had visited. There was a newly-painted proscenium at one end, and tables were distributed round the room whereupon the members regaled themselves with beer in white jugs, and grog from their own "stores." Altogether Uxbridge Street seemed a very "clubbable" place indeed, and that was about all. The West-end of the metropolis still awaits its secular propaganda on anything like a large scale.

I had projected a second visit to Jonah on the following Thursday evening, but matter more attractive cropped up in another direction; and, besides, the wind turned to the east, and I doubted whether that might not be as deterrent to the Tarlington Hall lecturer and audience as a mild downfall of rain!

IRISHISM.

In default of any recognised comprehensive title to cover the various degrees of Hibernian opinion, from full-blown Fenianism down to mild Home Ruleism, I adopt the above, which I heard coined by a gentleman who was waxing warm on the subject at the Temple Discussion Forum, and which seems generic enough for all purposes. I have to confess that, except as far as descriptive matter goes, my information on the subject of Irishism in London is defective. For obvious reasons the patriots of Erin do not care to lay bare their plans to me or anybody—it is not to be expected. I wrote to the head Secretary of the Irish Home Rule Confederation of Great Britain in Manchester, and received from him a prompt and courteous reply, simply referring me to the branch Secretaries of the Confederation in London, whose names, he said, I should find in the *Irishman*.

I bought the *Irishman*—(my newsvendor, by the way, must think me remarkably eclectic in my reading just at present)—and when I did not find what I wanted there, I of course at once understood that the reference was only a delicate way of declining to be " done." I am not so unreasonable as to be surprised at this. In a nascent political scheme, where success depends on things being kept "snug," I can understand the pertinacious newspaper correspondent being the greatest possible bore. He has got into the habit of looking at everything in the light of an article in a paper or a chapter in a book, and an else successful scheme might easily be blown upon and rendered abortive by one of these ubiquitous gentlemen. I hope that is a confession which will be appreciated by my Hibernian friends.

But if I did not find the addresses of local Secretaries in the *Irishman*, I found what was almost more to my immediate purpose—namely, announcements of the arrangements for the Amnesty Meeting in Hyde Park, and coming festivities for St. Patrick's Day. The first was as follows :—

"FELLOW-COUNTRYMEN IN LONDON.—We trust you will attend in thousands on Sunday in Trafalgar Square, and show to the world that we wish those prisoners to be set free. We have not had much time to organize, but we hope this will be made up by your energy. If there is no procession to start from your neighbourhood, come straight to the Square and fall in with the main body. On this day we are all Irish, without the least shade of political strife. Let every man bring as many friends as he can to swell the ranks. Do not stand on the footways or in little groups, but fall into line at once. Let every one who reads this report go to work at once among his friends, for it is a noble duty in a holy cause. Friends, we trust you will pardon us if this report is not so well drawn up as it ought to be, as we have but very little time. The meeting time in Trafalgar Square is half-past two. Do not stand particular about dining at the usual time if it would cause you to be too late. We request you will join any procession to the Square from your own district. But come whether you have processions or not. There will be several bands in the demonstration. The Irish National Brass Band on Clerkenwell Green, and the St. George's Temperance Brass Band have volunteered their services gratis (all honour to them!). We ask our countrywomen in London to aid us by their presence in the procession. We trust as many as possible will wear green rosettes, scarfs, or ribbons, and we most emphatically request men not to smoke in the ranks. Marshals will be appointed to direct the procession on the line of march. Last year's demonstration was so grand and so well conducted that everybody is acquainted with the order of march and the route to be taken. The different district processions will start from the same meeting-places that they did last year, and at the same time. Do not fail to be in Trafalgar Square, and march to Hyde Park, in the interest of the God-like virtue of setting the captives free.—We are, fellow-countrymen, yours truly—

"THE COMMITTEE OF DELEGATES APPOINTED TO CARRY OUT THE PROCEEDINGS."

The second as follows :—

"To THE NATIONALISTS OF LONDON.—A ball and concert will take place at Grafton Hall, Grafton Street, Soho, on Tuesday, March, 17, 1874. An efficient band will be in attendance. There will also be a Grand Panorama of the principal Irish Patriots and leading political events from 1848 down to the present time. *Chairman*, Mr. J. Ryan; *Master of Ceremonies*, Mr. J. Keane; *Secretary*, T. Dunne; *Treasurer*, P. Deering. Concert to commence at seven. Dancing at 9.30. Admission, sixpence; money taken at the door. The proceeds of the entertainment will be devoted to a National purpose."

Though having no connexion with Ireland, and owning no particular sympathy with the Fenian prisoners beyond that commiseration which all must feel with possibly well-meaning men suffering for their offences, I resolved to "demonstrate" on the Sunday like a real patriot. I took my station under the Reformers' Tree in the Park, and read *The Irishman* and the *Flag of Ireland*—two papers in which I found some sweetly loyal sentiments touching the Imperial Government in general, and the Ashantee War in particular. I wonder whether King Koffee takes in those two newspapers. He would be surprised to find his cause so warmly espoused against the British.

It was a balmy spring afternoon, and there was

already a good sprinkling of people in the Park when I got there. I only saw one patriot, and he wore a green riband with a gold harp embroidered on it, carried a sort of Field Marshal's baton in his hand, and had an artificial leg. Itinerant preachers were improving the occasion, and gathering large congregations from the enforced idlers; while the few police who were present occupied themselves in expelling the vendors of oranges from the Park. The way that an active and intelligent officer hustled a feeble old woman beyond the railings was edifying to see; but she was soon back again when the procession hove in sight.

We heard the sound of a patriot punishing a big drum in the distance, and presently saw what looked like the top of a bright green four-post bedstead struggling among the trees. This was the leading banner of the Emerald Isle; and really the procession was an imposing one in quantity, if not in quality. Men of all grades were there, each wearing his green badge or bit of shamrock, baskets of the latter being sold along the line of procession. The brass bands played excruciatingly, as usual. "St. Patrick's Day in the Morning" and the "Tramp Chorus" were the prevailing melodies; and the effect of the two, played by bands in close proximity, and a few fifes and drums coming in with another air, was exhilarating in the extreme. I fancy the computation of ten thousand people was quite within bounds. There were some score of banners and flags, and about half as many bands, representing I know not what societies. A great many females marched in the last batch, and all seemed to enjoy their outing amazingly. When they got to the centre of the Park—where even those many thousands interfered with nobody—there was some speechifying, which a very small fraction could hear, and no doubt enjoyed. We outsiders could only see it all in dumb show.

It was certainly the most imposing demonstration, and best deserved the name of any of the attempts I had ever witnessed. The working men were there literally " in their thousands," and if they did not do much towards getting their fellow-countrymen out of Portland, still they had a day's outing; and I could not help thinking how much wiser we were in 1874 than in 1866, since we let the patriots exhaust their energies in blowing trombones, beating big drums, and making speeches which nobody could hear, instead of pulling down the Park railings. Nothing could possibly be more orderly and decorous than the behaviour of the patriots; and by five o'clock the talkee-talk was over, and the only signs of the late gathering were stray patriots with green decorations, drifting along Oxford Street eastwards, and cheering one's heart with their merry brogue as they discussed, with the best of good-humour, the accomplished " meeting."

The circumstances of this Hyde Park demonstration brought home to my consciousness the fact that St. Patrick's Day was at hand, or else I do not think I quite knew when the festival of his saintship occurred; but the question of Home Rule had been somewhat occupying my attention, and I thought I might gain something on the subject if I attended some of the London celebrations. I referred once more to my two newspapers—*The Irishman* and *The Flag of Ireland*—and immediately found, as Wright used to say in "My Precious Betsy," apropos of "The Penny Satirist," that those publications would henceforth be necessary to my existence. The open undisguised way they sympathized with King Koffee, for instance, against the hated Sassenach was, as I have said, edifying in the extreme; and altogether the sheets are suggestive as to the perfect freedom of the press in the British Islands.

Well, I found in these savoury journals that there would be no dearth of doings in London—from a concert in St. James's Hall, and a West-end gathering of the Archbishop and Catholic clergy, down to the panorama at Grafton Hall, St. Giles's, with speechifying and singing. It was, I suppose, an evidence of my heretical tendencies that I deliberately chose the last, and resolved—like a true Irishman—to begin St. Patrick's Day *at night*.

I had some difficulty to find Grafton Street, Soho; and could not go to it again even now without asking. There was scarcely anybody there when I arrived, paid my sixpence, and passed into what had evidently once been a chapel; for the galleries, which I tried first, were still pewed, but downstairs the "flure" was covered with forms, and at the other end was a smartish little stage and proscenium, also locomotive. I first of all took my place in the gallery, but some lively Irish boys came in, and occupied themselves awhile in fighting, but ultimately took to spitting at one another from a distance, which was dangerous, so I evacuated and went downstairs.

I studiously wore a Tyrolese wide-awake, and garnished my button-hole with a sprig of shamrock, but I don't think the people liked the look of me. I feel sure they thought I was a policeman, though I cannot say that circumstance caused them to be at all particular in what was said or sung. The patriots did their singing and recitations themselves; but had a professional fiddle, cornet, and harp for the instrumental accompaniments. Occasionally these gentlemen tried to accompany the singers; but the melodies were of a character best left to themselves. "Biddy McCarthy" was most racily sung, and "The Rising of the Moon" and "My Brave Fenian Boy" were suggestive of something more than Home Rule. In fact, pikes were plainly mentioned, and whenever they were so the applause was vociferous. One fine young fellow in a stirring recitation, pined for a revival of Fontenoy, and several bright-eyed Irish girls trilled out their untutored lays in a manner that showed how essentially music is an Irish gift.

The singing went on a very long time, and then came the panorama of Irish patriots. The gentleman who read the description had such a very fine brogue, and all the audience were so exceedingly anxious to bear their concurrent testimony to the excellence of the heroes at once, that I failed to catch many of the names. I can only express a hope, however, that none of those gentlemen at all resembled his portrait, for a more atrocious misrepresentation of the human physiognomy than that series of portraits it was never my misfortune to behold. Had they been at all like the originals (which I am quite sure they were not) Mr. Gladstone would simply have made the most fatal mistake in amnestying such ill-favoured personages, and no amount of demonstrations ought to induce Mr. Disraeli to repeat the error. But excitement, not art, was what our Irish friends wanted; and they got it to their heart's content out of that hideous magic-lantern.

It was eleven o'clock before that exhibition was over, and then the "flure" was cleared for dancing. I only waited for the opening quadrille, which was danced by the younger portions, the old people solacing themselves with solitary jigs in the corner, after which I went out; and I confess I think the door-keeper was easier in his mind when he found I did not take a check to return.

My next experience on the Irish Question was at the Temple Discussion Forum, Fleet Street, where I found the subject of debate set down one evening thus:—" The Meeting of the Home Rule League in the Dublin Rotunda. Ought there to be an Irish party acting independently of all other parties in the United Kingdom? To be opened by Mr. Vaughan Dayrell."

The opener, one of those remarkable specimens continually met with in such associations, was an eloquent scholarly man, sparkling with wit, copious in classical quotation, and with frequent allusion to his own Oxford career. He opened decidedly in the negative, and took as his exordium the fact that the day on which he spoke, April 10th, was the anniversary of the occasion when his right honourable friend eating his supper at the other end of the room (Mr. Finlan) led the Chartist forces to Wimbledon Common and then ran away. He himself was on duty that day as a Special Constable, and narrated the raciest stories of his experiences when "alone in the Strand, in the execution of his duty." He had frequent recourse to a half-pint pewter of stout—begging to be excused whilst he took his "champagne"—and kept his listeners thoroughly amused, if not much edified on the subject of Home Rule, for nearly an hour. He apologized for his incoherence. He had made notes; but some rival orator—probably his right honourable friend at the other end of the room—had no doubt appropriated them. Mr. Finlan rose to reply, and, in measured terms, occupied some twenty minutes in personal recrimination, when he had to be called to time, and sat down angry, without having even approached the subject of debate. A herculean young man on the right of the chairman followed, and whilst bearing testimony to the individual excellence of the Irish, thought they were unreasonable in their demand for Home Rule. Mr. McSweeney rose on the Irish side, but he too got angry, being interrupted by the talking in the room, and could not be persuaded to continue. The consequence was that we only got two speeches at all *ad rem*—one from an elderly gentleman, who instanced the Hungarian Parliament at Pesth as a case of an *imperium in imperio* working successfully; and another from a young man, who, in a most lucid speech, pointed out that Ireland, with a population of 5,000,000 only, sent 105 members, or nearly one-sixth of the whole, to the House of Commons, and therefore could not reasonably complain of deficient representation.

Time and trains wait for no man—not even listeners to an Irish debate. I had to leave while this young gentleman was speaking, and without waiting for Mr. Dayrell's reply. And there my meagre experience of Hibernicism ends.

THE VICTORIA INSTITUTE ON ATHEISM AND PANTHEISM.

IN portraying the various phases of heresy in the metropolis my method has nearly always been to visit some heterodox gathering, note its more salient points, and either myself report in essence, or more frequently transcribe at length the utterances of my representative man or woman, adding such quotations as I could collect from published books or pamphlets of recent date on the subject in hand. I know of no better plan to get a view which shall be at once compendious and, as far as may be, exhaustive of unfamiliar faiths and practices.

In the present instance I exactly reverse the process, and on the principle that, occasionally at all events, *fas est ab hoste doceri*, take my illustrations of Pantheism and Atheism principally from the mouth of an assailant. After pursuing my former method to this advanced portion of my work, and giving full liberty of speech—some may perhaps even deem it licence—to the representatives of heresy and heterodoxy, I thought it might be useful in the way of comment, as certainly a relief in the shape of variety, to change my tactics, for once at all events; while such a variation might do something towards relieving the minds of my more sensitive readers by securing that, so far at least, the bane and antidote should go together.

The Victoria Institute, or Philosophical Society of Great Britain, which assumes as its motto the orthodox words, "Ad Majorem Dei Gloriam," meets at 8, Adelphi Terrace, Strand, and enumerates among its objects the following :—

"First.—To investigate fully and impartially the most important questions of Philosophy and Science, but more especially those that bear upon the great truths revealed in Holy Scripture, with the view of reconciling any apparent discrepancies between Christianity and Science.

"Second.—To associate men of Science and authors who have already been engaged in such investigations, and all others who may be interested in them, in order to strengthen their efforts by association, and by bringing together the results of such labours, after full discussion, in the printed Transactions of an Institution; to give greater force and influence to proofs and arguments which might be little known, or even disregarded, if put forward merely by individuals.

"Third.—To consider the mutual bearings of the various scientific conclusions arrived at in the several distinct branches into which Science is now divided, in order to get rid of contradictions and conflicting hypotheses, and thus promote the real advancement of true Science; and to examine and discuss all supposed scientific results with reference to final causes, and the more comprehensive and fundamental principles of Philosophy proper, based upon faith in the existence of one Eternal God, who in His wisdom created all things very good.

"Fourth.—To publish Papers read before the Society in furtherance of the above objects, along with full reports of the discussions thereon, in the form of a Journal, or as the Transactions of the Institute.

"Fifth.—When subjects have been fully discussed, to make the results known by means of Lectures of a more popular kind, and to publish such Lectures.

"Sixth.—To publish English translations of important foreign works of real scientific and philosophical value, especially those bearing upon the relation between the Scriptures and Science; and to co-operate with other philosophical societies at home and abroad, which are now or may hereafter be formed, in the interest of Scriptural truth and of real Science, and generally in furtherance of the objects of this Society.

"Seventh.—To found a Library and Reading Rooms for the use of the Members of the Institute, combining the principal advantages of a Literary Club."

Moreover it appends to its conditions of membership the very significant and characteristic one:—

"It is to be understood that only such as are professedly Christians are entitled to become Members."

My own attention had been first called to the Institute by the receipt of an invitation to become a member, after preaching my sermon on Positivism which I quoted above. For various reasons I felt bound to decline, although, of course, flattered by the suggestion; and I was glad when I saw advertised for discussion a subject which so exactly came within the limits of my present work, as Prebendary Row's Paper on "The Principles of Modern Pantheistic and Atheistic Philosophy, as expressed in the last work of Strauss, Mill, &c."

It was an assembly of "potent, grave, and reverend signors," of which I found myself making one in the handsome room of the Institute, very different from the squalid halls and motley assemblages in which I had recently been "assisting." I no longer needed to wear the brigand hat or forswear the sober livery of black clothes and white tie; and it was quite a relief to feel once more *in propriâ personâ*. By a peculiar arrangement, we each of us as we entered had placed in our hands a proof copy of the paper to be read; which, whilst it was in some respects convenient, rather resembled a prologue to one of the Tragedies of Euripides, wherein you are told at the outset all the plot of the ensuing drama; and anything like surprise or possible sensationalism is thereby at once obviated. We did not come to the

Victoria Institute to be surprised, but to be edified; and the staid, decorous, and eminently orthodox tone of my surroundings had already begun to exert its influence on me when Prebendary Row took up his parable and read, while we took up our proof copies and followed him :—

"The following passage from the 'Autobiography of the late Mr. J. S. Mill,' he said, "demands the earnest attention of all those who believe that there is a personal God, who is the moral governor of the universe: 'The world would be astonished if it knew how great a proportion of its brighest ornaments—of those most distinguished even in popular estimation for wisdom and virtue—are complete sceptics on religion, many of them refraining from avowal, less from personal considerations, than from a conscientious, though now in my opinion most mistaken apprehension, lest by speaking out what may tend to weaken existing beliefs, and by consequence, as they suppose, existing restraints, they should do harm rather than good.'

"The first question which strikes the mind on reading this passage is, Is the assertion true, 'that a large proportion of the "world's brightest ornaments" are complete sceptics on religion'? If so, it is of the most serious import. Mr. Mill has probably exerted a greater influence in the higher regions of thought than any writer of the existing generation. No holder of his philosophy can any longer entertain a doubt that certain portions of it are the philosophy of scepticism. The peculiar idiosyncrasies of mind which the Autobiography discloses, may have led Mr. Mill somewhat to over-estimate the sceptical tendencies of others. Yet the large number of writings which have been recently published of a sceptical tendency, is a sufficiently clear evidence that the principles of a pantheistic or atheistic philosophy are widely diffused among cultivated minds. Strauss, in his recent work, distinctly affirms that he is only acting as the spokesman of a wide range of pantheistic thought.

"I quite concur with Mr. Mill in opinion, that the time is come for speaking out plainly. In fact, unless morality is nothing better than expediency, there never has been a time when it has been right to profess adhesion to a system of thought which in secret we utterly despise. I fully concede that theologians no less than philosphers would do well to act on this opinion, and not to have an exoteric doctrine for the vulgar, and an esoteric one for themselves. But it is with the latter that I am now dealing. A sound philosophy requires that the too frequent example of the ancient philosopher, who acted the part of the high-priest of the god whose moral character he despised, and whose existence he disbelieved, should be utterly repudiated. What can be more degrading than the spectacle of an atheist Cæsar, dressed in the pontifical robes, uttering solemn vows to Jupiter in the Capitol? Persons capable of acting such a part must have a supreme contempt for the vulgar herd of humanity; and are at one in principle with the priests whose conduct they denounce. It is satisfactory to be informed that in the opinion of Mr. J. S. Mill, his father's prudential principle of not avowing his opinions to the world 'was attended with *some* moral disadvantages.' The italics are ours; in place of 'some' we would read 'great.'

"Before entering on the consideration of some of the principles of pantheistic and atheistic philosophy, to which I propose drawing attention in the present paper, it will be necessary to state what Atheism, as held by men of culture, really means. The son's account of the character of his father's atheism will clearly define its nature. 'Finding,' says Mr. J. S. Mill, 'no halting-place in Theism, he yielded to the conviction, that concerning the origin of things nothing whatever can be known. This is the only correct statement of his opinion, for dogmatic Atheism he looked on as absurd, as most of those whom the world have considered atheists have always done.' Atheism, therefore, as a philosophic theory, does not consist in the denial of the being of a God, but in the affirmation that there is no evidence that there is one. The moral value of the distinction between these two positions is *nil*, but the intellectual one is great, for it frees him who entertains it from the necessity of proving a negative.

"The following is worthy of quotation, as an illustration of the nature of the elder Mill's atheistic reasonings. 'He impressed upon me from the first that the manner in which the world came into existence was a subject about which nothing was known; that the question, "Who made me?" cannot be answered, because we have no experience or authentic information from which to answer it; and that the answer only throws the difficulty a step further back, since the question immediately presents itself, "Who made God?" It is almost incredible that such reasoning could have commended itself as valid to a man of the mental acuteness of the elder Mill; and it is quite a relief to be informed by the son that his father's atheism was rather moral than intellectual.

"I now proceed to examine some of the philosophic principles on which modern Pantheism and Atheism are based; and, first, their principle of causation. It is an accepted dogma of the Positive philosophy that a cause is nothing but an invariable sequence between an antecedent and a consequent, and that the notion of any efficiency in the cause to produce its effect is a fancy which has been exploded by the discoveries of physical science. This opinion is the natural outcome of a philosophy which teaches that the whole of objective nature, and even the fundamental principles of the mind, are nothing else but a bare succession of phenomena; and that a knowledge of any truth objectively valid for all time and space is unattainable by man.

"It strikes one at first sight as a strong objection against such a system of philosophy that language has been formed on the assumption that it is not true; its forms embody the universal experience of mankind, and have grown out of that experience. Now, nothing is more certain than that whenever we use words denoting causation we mean by them something very different from the mere invariable following of a consequent on an antecedent. If this is the true idea of a cause, nothing is more misleading than human language; for it is impossible to express the conceptions of this philosophy in it except by using it in a non-natural sense. One of the first duties which it owes to truth is to revolutionize human language, for, in its present forms, it is incapable of being the vehicle of accurate thought. If, therefore, this philosophy is a true representation of ultimate realities, one of its first duties is to attempt to construct a language capable of expressing them. At present it is a strong argument against the truth of this system of philosophy, that a few philosophers are committed to a particular theory on the one side; and, on the contrary, is the universal experience of mankind, as testified by the fundamental structure and the forms of language. . . . .

"We must now consider another most important principle on which this philosophy is founded—viz., its denial that the order and adaptations of nature are a sufficient ground for inferring the existence of an intelligent and conscious mind, which the philosophy of theism designates as a Personal God. The affirmation of certain systems of current philosophy is clear, and leaves no doubtful issue—viz., that we are not justified from the presence of order in nature in inferring the existence of an arranger; or from adaptation, of an adapter, or from apparent contrivance, of a contriver; or from the suitableness of the means by which a definite result has been brought about to effectuate it, of a designer. In one word, it is affirmed, when we see in nature results which elsewhere are unquestionable evidences of the presence of intelligent mind, all such inferences are invalid in the domains of nature; and that in making them we are only transferring the subjective impressions of our own minds into objective facts. On the contrary, this philosophy teaches that the order and adaptations of nature are not due to the presence of conscious intelligence; but of latent unintelligent self-evolution. To put the matter broadly: it is affirmed that intelligence has not produced nature, its order and adaptations, but that nature is the storehouse from which unintelligent law and latent forces have evolved all these wonderful phenomena. Non-life has generated life; unintelligence, intelligence; unconsciousness, self-consciousness; impersonality, personality; necessary law, freedom; latent forces, moral agents.

One aspect of pantheistic philosophy postulates the presence of unconscious intelligence in nature. But what is its nature, how it acts, or in what it is inherent, it leaves involved in a haziness which far exceeds that of any mystery involved in theism.

"Let us do these theories justice. It is affirmed that our conceptions of order and adaptation are essentially human, and have no validity when they are applied to anything which is not the product of the human mind. Also it is affirmed that all analogy fails between the works of nature and those of man; and that this renders invalid the conclusions which the theist seeks to draw from them.

"I reply that the objection is invalid, because, if true, it condemns us to universal ignorance. Our conceptions of law, force, and energy are human conceptions, the creation of our own minds. If this is a reason why they must be invalid in the one case, it is no less so why our reasonings respecting them must be invalid in the other. The objection is suicidal, and one which would render all philosophy impossible.

"But further: when we contemplate order and adaptation, we do not infer from it the presence of any particular form of intelligence, but of intelligence generally; just as when we speak of matter, time, and place we do not confine them to the special subjects from which we have derived our conception of them; but we apply them to phenomena generally. It is perfectly true that within the range of our experience, men and animals are the only beings who are capable of producing the results of order and adaptation. We have evidence that among these, different orders of intelligence exist. We are therefore justified in concluding that different orders and degrees of intelligence may exist in regions beyond our experience; though they may differ in some respects from that of men.

"I admit that there are a few cases in which order and adaptation have resulted from the action of that which, for want of a better term, we designate chance. Such, however, are so rare, and the instances so imperfect, that they are not worthy of consideration in the present argument. One thing is certain. As far as our experience goes, chance is only capable of producing such results on a very diminutive scale, and after long intervals of time. Yet the principle of chance is largely invoked in aid of the theories of this philosophy; though all experience affirms that it is incapable of producing the results in question.

"The all-important fact to be observed is that, as far as experience goes, lucky chances have no tendency to repeat themselves. On the contrary, the legitimate inference is that the occurrence of one once is a reason why we should expect it not to occur again. Whenever such a result takes place frequently, we cannot help inferring that this must be due to the intervention of mind. Let us take an example. If we were to throw up twelve dice into the air at haphazard, it is possible, though in the highest degree improbable, that they might all fall with their aces uppermost. But if the operation were repeated one hundred times, and the same result followed, there is no one who is capable of understanding the operation who would not draw the conclusion that the dice were heavily loaded as the highest of certitudes. The case is precisely similar with respect to the order and adaptations of nature. They are not only numerous but innumerable. It follows, therefore, that nature in every part is loaded heavily, and that that which loads it is the Divine mind.

"It will be objected that this philosophy nowhere affirms that order and adaptation have been evolved by chance action, but by forces working in conformity with immutable law. I reply that chance is only another name for the blind action of unintelligent laws and forces, and that the only additional factor introduced by the term chance, is that two or more of these forces or laws happen to intersect one another at a time and place suitable for producing a particular result, and without which concurrence the result could not have existed. When these do so at such a time and place that a particular effect is the result of their intersection, this is what we call a lucky chance. What I mean will be more easily understood by an illustration. Let us suppose a rock undergoing the process of disintegration. The action of water and of frost have opened in it several fissures. In accordance with another set of natural laws, the wind, or some other force, carries into them at this particular moment a number of seeds. These take root; fresh disintegration takes place. The operation is repeated; and thus the process is accelerated far more than it could have been by the action of a single force. This philosophy is compelled to invoke the aid of such lucky concurrences of forces in numbers numberless. Without them it would be powerless to impart to its speculations even the appearance of probability. In addition to this, it demands the right of drawing to any extent on the eternity of the past for an indefinite amount of time for the purpose of carrying on its operations. What is not possible in one hundred years may happen in one million. In this manner, with the bank of eternity at command, all things are possible.

"I submit that this mode of reasoning is not to solve the question, but to evade it. It gives no real account of the origin of those adaptations with which the universe abounds. On the contrary, there is something in the constitution of our minds which compels us when we contemplate an adaptation of complicated parts, exactly fitted to produce a suitable result, and observe that the result is brought about by the adaptation, to infer that it has been effected by the action of intelligence. Reason arrives at the conclusion that order and adaptation cannot have resulted from the action of unintelligent forces, but of intelligent mind. This will be the invariable inference, except where the exigences of a particular theory compel those who hold it to renounce the convictions of common sense. Let it be observed that I am speaking, not of some imperfect condition of the human savage, but of the fully developed intellect of cultivated men.

" The importance of this principle in reference to the philosophy of Pantheism and Atheism is strikingly brought before us in the celebrated work of Strauss, entitled 'The Old Faith and the New,' in which he professes not only to state his own opinions, but to be acting as the mouthpiece of a large number of German unbelievers. As this work has already gone through more than one edition in our language, besides the large number that it had previously gone through in Germany, it will be necessary to give it a special attention, for the purpose of exposing the unsound basis of its philosophy. The questions discussed in it are such that it is impossible to exaggerate their importance. They are as follows: In answer to the question, Are we still Christians? in the name of advanced thought in Germany, he answers in the negative. In reply to the question, Have we a religion? the answer is of a similar import. In answer to the question, What is our conception of the universe? his reply assumes the form of a material Pantheism, which differs in nothing from Atheism except in an illicit use of the language of Theism Lastly, wonderful to say, in answer to the question,

What is our rule of life? he announces himself a thorough-going German conservative, and utters a loud protest against the various forms of Communistic Atheism. It would appear that he and those in whose name he speaks are of opinion that the only effective mode to bar out the ocean is to demolish the old strongly-built sea-wall to its foundations, which has for ages past successfully repelled its billows, and in future to attempt to dam them out by substituting for it a thin layer of sand.

"The faith into which the author's philosophy has conducted him, and those in whose name he speaks, is that of the existence of a Cosmos, the sum total of all being, material, mental, and moral, including all existence and its laws, but which is void of personality, which is deaf to the voice of prayer; in which the place of volition is supplied by necessary and unyielding laws; of an intelligent Creator, by a self-developing power utterly unconscious, which to man is incapable of being the object of either hope or trust; which in the course of its self-development has evolved both the individual and the race, and will crush them again beneath the heel of iron destiny. This power will, through the endless whirl of the eternities of time and the infinities of space, go on evolving fresh worlds out of the ashes of preceding ones, and endless successions of systems and of galaxies, in which we as individuals shall take no part, to be again absorbed into the bosom of the mighty infinite. At death our self-conscious existence shall perish, never to be renewed. The atoms which compose us, after having been absorbed into the unconscious infinite, may be useful as materials for future life: but the hope and the destiny of the individual is eternal silence. To this, the only alleviation which this philosophy affords, is the consideration that while our conscious selves have utterly perished, the cosmos will go on evolving fresh forms of life and beauty throughout eternity, and will crush them again beneath the iron wheels of its chariot. No feeling of responsibility for the past need disturb us. Our destiny is non-entity.

"Such is the general sum total—the net result which this philosophy propounds to us in lieu of Theism. A few quotations from it will place its principles in a striking light.

"'The argument of the old religion was, that as the reasonable and the good in mankind proceed from consciousness and will, that, therefore, which on a large scale corresponds to this in the world must likewise proceed from an Author endowed with intelligent volition. We have given up this mode of inference. We no longer regard the Cosmos as the work of a reasonable and good Creator, but rather as the laboratory of the reasonable and good. We consider it not as planned by the highest reason, but planned for the highest reason. The Cosmos is simultaneously both cause and effect, the outward and the inward together.' Again : ' We stand here at the limits of our knowledge. We gaze into the abyss, we can fathom no further. But this at least is certain, that the personal image which meets our gaze there is but the reflection of the wondering spectator himself. If we always bear this in mind, there would be as little objection to the expression " God " as to that of the rising and setting of the sun, when we are all the time conscious of the actual circumstances.' After these and numerous similar assertions, the following utterance is remarkable : ' At any rate, that on which we feel ourselves entirely dependent is by no means merely a rude power, to which we bow in mute resignation; but is at the same time both order and law, reason and goodness, to which we surrender ourselves in loving trust. More than this—as we perceive in ourselves the same disposition to the reasonable and the good which we recognise in the Cosmos, and find ourselves to be beings by whom it is felt and recognised, in whom it is to become personified, we also feel ourselves related in our inmost nature to that on which we are dependent; we discover ourselves at the same time to be free in that dependence, and pride and humility, joy and submission intermingle in the feeling for the Cosmos.'

"Such is the substitute which this philosophy provides for a personal God. We are to feel all this for a being (if an infinite Cosmos can be called a being) who has neither personality, intelligence, nor will; who is the prey of inexorable law; who is incapable alike of affection and of thought; who, if he has children, has not made a single provision for their wants, cares not for them, and in due time inexorably devours them. Surely the theories of Atheism are rational compared with a Pantheism which offers such adulation to a Cosmos which can neither see, hear, feel, nor think, which is alike incapable of affections and intelligent volition. Truly, one is reminded of the mocking of Elijah, 'Cry aloud, for he is a god. Surely he sleepeth, and must be awaked.'

"One of the atheistic friends of our author, whose works he advises the reader not to glance at but to study, pronounces that it would have been better if the universe had never existed; and if no life had ever arisen in the earth any more than in the moon. This assertion is certainly not invalidated by Strauss's thin logic. 'If it be true,' says he, 'it follows that the thought that it would have been better if the universe had never existed, had better not to have existed likewise.' One can hardly help thinking that the following passage must have been written in irony :— 'Sallies of this kind, as we remarked, impress our intelligence as absurd, but our feelings as blasphemous. We consider it arrogant and profane on the part of a single individual to oppose himself with such audacious levity to the Cosmos whence he springs, from which also he derives that spark of reason which he misuses.'

"But I must now draw attention to some of the principles from which the author considers that these are natural conclusions.

"He begins with the conception of the Cosmos, which he defines 'not only as the sum total of all phenomena, but also of all forces and of all laws. The All,' says he, 'being the all, nothing can exist outside it; it seems even to include the void beyond.' After having pointed out the various changes through which its various parts have passed, he goes on to assert that this infinite Cosmos constitutes a unity. 'The Cosmos itself,' says he, 'the sum total of infinite worlds, in all stages of growth and decay, abides eternally unchanged in the constancy of its absolute energy amidst the everlasting revolution and mutation of its parts.'

"I have quoted these passages for the purpose of showing that the fundamental difficulties of this philosophy fully equal those of theism, against which it is in vain for it to urge that it enters into the regions of the unknowable. If the universe is the sum total of all phenomena, forces, and laws, a few questions may be propounded for its solution. Is it nothing but these? Are phenomena and laws possessed of an objective existence, or must something else underlie them? Are laws existences, or modes of existence, or what are they? Are its forces actually existent things, or qualities inherent in them? Again: 'the Cosmos is the sum total of infinite worlds.' It is therefore infinite, but consists of finite parts. Can it therefore be a unity? It follows, then, that that which is infinite is not absolutely unthinkable, and that some of the conceptions which are derived from our finite modes of being may be projected into it without violating any principle of sound philosophy. But further: this infinite universe consists of parts several of which are infinite; it follows, therefore, that an infinitude which is composed of subordinate infinities, can constitute a unity. But, as a crowning mystery, we are told that it abides eternally unchanged in the constancy of its absolute energy amidst the everlasting revolution and mutation of its parts. Surely a philosophy which admits a number of such positions among its fundamental principles may be asked to show a little modesty when it assails the difficulties of theism. The one contains unfathomable mysteries equally as the other.

"'But,' says our author, 'the Cosmos is a phœnix, ever recovering itself from its ashes.' Yes, surely, it is a consolatory truth for men who will never renew their personal existence, to be assured that their remorseless parent never had a beginning to its activities, and never shall have an end, but that it shall continue throughout the infinities of time and space to cast up the bubbles of phenomena, and devour them, to reappear again, in endless progression. Yet this is the god of this philosophy, who goes on endlessly reproducing himself, under the impulse of blind forces directed by equally blind laws, in endless forms of life and death, of reproduction and decay, throughout the dismal eternity of the future. Full well may Strauss's atheist friend satirize the folly of such a god. But, no: he is alike incapable of wisdom and of folly; though he contains in himself potentiality, and evolves into actuality all wisdom and all folly, all order and disorder, all growth and decay, all good and evil, all virtue and all crime. Verily such a god cannot be a phœnix, but a Proteus. Yet our author, and those in whose name he speaks, assert that they think it worthy of a reverent regard, and that to insult it is a blasphemy!

"There is an obvious difficulty which confronts this philosophy, of which it does not attempt to offer a solution. If the Cosmos is thus eternally reproductive, why may it not at some period during the infinity of future time reproduce our own personal existence, and even hold us resposible for what we have done in our previous state of being? To do so would only be to add one wonder more to the multitude of wonders which it is declared to be able to effect. Against this most serious contingency this philosophy has nothing to offer but its dogmatic assertion, that personal existence, after its fleeting phenomenal appearance, must sink into eternal silence.

"Let us now examine some of the processes by

which it attempts to account for the origin of the existing order of things. With respect to some of the processes by means of which it affirms the universe of matter to have been constructed, we need have no difficulty. They may have been the very means which the Creator has employed to effectuate His purposes; and to accept them as denoting the law according to which creation has been evolved is quite consistent with a belief in Theism. As all His manifestations with which we are acquainted are in conformity with law, and involve the use of means, so there is no difficulty in conceiving that God's creative work has been conducted in conformity with a definite law and order, and that He has made use of means in effecting it, instead of creating each separate existence immediately. On the contrary, it is highly probable that such would be the mode of His action.

"But this is widely different from the assumption that the Cosmos can have been built up by the action of blind forces without the aid of intelligence and will. Law, however convenient as a term, denotes nothing but an invariable mode of action. In itself it embraces no conception of energy or power, although nothing is more common, even in philosophic language, than to confound this conception with it. But it is impossible to build the universe without the energetic action of both these. Unless forces have an action given to them, they can effect nothing—confusion, not harmonious arrangement, will be the results of their operations. These can only be found in intelligence and will. As far as human experience extends, forces acting in conformity with blind laws, have never produced a single adaptation, order, or arrangement, but destruction only. This philosophy, for the purpose of enabling it to dispense with the directing power of intelligence and will, postulates an eternity of time, during which forces have acted, and affirms that this can produce all the results of intelligent volition.

"Having evolved the matter of the universe into planets, suns, and systems, by means which the Theist need not dispute, as long as they have an omnipotent intelligence at their back, energizing in and through them, our author is compelled to face the question of the origin of life. He is fully aware of the difficulty of the problem, and admits that it is no solution of it to say, that its absence may be accounted for in the lower strata, by the supposition that causes may have been in existence which have destroyed all traces of it. 'There was a time,' says he, 'when the temperature of the earth was so high, that living organisms could not exist on it. There was once no organic life on the earth: at a later period there was: it must consequently have had a beginning, and the question is, how?'

"Yes, truly; that is the question. Kant judged that it might well be said, 'Give me matter, and

I will explain the origin of the world ; but not, Give me matter, and I will explain the origin of a caterpillar.' Let it not be forgotten also that Kant bowed in reverence before the moral nature of man, and its authoritative affirmation of the obligation of the moral law. These mighty gulfs, however, the philosophy of Atheism and Pantheism has attempted to bridge over. 'Here,' says Strauss, 'faith intervenes with its miracle.' This philosophy postulates an operation no less miraculous—viz., the action of blind forces under the direction of blind laws, continued throughout an eternity of time.

"I need hardly say, that our author resolves all difficulties by boldly assuming the truth of the theory of spontaneous generation. Here let it be observed, that Atheism is obliged to use a word which implies the presence of will. He admits the uncertainty of previous experiments; but nothing daunted, he affirms, 'If the question of spontaneous generation could not be proved in regard to our present terrestrial period, this would establish nothing with respect to a primeval period under totally different conditions. The existence of the crudest form of life has however never been actually demonstrated. Life too, after all, is nothing but a form of motion.'

"On questions of pure physics I shall not enter. But it belongs to the present subject to point out the conditions of the problem which this philosophy has to solve ; and not to allow it to substitute an unreal for the true issue. That issue is not the one here stated. Before it can advance one step, proof positive of the truth of the theory of spontaneous generation must be given. It is no solution of the problem to take refuge in the assumed possibility, that it may have taken place under widely different conditions during the uncertain past. To do so is cunningly to assume the question at issue. Professor Huxley tells us that proof of the theory of spontaneous generation has yet to be given.

"But further: supposing a living being of the lowest type could be constructed in the laboratory, does this bring us one atom nearer to the point at issue? The real question is, whence comes living matter? and what is the distinction between it and non-living matter? There our opponents, being the judges, differ *toto cælo* from each other. Is there any evidence that matter which has never lived, can be made to pass into living forms? Till this can be shown, the mere formation of a being in the laboratory, which possesses the lowest form of life, proves nothing. The only adequate solution of this question on the Pantheistic and Atheistic side is proof positive that life is a mode of motion, and nothing else. This proof has certainly not yet been adduced, and even if it could be found, there is yet a further question which demands an answer—viz., how, whence, and where has originated this peculiar modification of motion which constitutes life; and how has it come into existence at the favourable moment for its existence? Had it not been favourable, the feeble germ would have been crushed by the mighty powers of nature in the struggle for existence. All this and much more must be answered before it can be proved that mechanical or chemical forces can become vital ones by any powers which they possess of self-transmutation.

"Our author endeavours to evade the question by concealing it behind a mass of scientific jargon. He says: 'Life is only a special—viz., the most complicated, form of mechanics. A part of the sum total of matter emerges from time to time out of the usual course of its motions into special thermico-organic combinations; and after having for a time continued therein, it returns again to the general modes of motion.'

"When we are famishing for scientific bread, it is cruel for philosophy to throw us a stone. As an account of the matter we are considering, part of the above sentence is unintelligible, and the remainder attempts to answer one difficulty by raising others far greater.

"The perusal of this work affords a striking proof that the philosophers in whose names it is written were far from being satisfied with their position, even after they had obtained possession of an inorganic cell, from whence they might commence the operation of creating the various forms of organic life, of which man is the crown. They felt deeply, in the words of our author, 'that no acorn ever produces a fig; that a fish always produces a fish, and never a bird or a reptile; a sheep always produces a sheep, and never a bull or a goat.' They have therefore hailed, as the rising of a new sun, the theory of natural selection as a means for constructing the worlds of life and organism, without the intervention of a Creator. For the use they make of it, it is possible that its author will owe them little thanks; but they are almost ready to forgive Mr. Darwin for his postulate of the original intervention of a God to infuse into inorganic matter the principle of life, in consideration of the greatness of his discovery. He is with them, the founder of the new age, in which the belief in the being of a God is destined to become an old wife's fable.

"Let it be observed, however, that the Darwinian theory, whatever be its merits or defects, is only a special form of a theory of creation by evolution. It assumes, in the first instance, a creative act, by which some cells had infused into them the principle of life. It then proceeds to account for the existence of every living form by the aid of two principles, designated natural and sexual relation, without any subsequent intervention of Divine power. Whatever may be thought of this particular theory, it is evident that a principle of evolution, by which I mean that all existing organisms have been gradually evolved from one another by the Creator's wisdom and power, through certain forces of which He possesses the absolute control, is as consistent with theism as any other theory of creation. The only theories which are essentially Atheistic and Pantheistic are those which lay down that God is not the author of the laws of nature, nor their contriver, nor the director of their operations, and that blind forces can produce the phenomena which result from the operation of intelligence, and that forces can exist independently of His constant energy. The old theory of creation was, that each species was produced by a separate creative act, the idea being that its progenitors must have started into being entire and complete. This may or may not have been the *modus operandi* employed by the Creator; but, as a theory, it leaves us in the dark how creation was effected, except that it was the result of the exertion of the divine will. A theory of development professes to give the law of progress and to account for some of the means through which creation has been accomplished. Whether it has been effected in this way, or in that, can only be determined by the facts of nature which throw light on the subject. To speak of creation out of nothing as an adequate solution of how creation has been effected is only a confession of our ignorance. The real point is, is the theory suggested an adequte account of the facts of nature? Are the means adequate to produce the result? Or must other agencies have contributed to it, and among them the direct intervention of God?

"There is, unquestionably, a tendency among religious men to charge every theory of creation by evolution with Pantheistic and Atheistic tendencies. This would be just, if it were a necessary part of such theories, that blind forces and laws are able to produce this result independently of the power and intelligence of a personal God. But where I ask, is the Pantheism and Atheism, if we assume that the Creator has followed a definite order and law in His creative acts, and has carried them on, as He does all the acts of His providence, by the use of means? Or if, instead of causing the first progenitors of a species to spring up from the ground, he has produced them out of beings previously in existence? Our present knowledge is very inadequate to determine how creation has been effected. This is a strong reason why we should avoid premature dogmatizing; but certainly none why we should not make it the subject of careful study.

"There are not wanting indications that in the formation of the universe the Creator has acted through the agency of means, and not by that which we designate direct action. Of this the evidence is considerable. Whether this be an entire account of the matter is quite another question. Still more clear is it that His creative acts have followed a sequence and order, and been constituted on a general plan. This latter point must be admitted even by those who refuse to admit the theory of creation by evolution. We might have hoped that the general acquiescence in the well-known illustration of Paley's watch, would have been a sufficient safeguard against wholesale denunciations of those who hold this theory as if it were destructive of Theism. As he observes, if a watch could be so constructed as to produce another watch by its mechanism, and should thus go on producing a succession of watches, each possessed of the power of self-reparation, we should feel the most profound admiration for the skill of the artist. Nor would it be diminished, if the mechanism could construct a first-rate chronometer; and this a succession of still more perfect instruments. The only point in which such a theory can be either Pantheistic or Atheistic is when it is assumed that such harmonies can have resulted from the action of blind forces, without the intervention of intelligence.

"Still more remarkable is it that such a theory should be suspected of Pantheistic or Atheistic tendencies, when we reflect that the mode in which God has created every individual is by a process of evolution. Yet surely it will not be pretended that He has not made each one of us, and every individual of every species. Yet He has unquestionably effected this by a process of evolution. The media through which He works may be very obscure; but this does not affect the fact itself. History also teaches that in man the evolution of more perfect from less perfect states, is the order of God's providential government of the world. The New Testament declares that Revelation has been communicated in a similar manner. Why, then, may not the Creator have created different species by producing one out of another by a process unknown to us? It is absurd to attempt to shut up all inquiries on this subject, by asserting that all such theories are either Pantheistic or Atheistic.

" Still it is undeniable that the Darwinian form of this theory has been widely embraced by the philosophic schools in question, as affording an apparent solution of some of their difficulties. The joy with which they have hailed its advent is very remarkable. It becomes, therefore, a duty thoroughly to examine into its ability to produce the results in question, and to estimate the difficulties with which it is attended. Yet it must not be forgotten that its author distinctly assumes the necessity of a Creator to infuse into matter the first forms of life, and to impress on it its laws. This difficulty can only be got over by Pantheists and Atheists by the exercise of a hearty faith in some unknown powers of the past or discoveries of the future. It follows, therefore, that the faith which they deride in connexion with religion and Christianity is essential to this philosophy. It demands the exercise of faith in the unseen—viz., the discoveries of the future or the unknown possibilities of the past, for without it it is destitute of even the semblance of proof. It would seem as if faith in the unseen is only objectionable when it is demanded in connexion with religion.

"It follows, therefore, that it is impossible for these systems to bridge over the interval which separates life from not life. There is also another interval which can be spanned by no arch—viz., the production of the power of sensation. According to these theories, there must have been a time when there was no sensation in that part of the universe to which we belong. There, therefore, must have been a time when the first being which was capable of sensation sprang into existence. Pantheism will, perhaps, affirm that the infinite Cosmos has ever possessed within itself sensation and intelligence. If so, particles capable of sensation must have existed in that fire mist out of which the present order of things has been evolved, the heat of which was sufficient to have sustained all existing matter in the form of gas. If so, their existence must have been very uncomfortable during the countless ages the matter of the solar and sidereal systems has taken in cooling. The alternative will doubtless be preferred, that a time once was, when the first being capable of sensation began to be. But a vast interval separates the sentient from the non-sentient, not a succession of trifling variations. The philosophy which attempts to construct a universe without the intervention of a God is bound to give us an account of how the first sentient being began to be.

"But there are several other states of being which are separated from each other, not by short steps but by vast intervals. Among these self-consciousness occupies a conspicuous place. It is obvious that it exists. It is as certain as any fact of time or space. We can all and each of us utter the mysterious word 'I,' and attach a distinct meaning to it. It is the most mysterious of words. Who shall fathom its profound depths? It is that which separates between self and not-self, person and thing. It is that which constitutes us a unity in the midst of plurality and change. As beings capable of self-consciousness, we feel that we have existed through long intervals of time, surrounded by and deeply interested in multitudes of things which are not ourselves. Not one particle of matter constitutes our present bodies which composed them twenty years since, yet we are the same. There must have been a time when self-conscious beings existed not. There must, therefore, have been one when a self-conscious being first began to be. Here then is an interval, the depth of which the imagination can but imperfectly fathom. It is not too much to say that no theory of evolution can bridge this over without the intervention of a self-conscious Creator.

"There is yet another interval. A being may be

a person, and yet have no conception of right or duty. I select this conception as representative of the whole moral nature of man, of which it forms the most remarkable characteristic. It is immaterial to my argument whether the utilitarian philosophy is correct in its analysis of the origin of the idea. I firmly believe that it is not. But the fact cannot be gainsaid, that vast number of minds, of the highest order, have a clear conception of duty quite distinct from any reference to utilitarianism. On the contrary, they feel the strongest obligation to sacrifice themselves to it in contradiction to the strongest dictates of expediency. There is something within us which says, let right prevail, even if the heavens fall. There must, therefore, have been a time when the first being, who was capable of feeling a sense of duty, who could bow before a moral law, and say, 'I ought,' began to be. The interval is one which separates the conception of duty from non-duty; of conscience from non-conscience; of a moral nature from the want of it. The difference is not one of degree but of kind. Between laws of motion and their modifications, and conceptions of duty, there is no one thing in common. When the idea of duty first originated a new order of being entered the universe.

"Even if the principle of the utilitarian philosophy is correct, that duty is the obligation to seek the greatest happiness of the greatest number, the argument is unaffected by it. The question still imperatively demands solution, how came it ever to be felt to be a duty, to seek the greatest happiness of the greatest number? When and how has this sentiment arisen? Of what form of motion is it the modification?

"Such are some of the gaps which must be bridged over by means of clear and indisputable facts, before a philosophy which has no other forces at its command but blind, unintelligent ones, can account for the origin of things. But supposing for argument's sake that these have been surmounted, the question at once arises, whether the Pantheistic and Atheistic theory of evolution is adequate to account for the existence of the various orders of beings which lie within these bounds. I will now examine some of the special agencies by which it has been attempted to be shown that the various forms of organized life have been developed without the agency of a being possessed of personal intelligence and power. The only principles which this philosophy presses into its service for that purpose are Darwin's two principles of natural and sexual relation.

"I by no means wish to affirm that these may not have been potent instruments in the hands of Omnipotence by which God has carried on His creative work. That they act within certain limits is an obvious fact. The question is, what are those limits? Are they the only agencies? Are they alone adequate to the work? Must not other principles, known and unknown, have contributed to it? Is their distinct and separate agency conceivable without Omnipotence at their back?

"We must begin by assuming that life has somehow originated in the earth. The problem before us is as follows: given matter and force acting in conformity with invariable laws, both alike destitute of intelligence, to evolve everything in the sentient universe, which bears the indications of the action of intelligence. Let us even suppose that one or more cells have been evolved from which our course of evolution is to commence which is ultimately to culminate in the production of man.

"There is one resource to which this philosophy flies in every difficulty, and which it uses with unbounded freedom—an infinite storehouse of past time. If a thing cannot be effected in one thousand years, it can in a million; if not in a million, it can in one hundred million. If the last period is inadequate, boldly multiply, for it is impossible to break the bank of the eternity of the past. With this agency at its command, all things are possible. Let us hear Strauss:—'Short steps and longest intervals of time are the magic formula by which actual science at present solves the mystery of the universe: they are the talismans by whose aid she quite naturally unlocks the portals, formerly reputed to fly asunder at the sole bidding of miracle.'

"Yes, truly: there is more truth in this passage

than its author probably intended to convey. The action of this principle is truly magical and talismanic; it is worthy of the deep consideration of those who invoke it, whether it can effect any results more real than the magical formularies and talismans of the 'Arabian Nights.' Little jumps, and infinite time to jump in, is all that is required to evolve all the order and adaptations of the universe, which exist in numbers passing all comprehension. The proposition that, if we have time enough to walk to a galaxy, compared with which the distance of Sirius is a speck, by taking steps of an inch long, we shall get there in the course of infinite time, may be incapable of being disproved; but it is absurd. I submit that this continual invocation of infinite time is not a rational solution of a difficulty, but an evasion of it.

"The truth is that physical science breaks this magic wand in the hands of the operator. While it tells us that the universe has existed a vast interval of time in its present form, it affirms that it cannot have existed for an indefinite one. The laws of its physical forces assign to it clear and definite limits, which it cannot have exceeded. It follows, therefore, that indefinite demands on a past eternity cannot be tolerated by a sound philosophy.

"Not only is this philosophy compelled to assume that a number of small variations must have taken place, which for any practical purpose it is impossible to distinguish from infinite; but it is compelled to take for granted that all those have been on the side of progressive improvement. Yet the history of man testifies that nature has made many failures and retrogressions. Human progress has been, unhappily, full of them. But these are easily got rid of by the theory of the destruction of the weakest and the survival of the strongest in the struggle for existence. Yet history informs us that some of the weak races of mankind have a remarkable tenacity of life.

"But if such a tendency exists in nature, this philosophy is bound to give us some account of its origin. Tendencies in nature on the side of progress are very useful ones. It is, therefore, a serious question, How got they there? For aught that appears, blind matter, force, and law might have produced tendencies suited to shiver systems to pieces, and not to construct them. Does not the existence of such tendencies imply the presence of superintending mind?

"But, says this philosophy, all that is necessary is to continue advancing by slow and gradual variations; and this glorious universe, with all its complicated adaptions, crowned by man, will appear at last! We need not care for the shortness nor the variety of the steps, nor for occasional movements in a backward direction; for have we not infinite time at our command? The cell with its lowest forms of life, or the intellectual or moral atoms diffused in yonder fire-mist, will in due time produce all the complicated organisms of living beings, with their wondrous adaptations, and at length a Newton, a Shakspeare, and a self-denying Howard.

"But, I ask emphatically, are such short steps all that is required? Shall we not be brought to a standstill by the absence of necessary conditions? Blind forces cannot effect their work except by the aid of things which, for want of a better name, we must call favourable chances, by which I mean forces intersecting one another at the right time and place. What myriads of forces must have worked in vain for the want of this condition of successful operation? Let me illustrate this by the example which Strauss has chosen as an illustration of the manner in which we may readily account for the production of the various organisms of nature. 'Let us suppose,' says he, 'a herd of cattle in primitive times to be still destitute of horns, only possessed of powerful necks and projecting foreheads. The herd is attacked by beasts of prey: it defends itself by running against them and butting with the head. The butting will be the more vigorous, the bulls the fitter to resist the beasts of prey, the harder the forehead with which he butts. Should this butting in an individual have developed into an incipient horny accretion, then such an individual would have the best chance of preserving his existence. If the less equipped bulls of such a herd were torn to pieces, then the individual thus equipped would propagate the species. Unquestionably there would be some at least among its descendants in whose case the paternal equipment would be repeated; and if on renewed attacks these very ones again survived, and, moreover, principally those whose horns were most developed, then little by little, by transmission of this weapon to the other sex, a completely horned species would be formed, especially if the other sex would of its accord give the preference to the males thus ornamented; and here Darwin's theory of natural selection is supplemented by the so-called sexual selection, to which he has recently devoted a special work.'

" Few of the operations of nature would seem to be more simple than the manufacture of a horn; let us, therefore, carefully examine the amount of time and lucky chance which this theory finds it necessary to postulate as necessary for its formation. This will give us a clear idea of the difficulties which must have been surmounted in the course of the evolution of man from an inorganic cell, if there was nothing but unintelligent forces to operate with.

" I. The theory before us presupposes a very favourable concurrence of circumstances with which to commence our operations. Nature has already kindly furnished us with a herd of cattle, with powerful necks and protruding foreheads. How long it must have taken to form these latter appendages this philosophy does not tell us. Having eternity at is command, it simply brandishes its magic wand and says, as indefinite a number of æons of past time as you require.

"II. Another favourable condition is provided all ready for our use. It seems that a horn cannot be grown on a hornless animal without the exercise of butting; accordingly, a number of beasts of prey are at hand at the proper time and place to offer battle to our unhorned herd—these, be it observed, are supposed to be fully equipped with all their weapons of offence. But suppose that these latter had come into existence at a different time and place, or that instead of our oxen being surrounded by beasts of prey, they had come into existence among a number of peaceful creatures, the whole operation of horn-growing must have come to a standstill. The concurrence of such favourable contingencies could only have occurred after the lapse of indefinite æons.

"III. The herd, when attacked, defend themselves by butting. It was fortunate that nature should have furnished them with this impulse. This looks like the presence of intelligence, for unintelligent nature might quite as well have provided them with a disposition to run away when attacked, as she has the hare, and there would have been no tendency to generate a horn. Such a disposition must have required the concurrence of multitudes of favourable circumstances for its formation, as well as that of indefinite æons of time.

"IV. The act of butting has a tendency to harden

the skull; this we know to be a fact. Still, a philosophy whose object is not theory, but truth, cannot help inquiring, Whence came this tendency? It might have been one in an opposite direction.

"V. We are next invited to assume that repeated acts of battery have not only hardened the skull, but developed a horny accretion. The remarks of our author might lead the reader to believe that all this could have been effected in a single generation of bull life. But it is quite evident that it could only have been the result of the struggles of protracted generations, who succeeded in transmitting to their descendants a gradually increasing horny appendage. If it were not so, bull life in those primeval ages must have been protracted to a period compared with which the age of Methuselah must have been as nothing. Let it be observed also, that the concurrence of every one of these favourable conditions must have been continually repeating themselves.

"VI. The bulls, says our author, who have succeeded in developing these horny appendages will have the best chance of preserving their existence. Still this is a chance only, but not a certainty, for many other contingencies might have destroyed them. Deaths from disease were probably not unknown in primeval times, and against this the possession of an incipient horn would have been no prevention.

"VII. We are next asked to assume that these

bulls go on continually fighting until all the less equipped ones are torn in pieces, in order that an individual with incipient horns may become the progenitor of a race. This philosophy, however, is utterly silent as to the number of years and of favourable contingencies it would have taken to bring about this result. It simply brandishes its magic wand, and the unhorned oxen disappear.

"VIII. It is necessary that the bull with incipient horns should procreate descendants similarly equipped. It is undoubtedly in accordance with natural facts that he should do so. Still this philosophy is bound to tell us how came this law into existence, for it has the appearace of being a result of that intelligence the existence of which it denies.

"IX. Our incipient horn has yet to grow into a longer one, and then into a longer one, until it attains its full length. For this purpose, these processes of fightings and buttings, and throwing out of small variations and survivals of the strongest, besides ever-recurring favourable contingencies, have to be repeated times without number. To evade these difficulties our only resource is again and again to brandish our magic talisman of infinite time.

"X. As yet this long and painful process has only led to the evolution of horned individuals, and not a horned race. We must therefore invoke the theory of sexual selection, and suppose that the horned females fall in love with the horned appendage of their male companions. It is not easy for us to say what are the precise ideas which cows entertain of beauty. We know however, that it is far from an invariable fact that the most handsome men and women unite in matrimony. Still, however, the assumption must be made, that the horned bull is irresistibly attractive to the horned cow before a horned species can be finally established by the forces at the service of this philosophy.

"It is hardly possible to go through these successions of indefinite æons of time, and of concurrences of lucky chances with gravity, and suppose that they constitute a true account of the past history of the race of long-horned oxen. But the consequence which I deduce from it is a perfectly grave one. Few operations of nature can have been more simple than the evolution of a horn. But if by the aid of these forces alone the operation must have been so complicated, involving indefinite æons of time, and the casual concurrence of multitudes of happy chances, for its accomplishment, what must we say of the period requisite for the production of the other peculiarities of the race of oxen? What must we say of the infinitude of them, which must have been necessary for the production of all the complicated organisms and adaptations of animal life? This philosophy affirms that the bodily, intellectual, and moral nature of the most highly gifted man has been slowly evolved by a few unintelligent forces in a long line of ancestry from a simple cell. Will it endeavour to compute the number of distinct species which must have been evolved in this long succession? the number of æons which must have elapsed before each stage could have been accomplished? or the number of happy chances which must have concurred before each step could have become a possibility? When it has done this, let it multiply these arrays of figures, which it is scarcely possible to embody in any finite conception, and present us with the result? Surely this philosophy has stumbled on the regions of miracle without observing it. Far more miraculous is this mode of evolving the universe than the intervention of an intelligent Creator.

"The number of intersections of independent forces, directed by nothing but blind laws, which this system is compelled to postulate, is alone sufficient to destroy its claim to be received as a philosophy. We know, as a matter of fact, that the occurrence of one lucky chance is a reason for expecting that it will not occur again; but this system is compelled to postulate them in endless succession. What right has it to make unlimited drafts on the infinite past, or the infinite future? What can positive science have to say to either of them? To affirm that blind forces can effect all things, if they have only sufficient time in which to operate, is not to propound a philosophy, but its negation. Our author, however, is not insensible to the difficulties with which he has to struggle. 'It was doubtless,' he says, 'no small achievement, when, in yon ape-like horde, which we must consider as the cradle of the human race, the thoroughly erect posture became the fashion, instead of the waddle or partially developed gait of the higher apes; but step by step it went on improving, and time at least was no consideration. . . . . More astonishing still does this progress appear, from the harsh scream of the ape to articulate human speech.'

" Yes, doubtless, vast is the gulf which separates the two, for it involves the entire interval which separates the rational from the irrational, the self-conscious from the non-self-conscious, the capacity of moral obligation from the absence of it. Strauss is well aware that without language as an instrument, all real thought is impossible. He therefore summons to his aid a race or races of intermediate beings, of whose existence the evidence is *nil*, and supposes that they have existed. He also observes that monkeys have a kind of language, although he candidly admits that, whatever else they are capable of being taught (and they can be taught many things), they have never learned to speak, even when they have been brought into the closest contact with man. Nor has our constant companion, the dog, with his half-rationality and his apparent desire to give utterance to his feelings, made the smallest approach to the use of articulate speech, although he has been the friend of man for thousands of years. If a Pantheistic or an Atheistic philosopher could educate either the dog or monkey to use rationally even the lowest elements of human language, he would do more to prove his theory than by millions of conjectures.

"But, adds our author, 'Ere that pre-human branch little by little elaborated something of a language, periods of immeasurable duration may have elapsed; but after he had once hit upon speech, in however imperfect a condition, the speed of his progress was vastly accelerated,' &c.

"I ask emphatically, is it reasoning, to have recourse to the magic talisman of infinite time, as the solution of every difficulty? Is it not more rational to invoke the aid of an intelligent Creator? If it be replied that an intelligent Creator belongs to the regions of the unknowable, does not an inexhaustible past eternity equally belong to them? Does it not leave the origin of intelligence utterly unsolved?

"Our author justly remarks, that if the power of thought fills us with astonishment, that of feeling is no less marvellous. 'A divine force,' says he, 'reveals itself in the sensations of the lowest animal as much as in the brain of a Newton.' After giving utterance to this great truth, a number of reasonings follow, for the purpose of proving that neither the one nor the other is divine. 'If,' says he, 'under certain conditions, motion can be transformed into heat, why may it not, under other conditions, be transformed into thought, into sensation, or even into self-conscious reason and will?' Why, indeed? Because the one class of phenomena are entirely different from the other. Any philosophy worthy of the name ought to give proof of its assumed facts, instead of taking them for granted, by asking others to prove their impossibility.

"This school of philosophy is forced to admit that there are certain organisms which are formidable obstacles in the way of elaborating the universe without the aid of an intelligent Creator. Of these, the eye may be taken as a crucial instance. 'It is formed,' says Strauss, 'not in the light, but in the darkness of the womb, yet it is admirably adapted to light which has had no concern in its formation.' A similar difficulty is well put by another writer, quoted by our author, respecting the instincts of animals. 'These latter enable them to perform from their birth, with hereditary finished art, to which the highest reason might have prompted them for their well-being, without any thought, experience, or practice on their part, or any instruction, example, or pattern.' Pantheism endeavours to account for this by assuming the presence of unconscious intellect in the universe.

"Let it be observed that our sole experience of intellect is as an attribute of conscious beings. If philosophy is to rest on a basis of fact, the existence of unconscious intellect diffused in the universe is a gratuitous assumption. No doubt many intellectual processes take place in our minds without leaving any trace on the memory; perhaps without emerging into direct consciousness. This is especially the case with such actions as have become habitual. But this affords no proof of the presence of intellect in a wholly different class of beings. If unconscious intellect can exist independently of any thinking subject, and aid in the construction of organisms, it follows that it must be inherent in every particle of matter of which they are composed. Also, that these unconscious intellectual atoms must have the faculty of acting in unison for the production of a common end; and from the various means by which it may be accomplished, of selecting the most suitable. The bare statement of such a proposition is its most effectual refutation.

"Next, our author invokes a theory of an unconscious absolute, which, 'acting in all atoms, and organisms, as a universal soul, determines the contents of creation, and the evolution of the universe, by a "Clairvoyant Wisdom," superior to all consciousness.' Such a theory may safely be consigned to the regions of dreary mysticism, though it is one which was hardly to be expected from one who imagines that he has escaped from the regions of the miraculous, by eliminating the conception of God from his philosophy.

"But to enable him to account for the production

of beings endowed with these faculties our author supplements these two principles by a theory of inherited habits, transmitted through a long line of ancestors, which have been gradually accumulated through indefinite successions of æons. 'It is not,' says he, 'the seeing individual which forms its own or its offspring's eyes by acting in concert with light . . . . . the individual finds itself put into possession of an instrument which its predecessors, during immemorial time, have gradually brought to an ever higher grade of perfection.' Again, 'It is not our present bee which plans its skilful constructions, neither is it instructed in them by a Deity; but in the lapse of thousands of years, since the lowest instincts were gradually developed into the various forms of Hymenoptera, the increasing needs produced by the struggle for existence have gradually fashioned these acts, which are now transmitted without effort as heirlooms to the present generation.'

"In the case of the eye there are two problems which require a definite solution, and we must not have our mental vision distracted from the point at issue by any phantasmagoria of words. First, the admirable adjustments and adaptations of the instrument itself—How come they? Secondly, How has this instrument, formed in total darkness, become perfectly correlated to the properties of light? There is one solution of these problems quite simple, and fully adequate to account for the facts—the existence of a

God of boundless power and matchless skill, and fully acquainted with all resources and the end to be attained, who has framed the mechanism and adjusted it to external nature.

"But there is also the solution of Pantheism and Atheism. Some of the simplest forms of life in the shape of cells burst into existence we know not how. These in the course of indefinite æons developed themselves into organisms of the simplest character, and these into others of endless variety, impelled by blind forces alone; these grew into more perfect forms in the struggle for existence. Though why, until life had become abundant, there should have been any struggle at all it is hard to conceive. A power of sensation originated somehow, but how or whence we have no means of telling. These beings gradually differentiated themselves—but how, whence, or where this power originated, or how each became possessed of another power, that of propagating its like—this philosophy is silent. After long courses of indefinite æons, a general power of sensation, diffused throughout the entire animal, concentrated itself in special senses, and produced the lowest form of eyes. Æon after æon rolled on its relentless course; variation arose after variation. Struggles for existence were ever ready to destroy imperfect specimens; at length one of the most perfect forms of eyes emerge. But all this leaves the problems with which we started utterly unaccounted for—viz., whence has originated the adaptations of the instrument itself; and how, being formed in darkness, has it become perfectly adapted to external light?

"With respect to the origin of instincts, our philosophers take refuge in a theory of transmitted habits during something like an eternity of time. Step by step they have grown from the smallest origin, and by gradual accretions have been handed down from remote ancestors until they have assumed their present form. But if this were conceivable, the question arises, How came habits to be thus transmissible? Is it the result of the action of blind forces or of intelligence? Again, why is it that the inherited habits of instinctive intelligence, which must have been possessed by multitudes of ancestors in the long line of man's pedigree, have not been transmitted to him; but in this respect he is utterly distanced by the inferior animals? Let it be observed, that it is not a single instinct which has to be accounted for, but numbers numberless, spread over the wide regions of animated nature, and each adapted to the external circumstances of the animal.

"The philosophy which we are considering is never wearied with urging the objection that our conception of a personal God is nothing more nor less than a magnified man. A very popular writer has recently had the bad taste to assert that the belief in a personal Gods differs little from a magnified Lord Shaftesbury. Such a question is one far too grave to be settled by ridicule.

"It is perfectly true, that as long as man is man he can only represent truth in human conceptions. No less so is it that multitudes of his conceptions are inadequate representations of the realities beyond. If our reasonings were to be confined to conceptions which are adequate representations of things, they would be few indeed. The truth is, there is a law of our intellectual being which compels us to transcend the limits of the finite, and to assert that there must exist something beyond our highest conceptions of it. It is the very condition of thought.

"But this philosophy affirms that the conception of a being who is at the same time personal and infinite involves a direct contradiction, and that a philosophy which asserts the existence of a personal God must be rotten at its foundations.

"It is perfectly true that we have no experience of personality except as an attribute of finite beings. Let us inquire what we mean when we affirm that we are persons. A being who is a person is one who can predicate 'I' of himself, who is conscious that he is distinct from all other persons, and non-persons, whose identity is preserved throughout all changes, and through protracted intervals of time, who feels himself to be a free agent, and is the subject of moral affections. There is no reason why an infinite being should not be capable of all these. The objection would be equally valid against introducing infinite quantities into calculations, because all our conceptions are finite. These, however, exist for the practical operations of mathematicians.

"There is no doubt that the habit of theologians of reasoning about the infinite in the abstract, and not in the concrete, has involved the whole controversy in serious difficulties. What do we really mean when we assert that God is infinite? I answer that He is a being who transcends our highest thoughts, and that He is something beyond which we cannot fathom; that there is no point of space where His energy is not present; that there is nothing which is possible which he cannot effect; nor any knowledge which He does not possess. His moral attributes ought to be designated perfect rather than infinite. The conception of infinite is quantitive, a moral one has nothing to do with quantity. Perfection, not infinitude, is properly applied to our ideas of justice, holiness, truthfulness, benevolence. The conception of a personal being, who in this sense is both infinite and perfect, plainly involves no contradiction; and is evidently not unthinkable, though our conception of Him may be inadequate.

Now, while it is a law of our nature that all our ideas must be human ones, there is no possible reason why they may not represent attributes of other beings as well as of ourselves. If 1 see an animal perform actions of a certain character, I am justified in drawing the conclusion that they are the results of intelligence. I infer justly that the animal mind possesses in these respects an intelligence similar to my own. If then, I can conceive of an imperfect form of intelligence, and reason on the fact, why may I not attribute our highest powers, freed from the imperfections with which they exist in man, to God? To assert that such an act is merely to manufacture a gigantic Lord Shaftesbury is not to appeal to reason, but to the worst feelings of our nature.

"Nothing more clearly shows the impotency of this philosophy to grapple with the difficulties in which it is involved than the necessity it is under to use language which contradicts the truth of its own assumptions. Our author endeavours to apologize for the practice: 'In so far as we speak,' says he, 'of a purpose in the universe, we are clearly conscious that we are expressing ourselves subjectively, and that we only express by it what we seem to recognise as the general result of the co-operation of the entire powers of the world.'

"In one word, all such expressions are blinds to enable us to impose on ourselves. A purpose in the universe is no purpose. It exists only in a delusive fancy of our subjective selves. Numbers of similar conceptions made use of by this philosophy can only exist as attributes of personality, and are utterly inapplicable to an impersonal something, whether we designate it Universe or God.

"Yet our author writes as follows:—'The general deduction from the existence of the universe appears to be, as a whole, the most varied motion or the greatest abundance of life; this motion or life specialized as one developing itself morally as well as physically, struggling outwards and upwards, and even in the decline of the individual only preparing a new uprising.'

"Such language is a plain stultification of the principles on which this philosophy is based. Still more remarkable is the following passage:—' From our standpoint the object of the terrene development seems much nearer its attainment now, when the earth is filled by men and their works .... than many thousands of years ago, and when she was still exclusively occupied by mollusca and cretacea, to which fish were added later, then the mighty saurians with their allied species, and, finally, the primeval mammals, yet without man.'

"What object? I ask; for an impersonal Cosmos can have none. Is man, then, the end of creation, its complement and crown? Is the purpose of an impersonal Cosmos getting near its realization? Unless this philosophy utters absolute nonsense, it has arrived at the same conclusion as Theism, that a purpose exists somewhere in the universe. Common sense must draw the conclusion that a purpose can exist only in a personal intelligence, *i.e.* in God.

"But there is a future which this philosophy must face, and which the mind of man, despite of all philosophy, will inquire into with the profoundest interest. What, then, are the destinies of the Cosmos?

What are the future prospects of man as an individual and a race? Let us hear the answer which it returns. 'Nevertheless a time must come when the earth will be no longer inhabited; nay, when we shall have ceased to exist as a planet. Then all which in the course of her development was produced, and in a manner accomplished by her—all living and rational beings and all their productions, all political organizations, all works of art and science—will not only necessarily have vanished from existence without a trace, but even the memory of them will survive in no mind, as the history of the earth must necessarily perish with her.'

"Surely this is a dark prospect which this philosophy unfolds. Man, as an individual, and as a race, shall pass into eternal silence; and no trace of him or his works shall remain in any mind. Still, if this is the inevitable destiny of the future, let us face it boldly and honestly; and not imitate the ancient philosopher, who wished, if the doctrine of man's immortality were not true, that no one should undeceive him while he lived. No; if this philosophy is true, the most cultivated intellects, the greatest moral elevation, and the lowest baseness of wickedness, shall alike rest in peaceful, but eternal silence.

"Again, 'Either the earth,' says the author, 'has missed her aim here—no result has been produced by her protracted existence—or this aim did not consist in something which was intended to endure, but has been attained at every moment of her development.' Let us take courage then, for the gospel of despair can only express itself in the terms of the gospel of hope. Nature then has an aim and a purpose! Aims and purposes are not attributes of an impersonal infinity, but of intelligence, personality, and will. It also announces that the infinite All perishes not, nor ceases from its perfection. 'The All in no succeeding moment is more perfect than in the preceding one, nor *vice versá*. There exists in it, in fact, no such distinction as sooner or later, because all gradations and successions, stages of contraction and expansion, ascent and decline, becoming and perishing, exist side by side, mutually supplementing one another to infinity.' This then is our consolation. Though we perish, the mighty All remains unchanged in its perfection. The elements of which we are composed may, during the evolutions of eternity, help to build up glorious galaxies, though of ourselves, as conscious individuals, there shall be no resurrection.

"There is something in human nature too strong for the reasonings of Pantheistic and Atheistic philosophy to crush. Danton, when questioned at his last trial as to his abode, replied, 'My abode shall soon be annihilation; but I shall live in the Pantheon of History.' This philosophy teaches that even this hope is only a fond delusion. What are the substitutes it furnishes to satisfy the eager cravings of the human heart? Ah! a reverent regard for a Cosmos for which it is impossible to feel either reverence or regard. The memory of a departed wife, to be to us in place of a religion; the worship of humanity, typified in a female form, the destruction of which humanity is certain. This is its substitute for a personal God, the moral governor of the universe which He has created—whose attributes are justice, mercy, and truth; whose providence embraces all His works; who shall continue reigning for ever and ever. Religion teaches an hereafter, which shall give a scope for the exercise of man's mighty powers which is denied him here. But this philosophy affirms that one destiny awaits the holiest and the most abandoned, the man of the most disinterested benevolence and the most refined cruelty, a Nero and a St. Paul—a silence from which there shall be no awakening—the conscious being of both alike shall be swallowed up in the infinite Cosmos. The only conclusion of such a philosophy must be, let each man enjoy life as he best can, for we shall die to-morrow, and sleep for ever the sleep of unconsciousness. The best safeguard against such a philosophy is, that human nature will refuse to accept it as a true account of its aims, its aspirations, and its destinies."

I have quoted largely from the above paper, in the same way as I have done with those utterances of a different character which I have from time to time reported.

Under the conditions of membership prevailing in the Victoria Institute, it was not, of course, possible to have any great collision of opinion. There was, in fact, some danger lest we should altogether renounce the dialectical method in favour of a stagnant mutual admiration. The chairman, while admiring the paper on the whole, thought Mr. Row had scarcely grasped Darwinism, which he defended. Mr. Darwin, he said, admitted God *plus* natural selection, but in such a way that it appeared to the speaker, he was rather polytheistic than atheistic or pantheistic. An inoffensive gentleman asked whether Mr. Row believed in the evolution of man; whereupon Mr. Row, who was as lithe and active as his querist was stout and phlegmatic, flew at him and hit out cruelly—in an intellectual, not a physical way, of course—saying he had made that perfectly clear in his lecture, and half insinuating that the adipose gentleman had been asleep. One gentleman just behind me had slept all through the paper, and snored so loudly that we had to stir him up with the point of an umbrella; but it was not this one: and he sat down again with a look of personal injury on his countenance which it was painful to witness. A fresh-looking gentleman, who seemed to carry weight with the meeting (but whose name I cannot chronicle, as the chairman omitted to name any of the speakers who were members), then took Mr. Row to task on the subject of the dice and lucky chances, which he set down as a "mathematical heresy." It was quite refreshing to find some heterodoxy in so august an assembly. Dr. Irons, whom I knew by sight, said it was sad to find Strauss and Mill so popular, and asked how it was that such was the case when Christianity had been in possession of the world so long? Why would men accept a "thin theism" in place of dogmatic Christianity?—It was because they saw we were ourselves afraid of dogma.

This was all the discussion—if so it could be called —which we had; and by-and-by even this flagged, and blushing disputants had to be fished out from among the visitors. Last of all, and very much the least, my turn came; and if I quote myself it is only to chronicle the impression left upon my own mind at the moment. I told those orthodox Victorians that I had just concluded a personal examination of all the Atheistical and Secularist meetings I could find in London; and I thought it was a great pity men of Mr. Row's calibre did not go and discuss matters with the representatives of those systems on their own platforms, instead of leaving the defence of Theism to the feeble ninepins that had been bowled over so triumphantly. In his reply he confined himself to my speech, and agreed with me that Christianity suffered more from its weak defenders than its most powerful opponents.

It may not be out of place to append to the above a brief account of Pantheism, extracted from the Secular Almanac for 1874 :—

"By Theism we mean the recognition of a principle apart from nature, independent of nature, yet moulding, regulating, and sustaining nature. This principle is supposed to be spiritual, and to be able to communicate to dead matter vital and organic energy. On the contrast between the spiritual and the material Theism is fond of dwelling. Both literally and substantially Atheism is simply the denial of Theism, but it is not the necessary rejection of a formative or procreant force in the universe, which many Atheists are the foremost to admit. The spiritual, whatever meaning may be attached to the word, Atheism consistently renounces and persistently denounces. That ascription to the universe itself of those attributes which the Theist limits to an infinite and spiritual principle is Pantheism, whereof, however, as of Theism and Atheism, there are numerous varieties. By way of distinction, I call the Pantheism in which I believe, and have long believed, Pantheism poetical and passionate. For Pantheism the distinction between the material and the spiritual is wholly meaningless. Pantheism propounds and defends the unity of substance, a unity carrying us into depths where the material and the spiritual lose their customary signification. Conscious substance, acting eternally and instinctively, such is the universe to the Pantheist, who everywhere beholds supreme order, but not in the rationalistic sense. All things, according to him, not merely flow from the substance conscious and One, but are essential portions thereof. He thinks that nature creates, not with plan or purpose, but from interior and irresistible necessity. Hence he takes a cosmical not an ethical view of the Cosmos and all its relations; and instead of puzzling himself about Providence, he tries to identify himself to the utmost with the universal life. Of this universal life he does not pretend to know anything. It is to him an impenetrable mystery, whose common veil is form, whose higher veil is beauty, whose highest veil is symbol. Sympathizing with the universal life, Pantheism sympathizes with all its manifestations, with its minutest expressions, with its tiniest embodiments, and it finds nothing specially miraculous simply because it finds everything miraculous. Free from intellectual disdains, Pantheism is equally free from the ambition to solve problems. There are, in truth, no problems in the universe; it is only ethical Theism which encounters problems, and perplexes itself with them. One of the figments on which Pantheism makes war is the notion that man is ceaselessly progressive. The tides of life ebb and flow in human destinies as in the entire sum of existence, and they have no reference to remote results and final triumphs, either in the development of mankind or in development generally. Nevertheless, though Pantheism scorns theories and abstractions, it is intensely idealistic. As nature is the symbol of symbols, so is she likewise the idealist of idealists, striving evermore toward the unattainable. As the son and adorer of nature, the Pantheist idealizes his own being, idealizes whatsoever comes within the sweep of his phantasy.

"Next to the living universe, it is with the great Pantheistic philosophies, the great Pantheistic religions of olden days, and of Oriental climes, that he loves to hold converse. It is the hope of still sublimer Pantheistic philosophies, still sublimer Pantheistic religions, than those of the past which cheers him. But while he is always willing to bear testimony to his faith, he is never inclined to take either a proselytizing or a polemical attitude, knowing how little his puny efforts can either help or hinder. He is persuaded that the only demonstration of the Pantheistic evangel which he can give to his brethren is the nobleness and heroism of his own deeds. Democracy he views not as man's ultimate condition, but as the path to the Theocracy, for with the Theocracy man began, and to the Theocracy he must return. Pantheism at present is not much more than an aspiration. The war between Theism and Atheism must be fought out before there can be a magnificent and exuberant Pantheistic revival. So gross are the inconsistencies, so crass the imbecilities, so debasing the tendencies of Theism, that Atheism would have an easy victory over it if the European world had not been for two thousand years under the empire of Theistic influences. Theism must perish as slowly as Polytheism perished—perish from the assaults of Atheism, perish from its own exhaustion and corruption. The Polytheism of the Greeks and the Romans was an imperfect Pantheism. In its deification of the individual objects of nature it overlooked or did not comprehensively behold, as the Indian and Egyptian religions beheld, Nature, the Mighty Mother herself. Pantheism revels in the illimitable; but art, in which the Romans, and especially the Greeks, excelled, is limitation and self-limitation. To say that Pantheism is the most joyous of creeds would not be enough to prove its superiority. Its disciples, however, deem it the truest of creeds, because the most natural. Having its birth in the fetishism of the savage, it ascends and ascends, it expands and expands, till the Pantheistic religions and the Pantheistic philosophies are as rich in symbol and suggestion as the universe itself. Logical Pantheisms, such as those of Spinoza and Hegel, are by no means attractive. To be fascinating Pantheism must wear a poetical garb, such a garb as Shelley could have given it, and in his gladder and grander moments really gave it; and it would not be wrong to call Shelley the laureate of Pantheism, for his professed Atheism was little more than a cry of anger and anguish, or a caprice. Whoso lives poetically and rejoicingly in nature, venerates nature as holy, loyally submits to nature, evermore idealizes nature, is substantially a Pantheist, even if he is regarded as an Atheist by others and by himself. However, the vast Pantheistic temple, the universe, is, with its starry dome ever open, whether the worshippers there be many or few."

AN ATHEIST'S FUNERAL.

To those who believe in special providences there might appear something significant in the death of Mr. Austin Holyoake at the very time when the last sheet of this book was going through the press.

It was in the following words that the *National Reformer* announced the departure from this life of one who was in many respects foremost in the ranks of Advanced Thought in London, Austin Holyoake:—

In Memoriam.
"GONE BEFORE."
AUSTIN HOLYOAKE,

Died April 10th, 1874.

AGED FORTY-SEVEN YEARS.

"This world is the nurse of all we know;
This world is the mother of all we feel;
And the coming of death is a fearful blow
To a brain unencompassed with nerves of steel."

"I have lost a friend; the movement has lost a worker. Nearly a quarter of a century since our first meeting, and fourteen years of the closest friendship and communion, death has closed a well-filled common page, in which no word of quarrel or mistrust has ever figured between us. For quite three years death has waited very near, and the ending is no sudden shock; but it is none the less painful to lose one trusty counsellor and loyal co-worker from a circle so narrow. This journal has owed much to his labour; our movement is greatly debtor to his loyalty. Not my pen can tell the story of his life, but he died as true and brave as man could die. His 'Sick-room Thoughts,' which appear in another column, dictated to his wife and revised by himself, were—at his own request, and in any event—to have been published this week. Two days before he died I received the MS. from his own hands to give to the compositor. This is now become the voice from the tomb, the last utterance of his thoughts. He identified himself with my cause, made his foes mine; and if this my tribute to the dead be poor and weak it is from my lack of power to make mere words the translators of my emotions. "CHARLES BRADLAUGH."

I could not help noticing as adding to the pathos of this touching "In Memoriam" the omission of those two words which form its complement to the Christian. To the believer in an immortality and future reunion it reads "Not lost, but gone before"— to the unbeliever, only "Gone before." Probably no such speaking symbol of the difference between the two systems could be instanced as the negative one of the quiet elimination from thought and speech of the words "Not lost." Even suppose it be but the wish which is father to the thought, there is surely more comfort in realizing the exquisite words of Keble—

> 'Tis sweet, as year by year we lose
> Friends out of sight on earth, to muse
> How grows in Paradise our store.

The following are the Thoughts in the Sick-room referred to above:—

"April 8th, 1874.—All those persons who have taken the trouble to read what I have written in the *National Reformer* for some years past, and also published in pamphlets, will know what my opinions on death and immortality recently were. Those views were formed when I was in perfect health, and after years of reflection and inquiry. I am now about to state how my views remain after protracted suffering.

"Christians constantly tell Freethinkers that their principles of 'negation,' as they term them, may do very well for health; but when the hour of sickness and approaching death arrives, they utterly break down, and the hope of a 'blessed immortality' can alone give consolation. In my own case I have been very anxious to test the truth of this assertion, and have therefore deferred till the latest moment I think it prudent to dictate these few lines.

"I was born of religious parents, my mother being

especially pious, belonging to that most terrible of all sects of the Christian body—the Calvinistic Methodists. From my earliest childhood I remember being taught to dread the wrath of an avenging God, and to avoid the torments of a brimstone hell. I said prayers twice a day, I went to a Sunday-school where I learnt nothing but religious dogmas, and I had to read certain chapters of the Bible during the week. My Sundays were mostly days of gloom; and I may sincerely say that up to the age of fourteen I was never free from the haunting fear of the devil.

"About this period new light began to break in upon me. Robert Owen and his disciples first appeared in Birmingham, and attracted much attention. My eldest brother and sisters went to hear the new preachers, and what they had heard they came home and discussed. I listened with all the eagerness of an enthusiastic boy, and from that hour my mental emancipation set in.

"My belief in the infallibility of the Bible first gave way. Soon after commenced my disbelief in the possession of any special knowledge on the part of the preachers of the Gospel, of the God and immortality of which they talked so glibly. But it was years before I thought my way to Atheism. It cannot therefore be said that I never experienced religious emotions.

" For twenty years past my mind has been entirely free from misgivings or apprehensions as to any future state of rewards and punishments. I do not believe in the Christian Deity, nor in any form of so-called supernatural existence. I cannot believe in that which I cannot comprehend. I shall be accused of presumption in expressing disbelief in an idea which has commanded the faith of some of the best intellects for centuries past. This I cannot help. I must think for myself; and if each of those great men had been asked to define his God, it may safely be predicted that no two would have agreed. I may also be reminded that 'the fool hath said in his heart there is no God.' This would imply thought, and it is doubtful whether *a fool* ever thought upon the subject at all; but his idea of a Deity, if it could be got at, would no doubt be as coherent as most other men's. Many fools have written and spoken as though they had penetrated the secrets of the inscrutable, and many wise men have lost their reason in endeavouring to solve the insoluble; and the world remains just as ignorant on the subject as it did at the earliest dawn of civilization.

"I do not believe in a heaven, or life of eternal bliss after death. There is nothing in this world to induce me to give credence to the possibility of such a state of human existence. Wherever there are living organisms there are suffering and torture amongst them; therefore analogy would go to prove that if we lived again we should suffer again. To desire eternal bliss is no proof that we shall ever attain it; and it has long seemed to me absurd to *believe* in that which we wish for, however ardently. I regard all forms of Christianity as founded in selfishness. It is the expectation held out of bliss through all eternity, in return for the profession of faith in Christ and Him crucified, that induces the erection of temples of worship in all Christian lands. Remove this extravagant promise, and you will hear very little of the Christian religion.

"An eternal hell seems to me too monstrous for the belief of any humane man or sensitive woman; and yet millions believe in it. Like heaven, it is enormously disproportionate to the requirements of the case; as man can never confer benefits deserving an eternal reward, so it is impossible for him to commit sins deserving eternal punishment. The idea must have had its origin in the diseased imagination of some fanatic; but it has been carefully cherished and improved upon by priests in subsequent ages, till it is now incorporated in the creed of all Christian churches. Father Pinamonti's 'Hell Open to Christians,' and the Rev. Mr. Furness's 'Sight of Hell,' show to what a fearful extent this diabolical idea can be used in warping and stultifying the minds of the young.

"As I have stated before, my mind being free from any doubts on these bewildering matters of speculation, I have experienced for twenty years the most perfect mental repose; and now I find that the near approach of death, the 'grim King of Terrors,' gives me not the slightest alarm. I have suffered, and am suffering, most intensely both by night and day; but this has not produced the least symptom of change of opinion. No amount of bodily torture can alter a mental conviction. Those who, under pain, say they see the error of their previous belief, had never thought out the problem for themselves.

"I cannot conclude without expressing the gratification I have received from my connexion with the *National Reformer*. My work on it has indeed been a labour of love, and my association therein, with my esteemed friends Mr. Bradlaugh and Mr. Charles Watts, for the past eight years, has been of the most harmonious nature. My extreme regret now is, that I cannot do my full share in the work the 'Trinity' have hitherto performed; but I must bend to inevitable fate, and content myself by knowing that an abler and better man may be found to take my place. However, of this I am sure, that my colleagues will never meet with a more faithful and ardent friend.

"To the true courage and patience of my dear and devoted wife I owe my present tranquillity. In my little son and daughter I have all a father's hope and confidence, and it softens the pain of parting when I contemplate leaving them with one who has all the—— [Mr. Austin Holyoake commenced the dictation of this last paragraph a few hours before he died; but, being soon exhausted, had to break off, and was not able to resume it.]"

It was soon after noontide, on a genial spring day, when I set out for the beautiful northern suburb of Highgate to attend the Atheist's funeral. Emerald buds decked each living bough, and seemed to realize Sydney Smith's idea when he pointed to the crocus peering above the mould and said, "The resurrection of the world!" For him who was to be borne to his last resting-place, and for those who would follow him there was no resurrection realized, even in conception. It was the heathen notion of the eternal farewell that was to be embodied there in the quiet sleeping-place. It was for them no cemetery—no sweet place of repose—but veritably the Necropolis, the City of the Dead.

A motley throng, representing the most advanced Free-thought of London, had gathered round the open grave, which was of course in the unconsecrated and less frequented part of the cemetery—as quiet and retired a nook as one could wish to rest in when "the fever called living is over at last." There were many faces I had seen of late on London platforms; many voices I had heard in hot debate were hushed to silence in the forced solemnity of that gathering round the grave.

Doubt as we will, that same grave will make us serious. Though why should it do so, if it were only something akin to yon clods, something far inferior to the germs of that budding hedgerow yonder —we were committing to the earth?

At length a procession of the hearse and seven mourning coaches, followed by one private carriage, made its appearance at the lower entrance of the cemetery, and having finally halted, the remains—if so we dare write it—of the dead unbeliever were borne to the grave, the mourners following bareheaded in double line. Behind the coffin were three brothers and the little son of the deceased. Who could help surmising the effect on the child of such a sepulture for his father?

When the body was lowered into the grave Mr. Charles Watts, in a voice broken with emotion, read over it the form of service written by Mr. Holyoake himself, and quoted at page 179 above. Mr. Bradlaugh, who, man of iron nerve as he is, could not quite control the quivering nerves of his rigid face, spoke as follows, and then the brief ceremony was over:—

" Here we pay farewell tribute to the last remains of my staunch friend, and your most loyal brother and true servant to the cause of human progress. Death came to him so slowly and yet so certainly, and with such constant menace, that it needed great courage to await the end so long and so bravely as he awaited. Around his grave we are gathered, each reverently placing on his coffin our testimony to his fidelity; trusting that thereout our children's memory will weave an enduring wreath of immortelles to mark at least his life, even when his tomb shall be forgot-

ten. He has left us two legacies—one, the benefit of
which enures to all who desire thought free and true—
this is, the tendency of the labour of his life. The
other legacy, involving some duty, was an unwilling
one—he would not have left it to us willingly as any
burden. His last recorded words, broken short like
some death-marking granite splinter, remind us of
this second legacy—his wife, his boy, his girl. To-
morrow can alone tell whether his little ones shall
have to be glad or sorry that their father died believing that the party whose minister he had been would
try to smooth the life path his death has made for
them so rugged. Of the dead and to the dead I can
say nothing; a quarter of a century's recollections,
and fourteen years' unbroken friendship are now in
that grave.

He did well; he did his best;
No more weary, now at rest."

With the one last lingering gaze upon the coffin-
lid, which seemed so instinctive at such a moment,
the hopeless mourners withdrew, and left him whom,
in thought, they had lost for ever. There were few
around the grave except those who shared the sentiments of the buried; but I heard one rough woman,
evidently uninitiated, thus criticise to her companion
the two addresses she had listened to:—"It *was*
beautiful. And they call them Infidels! They
might put many of our Christians to shame." It was
another of the many cases I have noticed, and some

of which I had cited, where men are so vastly better than their creeds; and I believe if hearts could have been analysed that spring afternoon, a gentler scepticism would have been found there than was often admitted, and which contained the germs of hope within it. The *genius loci* must have inspired so much; though who shall say how evanescent it was, or how soon, after they had turned their backs upon that grave, it relapsed into the old unhappy negation? To me it seemed a strange and significant commentary upon my then concluded work of examining the ranks of the unbelievers. It needed only the adoption of the new system, cremation, to have reproduced exactly that funeral scene so graphically described in Lord Lytton's "Last Days of Pompeii," with its

SALVE ETERNUM.

Farewell! O soul departed!
Farewell! O sacred urn!
Bereaved and broken-hearted,
  To earth the mourners turn!
To the dim and dreary shore
Thou art gone our steps before!
  But thither the swift hours lead us,
  And thou dost but a while precede us!
                  Salve! salve
Loved urn; and thou, solemn cell,
Mute ashes! farewell, farewell!
                  Salve! salve!

  *   *   *   *

Ilicet—ire licet.
The spark from the hearth is gone
  Wherever the air shall bear it;
The elements take their own——

  *   *   *   *

As I sat in the quiet sleeping-place of God's Acre, after the rest had gone, and read over again a kindly letter the dead man had a short time since written me, the utter hopelessness of mere negation seemed to come so forcibly upon me as to carry its own assurance that it could not be true. God would be an austere man, and life the cruel infliction of a tyrant, if all ended in that grave yonder. And as I wended my way back to the Great City, there seemed to echo and re-echo through my mind those sadly beautiful lines of Clough's in reference to the resurrection, with which I once concluded a sermon on "The Sorrows of Scepticism:"—

> Eat, drink, and die, for we are souls bereaved.
> Of all the creatures under heaven's wide cope
> We are most hopeless, who had once most hope,
> And most beliefless, that had most believed.
>   Ashes to ashes, dust to dust;
>   As of the unjust, also of the just—
>   Yea, of that Just One too!
> It is the one sad gospel that is true—
>   Christ is *not* risen!
> Weep not beside the tomb,
> Ye women, unto whom
> He was great solace while ye tended Him;
> Ye who with napkin o'er the head,
> And folds of linen round each wounded limb,
>   Laid out the Sacred Dead;
>   And thou who bar'st Him in thy wondering womb;
> Yea, daughters of Jerusalem, depart;
> Build up as best ye may your own sad bleeding heart!

THE END.

www.ingramcontent.com/pod-product-compliance
Lightning Source LLC
Chambersburg PA
CBHW022105290426
44112CB00008B/560